For Jen

Author's Note

This is a true account of my experience of being forcibly taken from my home as a teenager and sent to a "therapeutic boarding school." These so-called "schools," many of which are still in operation across the United States today, offer desperate parents what must seem like a miracle cure for children they have deemed "troubled," a term that is very loosely defined and includes what some would call typical rebellious teen behavior. It is my opinion that the methods these schools employ are, at best, debasing and, at worst, completely destructive. I hope to start a conversation for those who have been hurt by these institutions and not known where to turn. If by telling my story I can convince one parent to avoid this dangerous path, I will feel like I've accomplished something.

In recounting my story, I primarily relied upon my own recollections, personal letters, and journals, as well as conversations with others who shared this experience or portions of it with me. I want to stress that this is my story and my story alone—I do not purport to speak for my former classmates, friends, or acquaintances from this period of my life; nor do I mean to imply that they reacted to these experiences in the same manner that I did. In fact, I am aware that there are some individuals who credit their time at Carlbrook for improving or even saving their lives.

AUTHOR'S NOTE

Given the sensitive nature of the material presented in the book, I have changed the names and certain identifying characteristics of individuals. In some instances, I also have created composite characters and altered the timing and/or locations of events. I left only two names unchanged: my own, Elizabeth Gilpin, and that of the institution that forever changed my life.

Everything can be taken from a man but one thing: the last of the human freedoms—to choose one's attitude in any given set of circumstances, to choose one's own way.

—Viktor Frankl, *Man's Search for Meaning*

STOLEN

Prologue

SOMETIMES I THINK I was born afraid of the dark. Hall lights, bedside lamps, a flashlight hidden beneath the covers—nothing made me feel safe in the middle of the night. The setting sun filled me with dread, and twilight came with an impossible choice. Waking life and dreaming life were both unbearable at night. I was afraid of my own shadowy thoughts and even more terrified of the faceless man who haunted me in my nightmares.

Inside my picture-perfect brick house on my quiet Southern street, where the hand-striped walls matched the custom-tailored curtains, was my pink room. It was perfectly appointed, the sheets and pillowcases mono-grammed with my initials: E.L.G., written in cursive. I would lie in my bed night after night, paralyzed with fear but too embarrassed to admit it.

I had been right to fear the dark. The faceless man came for me after all, only in real life he had a faceless partner. They kidnapped me from my own home in the middle of the night, and no one stood in their way.

At fifteen, I was angry and defiant, in trouble more often than not. So my parents hired the man from my nightmares to take me away.

This is what I remember from the night my whole life changed:

First, there's light. Bright and blinding, it shoots fear through my body before my brain knows how to react. My vision is fuzzy and there are shadowy faces leaning over me. I blink. Two strangers come into focus, and their hands clasp around my wrists and ankles, holding me down. My brain is hazy, hungover. I can't move and I'm terrified.

"What's happening?" I say. "Who are you?"

The strangers in my room are adults. A man and a woman, large and dressed in black. I'm wearing powder-blue pajama pants and an enormous white T-shirt bearing the logo of a youth tennis camp. I'm fifteen years old and my nightmare is coming true.

"Let's go." The man is pulling me from my bed.

"No." I kick my legs wildly.

"I'm not asking."

I realize that I'm screaming. That I've been screaming this whole time. The shock has made me inarticulate and wild, my voice like an animal's. I focus and call out for help. Again and again I scream for someone to come save me. The strangers don't try to stop me. They understand it doesn't really matter.

"Your parents know we're here," the woman says. "And you're coming with us."

"Fuck that."

She grabs my shoulders and yanks me from the bed. I reach for a pillow to fend her off.

"Where are you taking me?"

I'm on my feet now, still trying to wrestle away from my kidnappers. I'm not wearing shoes. I need to pee.

"There are plenty of bathrooms on the road," the woman says in response.

The man tightens his grip as he drags me out into the hall. I understand now why my mom chose this weekend to take my brother and sister out of town. How long has she been planning this? Did she have "Elizabeth gets kidnapped" written down in her calendar?

"Ow." Beefy fingers dig into my flesh. "You're hurting me."

The strangers march me down the long corridor, past studio portraits of three well-groomed, blond children. With manufactured smiles, we could have been in the stock photo that came with the frame. I see

2

another figure looming in the shadows, right by the front door. It's my father. He's in his pajamas, standing tall and calm with his arms folded across his chest.

Has he slept? Did he brush his teeth and get into bed? Did he set an alarm for the arrival of his daughter's kidnappers?

I look at him now, my eyes wet and pleading. I want him to intervene, to tell my abductors there's been some kind of misunderstanding.

It's okay, my daddy is just trying to scare me.

And it's working. I'm terrified, desperate to stop whatever has just been set in motion.

"Why are you doing this to me?" I ask when I reach the door.

My father says nothing. He just stares at me with unblinking eyes. If those irises contain any emotion at all, it's resolve. His mind is made up: This is what I deserve.

Finally he mouths a single phrase: *I'm sorry.*

And that's it. The strangers drag me through the front door. A black SUV is parked in the driveway, taking up the spot normally occupied by my mom's car. I tumble into the backseat and pound on the reinforced window. I scream and flail as the car pulls out of the driveway and takes me away, forever.

I don't know it then, but I will never set foot in that house again. As the SUV logs mile after mile on the highways of South Carolina, I sit so silent and angry that the female escort joins me in the back, afraid of what I might do. I feel all hope slip away as we cross the state line and head toward the mountains.

There is another nightmare waiting for me deep inside the woods of Appalachia, a mean and twisted version of reality. And something unimaginable after that. I lost control of my own life the moment those strangers pulled me from my bed, and it would be many years before I'd get it back.

PART I

Chapter 1

My mother has a saying that nothing good ever happens after midnight. Growing up, I must have heard those words a thousand times. Always in the same tone of voice, her high Southern lilt dropped down an octave, less proverb than warning. And really, I should have listened. My whole life might have turned out differently if I'd only bothered to heed her advice.

Or at the very least, if I hadn't tried quite so hard to prove her wrong.

It was about 12:15 when the cops arrived to bust up our little party in the woods. It wasn't exactly a rager, just a dozen teenagers hanging out by the train tracks on a Friday night. Enjoying the fresh South Carolina air and a case of Bud Light.

I was sitting on Nick's lap. At fifteen, how good I felt at any given time was directly related to my proximity to my crush, this tousle-haired junior who wasn't exactly my boyfriend. I'd been sharing his foldout chair for most of the night and my head was spinning, though I'd had only a single beer. I was drunk with infatuation—and that made it all the more annoying when the cops showed up.

"Oh, shit!" someone said. "Cops."

I leapt off Nick's lap.

Headlights flashed from the other side of the tracks. They blinded us as we scattered and made a run for the row of cars parked on the road.

I dashed across the clearing. I must have reached the cars before Nick because I didn't see him anywhere.

As I looked around frantically, I felt someone grab my arm and push me into the passenger seat of the nearest car. I scrambled to close the door as the engine started up. We peeled out of the woods in a cloud of dust and screeching tires, and careened alongside the tracks for a few frenzied minutes.

"Fuck. That was close."

It was Jason talking. I'd known him for years, even though I was a freshman and he was a junior. He was in the same class as Nick and my brother, Philip. He and Philip were friends, but it was my father who knew him best. My dad, a surgeon and a sports buff, was the unofficial team doctor for the school football team, and Jason was the star player. If I were any other girl, I would have been thrilled to find myself in the passenger seat of that silver 4Runner.

"Are we sure they're gone?" Rebecca said from the backseat.

I looked around. It was just the three of us in the car, and the road behind us was dark. Either the cops were on the trail of another group or they hadn't bothered to follow us at all.

"I think so," Jason said, grinning with adrenaline. "Man, that could have been bad."

As we drove, Rebecca fielded calls from the other cars.

"Cool. I'll tell them," she said. "So everyone's going to Hannah's."

"Everyone?" I said. "So they all got out okay?"

"I think so, yeah."

Okay. So that must mean Nick isn't hurt or in prison.

But it also means he left without me.

"Jason," Rebecca said, "did you hear me? I said Hannah's house."

Jason nodded. But he was driving in the wrong direction.

"Are you, like, lost?"

He glanced at Rebecca in his rearview mirror. He raised an eyebrow and smiled. "No, I'm not lost."

"Then where are you going?"

"I'm making a stop," he said. "We should pick up weed."

Rebecca shrugged and leaned back. Jason was driving farther away from the area we all lived in. He seemed to be heading downtown, near the college.

"Um, how much longer?" I said.

"Close. Like half a mile. I know a spot."

We had just escaped a close call with the cops. Wasn't that enough excitement for one night? I wanted to get back to Nick, but I couldn't exactly say that. I couldn't claim I needed to be home for curfew either. Everyone already knew I was spending the night at Melanie's, which was basically like saying, "Drop me off sometime before the first bell on Monday." Melanie hadn't had a curfew since middle school—the year her mom got sick and her dad became permanently overwhelmed. Now that it was just her and her father, she basically lived without rules. She didn't have to worry about coming home a little tipsy, or not at all. Which meant that for tonight, neither did I.

We pulled onto a darkly lit block just as my phone rang. It was Nick. Sure, he'd abandoned me, but at least he was checking in.

"Hey," I said. "You going to Hannah's?"

"Already here. Where are you?"

"I'm with Jason and Rebecca. Buying weed."

"Seriously?" Nick said. "Where?"

Jason shifted to a slow roll. He stuck his hand out the window and held up his pointer finger.

"What are you doing?" Rebecca said.

"That's the sign," Jason said. "A number one."

"Some shady house," I said into the phone. "Where Jason knows *the sign.*"

"Bullshit." Nick laughed. "He's gonna get played."

As ridiculous as it seemed, Jason was right. He knew the sign. A minute later, a twentyish guy in a hoodie came outside.

"Yo," the dude said, glancing around. "How much?"

"Let's do an eighth."

"Forty," the guy said. "I'll be right back."

The guy headed back inside to retrieve his product. Jason pulled two crisp twenties from his wallet.

"Wow," I said. "That actually worked."

"We'll see," Jason said. "Sometimes they try to rip you off. Especially if they think you don't know what you're doing."

So maybe that's what "the sign" is for. To identify chump teenagers who don't know what they're doing.

The guy came back and passed a baggie through the window. Jason started to open it right there in the car.

"What the fuck are you doing, bro?"

"Checking the quality."

"No, man," the dealer said. "Pay me and get out of here."

"Chill. I just gotta check it."

"Give me my fucking money and go check it somewhere else."

"Then you'll have my money and I'll have shit weed."

"What are you trying to say?" The dealer leaned forward, attempting menace. "You insulting my product? Punk-ass kid."

By then, Jason had the bag open. He sniffed it and shook his head. It was dirt weed after all.

"Fuck this," he said.

The next few seconds were a blur. Jason put his car in gear. The dealer jumped onto the 4Runner's running board and grabbed the rack attached to the roof. Suddenly Jason was driving, the guy was clinging to the car, and none of us knew what to do next. Jason pounded his window, trying to shake the guy off, but he wouldn't let go. I screamed for Jason to slow down, Rebecca just plain screamed, and Nick was still on the phone, asking for an explanation.

"Elizabeth. Talk to me."

And then: silence. Not the relative quiet of turning the volume knob down or a temporary lull in the mechanisms of the world. This was a truly empty sound, the kind of silence you're not supposed to come back from. But I guess I'm just lucky that way.

"Oh my god, oh my god, holy shit."

After the sonic cocoon of total unconsciousness, Rebecca's shrieking was especially alarming. I opened my eyes slowly. The first thing I saw was the splintered windshield of Jason's 4Runner. Then it was a clump of my own hair suspended in the spiderwebbed glass. It took a moment to realize those images were directly connected. The third thing I saw was the imprint of my own head in the glass. I had caused the windshield to crack when I slammed halfway through it.

"What happened?" I said.

"We hit a tree," Rebecca said. "You don't remember?"

I shook my head.

Good sign. Probably not paralyzed.

Jason turned to me. We were all still in the car. His eyes were wide like a frightened puppy's. But he and Rebecca both seemed untouched.

"Oh my god," he said. "Are you okay?"

"I think so."

I did a quick check to make sure that was true. I was able to look around without any trouble, and none of my body parts seemed to have been displaced. In fact, I couldn't find more than a few minor wounds anywhere. There were cuts on my hand and a little blood on my temple. But my worst injury was a swollen finger, probably broken but maybe just sprained.

I was okay. Completely, astonishingly, okay. In retrospect, it was nothing short of a miracle that I got through that accident with a few surface wounds and a haircut. At times it feels like I was given nine lives, like a cat. I should have counted my blessings and vowed to stay out of trouble. But I wasn't exactly in a blessing-counting frame of mind back then. I was moody, hormonal, and angry at the world, and I'd been that way for years. I couldn't waste my time feeling all lucky to be alive when there were pressing questions on my mind.

11

Like, *How am I going to spin this so my parents don't freak out?*

And, *Is this going to keep me from meeting up with Nick?*

I wondered how much of the accident he'd heard. I picked up my phone from the floor, but there was no longer a voice on the other line.

"Thank God," Jason said.

Amazingly, he was able to start the car. We made it a few blocks in the totaled vehicle before it died.

At least we were away from the scene. It didn't seem like anyone had bothered to call the cops. We walked a little farther down the street while Jason called around until he found someone sober enough to come pick us up.

"Are you sure you're feeling all right?" Jason said.

"Yeah, I'm fine."

Jason's friend arrived quickly and we all piled into his car. When he asked where I was going, I gave him Melanie's address.

"Don't you want to go home?" Rebecca said.

I shook my head. In truth, I was hoping I might be able to keep the accident a secret from my parents. Since I was alive and relatively unhurt, I didn't see any reason for them to be involved. In my naive fifteen-year-old mind, I thought this would keep me out of trouble. Melanie wasn't back yet, but I knew where to find the spare key. I let myself in and tiptoed up the stairs. I shut myself in her room and immediately called Nick. I had three missed calls from him, and his voice was frantic when he answered.

"Elizabeth! Are you okay?"

"Yeah," I said. "Jason crashed into a tree."

"I heard. We drove around looking for you guys."

"Really?" My heart skipped a beat.

"Crazy night," Nick said. "You sure you're all right?"

After we hung up I decided to check. I walked into the bathroom, suddenly worried I was missing an eyeball or bleeding from my stomach. Maybe I was dying and had been too shocked to realize it. My face looked totally normal, though. The damage amounted to a single scratch etched across my forehead, right at my hairline. No missing limbs, no gaping wounds.

I ran my hand through my hair. Small pieces of glass rained down almost delicately, but there was hardly any blood. Just hair and glass and whatever was going on with my swollen finger.

I washed my face and changed into some pajamas, even though I'd promised Nick I'd stay awake in case I had a concussion. When Melanie got home she offered to stay up with me. She was too drunk to keep her eyes open and passed out. It was a little before dawn when I decided to rest for just a few minutes. I made a bed for myself on the couch and realized just how exhausted I was.

Fuck it. If I fall asleep, I fall asleep. Whatever happens next is out of my control.

It felt almost like I was daring the universe, playing a game of chicken with God. I simultaneously had a death wish and believed I was invincible. No matter how recklessly I behaved, things always seemed to work out fine.

I woke up in the morning feeling shockingly normal. It seemed I didn't have a concussion after all. It dawned on me that I might actually get out of this situation without having to tell my parents. I wasn't brain-dead and I wasn't bleeding. The only hitch was my swollen finger, which had doubled in size overnight. I knew I needed to go to the hospital, but that meant dealing with my father, a strict disciplinarian. Melanie and I brainstormed on the drive over until we'd settled on a lie.

"I slipped last night," I said.

My dad looked at me. "At the football game?"

"Yeah. In the bleachers while I was trying to get back to my seat."

"Did you get hurt anywhere else?"

I shook my head. "Nope. Just my finger."

As I said it out loud, I realized how utterly *sane* I sounded. My lie was perfectly reasonable, much more so than the truth. My father didn't even think twice.

"Okay," he said. "I'll have the nurse come in with a splint."

"Thanks." I smiled. "Hey, Dad, is it okay if I stay at Melanie's again tonight?" There was a house party that night and I wanted to go.

I was relieved that my dad didn't object, because I figured Nick would be at the party, and I hoped my brush with death might have made him realize how much he didn't want to lose me. I waited for him to show up, but he never did.

Jason wasn't there either. I figured he was probably grounded. *It's a lot harder to hide a totaled car than a swollen finger.* My father, however, did make an appearance at the party. He showed up, red-faced and screaming, to drag me away.

My small town in South Carolina was close-knit and news got around. Which is a nice way of saying my town *fucking loved* to gossip. I didn't tell my parents about the accident, and neither did anyone who had actually been in the woods that night. None of us wanted to get in trouble. It was Jason's girlfriend's mom, of all people, who ruined everything. Not that I blame her. She was a mom and was probably genuinely concerned. But her daughter Mary had ulterior motives.

To explain: Mary and Jason had an on-and-off relationship. She suspected he was hooking up with someone else. When she heard about the accident, she figured there was a good chance the girl in question was also in the car. Mary's instincts were correct. Jason had been cheating. It just wasn't with me.

"Elizabeth!" he yelled.

I heard my dad's voice and froze. He stormed into the living room, eyes blazing. He grabbed my arm and marched me through the house. He was too angry to actually look at me, but the rest of the party made up for that. All eyes were on me as we walked out the front door and headed for the car.

"What the hell is wrong with you, Elizabeth?" My father slammed the car door shut. "You're unbelievable. Do you know that?"

"No. I don't." It was a stupid response. But what else was I supposed to say?

"Of course not. Because you only ever think about yourself."

Oh yeah? How would you even know? It's not like you're ever home.

"I'm taking you to the hospital and ordering a drug test."

I felt tears welling up in my eyes. This kind of interaction was becoming more and more normal for me and my father. There was a time when the two of us really got along, but it had started to feel like nothing I did would ever be good enough.

My dad and I came from two very different places. He was raised in a military family without much money. His mother worked as a schoolteacher while raising four boys. All four of them joined the armed forces at eighteen before attending college on the GI Bill. My father went immediately from the Navy to med school where he trained as a surgeon.

He knew nothing but hard work and discipline. In his world, teenagers had jobs and responsibilities. They didn't get into car accidents on the weekends because there was no time for late-night parties.

It wasn't like I was a slacker, not by any means. I went to swim practice in the mornings and soccer practice in the afternoons. On the weekends, I traveled around the South for tournaments and meets for the premier teams I joined in addition to my school teams. And when I wasn't playing sports I was studying with the aid of tutors to ensure I'd get into a good college.

These things were luxuries, undoubtedly. I can see now how lucky I was that my family could afford to send me to tournaments and hire SAT tutors. But to my father, whose hard work afforded me my lifestyle, it meant there was little room for error. Any time I misbehaved, my dad saw it as a sign that I was ungrateful.

On top of that, he seemed to think I was some kind of drug addict and alcoholic. He drove us to the hospital and parked in his designated spot by the entrance. When we got inside, I stormed off to pee in a cup. I was pretty sure I was in the clear. All I'd had to drink was a little Bud Light, and it had been months since I'd smoked any weed. But I knew nothing about drug tests and was suddenly paranoid.

How long does marijuana stay in your bloodstream? A week? A year? Forever?

Before I left the stall, I made a last-second decision to add a little toilet water to the sample. I figured if there was any marijuana still in my system, this would dilute it. Really, I was a fairly innocent kid, all things considered. But no one, least of all my parents, wanted to believe it.

We waited in the lobby, both of us silent. I could feel the wall of anger thickening between us and I started to cry. My dad refused to show any sympathy, so I went outside to call my mom.

"He didn't even ask if I was okay! I could have *died*."

"Calm down," my mom said. "I can barely understand you."

"All he cares about is a stupid drug test."

"Well, he has his reasons. You did get in a car accident and lie about it."

"Why does he hate me so much?"

"Elizabeth, your father doesn't hate you."

Deep down I knew she was right. My father didn't hate me; he was just fed up with my behavior. But it was so hard to feel any love through my fog of misery. Some days I woke up convinced there was no point in trying because my life didn't matter. Other times I felt things so intensely I thought I might explode. Emotions rolled through me like a storm, a series of electric charges outside of my control. I often felt white-hot rage course through me like a sudden burst of lightning. I don't know where it came from, and I can't remember when it started. Maybe it had always been there, anger and fear, part of me from the start.

I didn't need a drug test. Or an MRI. I needed someone to tell me what was wrong with *me*, as a person.

In retrospect, what I needed was someone to diagnose my depression.

My dad came storming out of the hospital, looking madder than ever. He unlocked the car without saying a word and remained silent the entire drive home. I knew that meant I'd passed the test. It also meant that instead of being relieved his daughter wasn't a drug addict, my father was furious because he'd been wrong.

I jumped out of the car as soon as we got home and headed straight to my room. I was angry and overwhelmed, and I just wanted to shut out the world. But I heard the front door slam and the beginnings of an argument brewing between my parents. On top of that, my brother was yelling at me from the hallway. Clearly, the gossip had reached him and he was convinced I was a slut.

"Is there anyone in my grade you haven't blown?"

Shut up. I'm not a whore. I'm not a drug addict. But hey, the rumors say I am. So maybe I should just accept it and lean in.

Chapter 2

I WAS FOURTEEN when my next-door neighbor shot himself to death on a quiet summer afternoon. One pull of the trigger and it was all over for Dr. Winston. I imagined his body in his favorite armchair while his wife of five decades made lunch in the other room. Before that day I don't think I'd spent one single second wondering what my neighbor's life might be like. But in the aftermath, I couldn't stop.

For years, Dr. Winston was just the old man on the other side of the fence. He was kinder than Mrs. Winston, in my opinion, but it wasn't like I knew either of them very well. They mostly kept to themselves like a typical elderly couple. I usually saw him in the garden, either reading the newspaper or tending to his plants. He was nice to me the summer I became obsessed with gymnastics. When my heroes were Dominique Dawes, Kerri Strug, Dominique Moceanu, and the rest of the seven women who won Olympic gold for the United States.

Our properties were separated by a brick wall, low enough that I could use it as a balance beam. I spent hours out there jumping back and forth, trying out new tricks until I learned to stick the landing. My mother came out a few times to chide me for disturbing the neighbors, but Dr. Winston always sent her away.

"Doesn't bother me," he said before smiling at me. "Nine-point-six on that last routine."

I had long given up backyard gymnastics by the time that summer rolled around. I was no longer a kid, I was a moody teenager. At my lowest moments, I suspected I felt something akin to the darkness Dr. Winston must have been grappling with. He was the first person I knew who committed suicide. He confirmed what I sometimes secretly suspected: that maybe it's easier to just give up. How many times had he thought about it before he pulled the trigger?

Most of my life, I've had a morbid side I've managed to keep hidden under soccer uniforms and perfectly selected outfits. Outwardly, I was the last person you would expect to see at a cemetery in the middle of the night, but that was exactly where I sometimes went. There was a graveyard near our house that I liked to visit after everyone else had fallen asleep.

It was a strange kind of bravery, especially for a child who hated the night. It was a five-minute trip from my house to the cemetery. I always ran the whole way, feeling in control and alert. Once I got to the graveyard, I felt okay, almost understood. I looked at all the markers and wondered about the people buried beneath the ground. Had their lives been happy? Had they welcomed death like Dr. Winston? Or were they somewhere in between, constantly wondering if it was all worth it, like me?

My answer to that question could change from moment to moment. I wished I could ask Dr. Winston how he knew it was time.

So I decided to hold a séance the week after he died.

Which really wasn't very Christian of me at all. I was aware that the Bible explicitly warns against communicating with the dead. I'm sure my mom had entire verses about the evils of necromancy committed to memory. She was a woman who read the Bible every night before bed with a yellow high-lighter in hand. Surely, she'd be horrified to know I was planning to hold a séance in her own backyard; and that, honestly, was part of the appeal.

I scheduled the séance for Friday at midnight. My friends Stacey and Caitlyn were spending the night and they were both game for a little black magic. Not that we actually knew what we were doing, of course.

Our collective knowledge of how to hold a séance started and ended with *The Craft*.

"Do you have a Ouija board?" Stacey asked.

"No. Do we need one?"

"I don't know." She shrugged. "Probably not."

Short one Hasbro-branded divination tool, I decided we should find something that had belonged to Dr. Winston. Some object he had touched or a talisman to connect his spirit to the physical world. Without breaking and entering (and giving Mrs. Winston a heart attack), our options were limited to whatever we could find in the yard. I figured a few flowers from his garden would do just fine.

Once I was sure my parents were asleep I snuck over the fence. My friends kept watch while I swiped a few gardenias. I did know how crucial candles were for setting a séance-y atmosphere, and I'd taken a few from my mother's closet that afternoon. I don't remember seeing any Yankee Candles in *The Craft*, but Dr. Winston probably wasn't all that picky.

And who doesn't love the smell of pumpkin spice?

My friends and I took our séance stuff to a corner of the yard and sat down in a circle. We held hands and closed our eyes, so better to summon the spirits. I called for a moment of silence to channel the gods before I began to hum.

"Hmmmmm. Hmmmm. Dr. Winston, we are calling you back from the dead.

"Hmmmmmmmm. Can you hear me, Dr. Winston? We have these flowers from your garden.

"We're outside your house and we'd like to talk to you."

Stacey and Caitlyn added their own humming. "Hmmmmmmmmm. Hmmmmmmm."

"Dr. Winston, we wish you no harm. I'm sorry there's no Ouija board. I just want to know why you killed yourself."

"Hmmmmmmmmm. Hmmmmmmmm.

"If you're here right now, show us a sign."

Signwise, I was thinking maybe an object might topple over un-expectedly or the candles would go out. I would have taken a slight breeze as proof positive that the séance had worked, but the spirit of Dr. Winston wasn't fucking around. The words had hardly left my mouth before everything suddenly went dark. All the lights in my house, all the lights in his house. I jumped up and ran around so I could see the rest of the street. Pitch-black. Dr. Winston had shut down the power on the entire block.

"Holy shit," Caitlyn said.

"Oh my god." Stacey held her hand over her mouth. "Did that actually just happen?"

All three of us started screaming and laughing at the same time. We ran into my house and booked it straight up to my room. I locked the door and Stacey made sure the windows were shut. We kept laughing for a long time. *Yes, that actually happened.* For my friends, that was the end of it. Séance achieved. I began to regret running off like that. I might have played it off like a game, but my intentions had always been serious. If Dr. Winston really was communicating from the great beyond, what was he trying to say by blacking out the whole neighborhood?

Was he answering my question? Was it a warning, that it wasn't my time?

Maybe Dr. Winston knew what was in store for me over the next few years. Perhaps he was trying to scare me off. To shake me loose from having such an ambivalent relationship with death. Or maybe it was a much simpler message.

Listen to your mother, kid. Nothing good happens after midnight.

On the Monday after the accident, I woke up with a headache—but this was nothing new. I'd had migraines my whole life that were usually so severe they'd keep me home from school. Added to that was the fact I'd slammed my head into a pane of glass and had spent the rest of the weekend sobbing, so it was hardly a surprise that I didn't feel great.

I was almost glad for the headache, though, because there was no way

I could handle going to school. By then, most everyone had likely heard about my dramatic weekend and all the rumors that went along with it.

"Mom?" I came out of my room crying.

"What's wrong?"

"I think I have a migraine."

"Did you take your pill?"

"Yeah," I lied. "But my head still really hurts."

"Maybe we should take you to the hospital." Her voice was soft. "You could have a concussion."

She called my dad and took me to the hospital for an MRI. The scans came back clean, but my headache persisted. Truthfully, I might have played it up a little, but I was enjoying the extra attention. Back at home, my mom stayed by my side all day. She made me tea and sat with me on the couch, watching *SVU*.

Growing up, my mother was always there for me in my worst moments. An outsider looking in would probably see no reason why I lashed out at her so much. She was around as an everyday presence, taking me to tournaments and dropping me off at school. She dedicated her whole life to her family. But there were four of us to take care of, and sometimes it felt like I just wasn't seen or heard.

It wasn't surprising that she put her fear and anger aside to take care of me after my accident. I also knew that as soon as my dad was home and I was out of earshot, she'd be on his side, listening to him vent about my behavior and calming *him* down.

She was the constant peacemaker in our household. Since my brother and I inherited our temperaments from my dad, there was often a lot of peacemaking to do. When my father was home he was usually so exhausted and on edge that any little provocation would set him off. If he yelled, my mom would take his side, reminding us how hard he worked. If my brother was in a bad mood, she was there to comfort him, even if he was taking anger out on me. Sometimes it felt like a competition; three people with fiery temperaments fighting for one woman's attention. Add to that the baby sister who could do no wrong, and it's not hard to see why I started building up resentment.

I think I was seeking attention any way I could, and usually that meant being the loudest and most volatile person in the room. My anger was outsized and explosive, but it didn't always work. Usually, I just ended up in complete turmoil, and when my anger lessened I felt depression in its place.

Which was exactly what happened the week after the accident. When I woke up on Tuesday, I pretended my headache had gotten even worse. The thought of going back to school was still too unbearable. I felt tired and heavy. It was like a fog had crept in, some airborne misery that got in through my lungs and was spreading throughout my body.

I stayed shut up in my room all day. I stared at the posters on my wall. All my heroes were there: Mia Hamm, Tara Lipinski, Brandi Chastain the moment she famously whipped off her shirt after winning the World Cup.

Why hasn't Nick called me? He doesn't love me. Nobody does.

I felt isolated and disconnected. From my family, my friends, even myself. And it only got worse as the week went on. Every morning began with tears and claims that my head still hurt. In reality, I had stopped feeling anything at all. I had a test for those times it got really bad, to see if I could even register pain. I don't remember when I learned about the salt-and-ice-cube trick, the cold burn that comes from mixing salt and ice. I'd tap the salt out onto my arm and hold an ice cube over it until it melted. The pain should have been excruciating, but I hardly felt a thing.

On Thursday night I overheard my parents fighting. I knew it was about me. They were in the driveway, trying to be quiet, but I could hear every word from my window.

"Let her rest, Bill," my mother said. "You're too hard on her. That's probably why her headache won't go away."

"She doesn't have a headache."

"She's been sick all week. Her head's pounding. She flew through a windshield, for crying out loud. Of course she does."

"I saw the scans," my dad said. "Her head is fine."

"Stop it."

I ran my finger over my most recent cold burn.

"She's lying to us, Evelyn." I heard the anger in his voice. "How am I the only one seeing that her behavior just keeps getting worse?"

I pushed down on the wound as hard as I could. I felt nothing. No physical pain, no emotional pain. I was just empty. I wanted to be gone from my body altogether. I didn't even hesitate as I picked up the bottle of migraine medication. Without counting the number of pills, I tilted it back and swallowed it down with a swig of orange juice. I had no idea what would happen to me, if I'd die or if I wouldn't feel anything at all.

Whatever happens is for the best.

I wrote two letters. One was for my parents and the other was for Nick. To my parents, I confessed how sad I felt all the time. I knew they saw me as a disappointment and I was sorry for letting them down. But it wasn't like I was trying to be a problem.

I don't know why I am the way I am, okay? Maybe I was just born fucked-up.

To Nick, I simply asked why he didn't love me. Was it him or was it me? Maybe I had been born unlovable too.

I folded the letters in half. I wrote "Mom & Dad" on one and "Nick" on the other. Then I shut off the light and got into bed. The darkness made me shudder, yet I was completely calm about the pills in my stomach. For the second time in a week, I was about to go to sleep without knowing if I'd wake up in the morning. I whispered a prayer, more out of habit than any last attempt to save my immortal soul. It was a version of the same thing I said most nights.

Dear God, please protect my family. Mom, Dad, Philip, and Emily. Grammy and Poppy and Granddaddy Ed. Please don't let anything bad happen to them. I know I tell my parents I hate them, but I don't mean it. When I say I wish they were dead it's just because I'm angry. God, please help me find happiness and love. That is, if I wake up tomorrow. And please help those without food get food, those without homes find a home, and the people at war stay safe.

I know there are people less fortunate than me. I'm sorry for saying things I know I shouldn't say. Please forgive me.

I realized as I prayed that my mother was probably downstairs doing the same thing. Her hands clasped together, eyes closed. While I was apologizing for my flaws and asking God to help the needy, she was praying for her children—especially for me. She was asking God to keep me safe. To keep me alive.

Maybe it worked, or maybe I had used up another cat life. Either way, when morning came the sunlight woke me up just like it always did. I wasn't dead or in the hospital, I was still in my perfect pink room, staring at my Mia Hamm poster. The pills didn't seem to have done much damage at all.

Ironically, my only problem was that I now had a pounding headache.

Chapter 3

THE DAY MY family moved back to South Carolina was the day I started talking about getting the hell out of South Carolina. I was about six years old, a California kid at heart feeling suffocated by the smallness of my new Southern town. I remember wanting to go to boarding school as soon as I learned that such a thing existed. My parents weren't opposed to the idea. It was casually floated that I might go away for high school, but for whatever reason I remained at home for what turned into a pretty tumultuous freshman year.

The topic of boarding school was reintroduced after the accident. I think my parents realized that keeping me at home had been a mistake. I was more eager than ever to leave all the fighting and gossip behind.

Episcopal was a historic prep school in Alexandria, Virginia. It catered to the well-heeled, blue-blooded set: kids who played sports and excelled academically and went off to good colleges. It wasn't New York or Los Angeles, like I wanted. But the DC suburb wasn't South Carolina either.

So when my mother picked me up one afternoon and told me I had an appointment with an "educational consultant," I didn't think twice. I figured it was the next step in the process of getting me into Episcopal. As the appointment progressed I began to suspect that something else was going on. Like usual, my anger got the best of me that afternoon. And that sealed my fate.

A woman met us in the waiting room outside her office and introduced herself as Lynn Anne Moore. She wore khaki slacks, brown loafers, and a pale blue sweater set—the uniform of the Southern WASP. With her tight, judgmental smile and a *bless your heart* attitude, people like Lynn Anne were exactly the reason I was so eager to get out of South Carolina.

Lynn Anne led me into her office. It was blandly tasteful, with watercolor paintings on the walls and a bouquet of yellow flowers in a blue ceramic vase. She sat behind her desk and gestured for me to take the armchair on the other side.

"Good afternoon, Elizabeth."

"Hi." I smiled, trying to make a good impression. "Nice to meet you."

I was expecting a conversation or an interview. I thought Lynn Anne was screening me for Episcopal or looking to match me with a similar school. She hardly asked more than a few cursory questions before she brought out the tests. One, three, five, a million. I lost count as Lynn Anne administered psychological tests for the rest of the entire afternoon.

I tried to go with it at first. I knew something wasn't right when she pulled out a stack of painted cards. Like everyone else in the universe, I knew an inkblot test when I saw one. While I wasn't exactly an expert on the methods of Dr. Rorschach (or even the spelling), I was pretty sure Episcopal didn't much care whether I saw a bat, a butterfly, or a pile of shit.

"How much longer is this gonna take?"

"Why?" Lynn Anne said. "Does it make you uncomfortable?"

"Not really. I'm just kind of hungry."

And bored. Not to mention pretty sick of looking at your condescending face.

"Let's get through it then."

The next test was like a less abstract version of the Rorschach. Instead of amorphous blobs, the cards showed drawings of people in ambiguous situations. An anguished man standing next to an impassive priest. A child reading with his eyes closed. The back of a weeping figure, collapsed over a bed frame with her hand pressed to her forehead.

"Maybe she has a migraine," I said about that one.

The next card depicted a half-naked woman and a disheveled man. The woman was lying in bed, lifeless or maybe dead, and the man was standing with his face turned away.

"It looks like the man just did something to the woman," I said.

Lynn Anne nodded, waiting for me to say more.

"Like he hurt her or . . . something."

She nodded and jotted down a note. I tried not to think about what she might be writing. We still had half the stack to get through, and I started giving increasingly stupid answers.

"They're stealing his wallet."

"That's a woman asking her boyfriend if she looks fat."

"Whoa. This guy kinda looks like my friend Jason."

Lynn Anne didn't seem amused, and I was getting punchy. She slid a thick questionnaire and a number 2 pencil across her desk.

"Last part," she said. "Take all the time you need."

For me, what's right is whatever I can get away with.
True.

I think I'm superior to other people.
False.

When having a good time with my friends I can get pretty drunk.
True.

I'm very good at making up excuses to get myself out of trouble.
True. What teenager isn't?

I enjoy thinking about sex.
False. Mind your own fucking business.

I think success is based on survival of the fittest and am not concerned about the losers.

True. I'm an athlete. That's the whole point.

I do what I what, when I want, without worrying about the effect I have on others.

True? I don't know. It's not like I want to hurt anyone.

I don't see anything wrong with using others to get what I want.

False. What the fuck?

If I hurt someone's feelings, I feel a sense of remorse or guilt.

True. Come on. I'm not a monster.

My answers were a mix of vague honesty and I-don't-give-a-fuck. I suppose I just didn't think any of it mattered. It simply did not cross my mind that I was filling out a questionnaire to determine whether I was a psychopath. Or that every dumb or sarcastic answer I gave about an inkblot could—and would—be used against me.

Fifteen-year-old me had no idea that Lynn Anne Moore had all the power in the world that day. It certainly never occurred to me that she could use her power to ruin my life.

I was out of there the second I finished bubbling in my last true/false statement. I was hungry and mad that I'd wasted an afternoon. My mother was waiting for me in the lobby. She sat on the couch with her legs crossed politely, reading a magazine as though things were completely normal.

"Hi," she said. "How did it go?"

"Pretty bad. Can we leave now?"

I pushed through the doors without waiting for my mom. I stood by the car, getting more pissed off by the second. She was still smiling, but I could see a strain starting to form in the creases around her mouth.

"What's wrong, sweetheart?"

"Seriously, Mom? What's wrong?" My fists balled up in anger. "Why do you make me do stupid shit like this? Do you hate me or just think I'm crazy?"

"You're my daughter," she said. "I could never hate you."

"So you think I'm crazy, then. Good to know."

"You're not crazy, Elizabeth."

"Then why did you make me take all those fucking tests?"

She sighed. She had failed to calm me down, and I could tell she was bracing herself for an outburst. So I gave her one.

"Will you just take me to Episcopal already?" My voice rose. "Or are you trying to send me to one of those military schools that Dad always threatens Philip with?"

"Elizabeth. Calm down."

"Why?" I was yelling now. "Why am I even here? Those tests were for crazy people, Mom."

"Lower your voice."

"No!"

"You're making a scene," she said.

It was true. Lynn Anne Moore heard the noise and came marching toward us as quickly as her loafers would carry her.

"Elizabeth Gilpin," she said, scolding me, "don't disrespect your mother."

"Mind your own business," I said. "You don't know anything about me or my family."

She gave my mom a pointed look, which only infuriated me further.

"I fucking hate you both," I said.

Dark clouds were gathering inside my head. I didn't hate my mom and I knew she didn't hate me either. I just felt so misunderstood. In retrospect, I realize there was no way she could have understood me when I didn't even know what was wrong myself. All I could feel was raw emotion, that lightning bolt of rage, and once it struck there was no room for any other feeling.

I shoved past my mother to get inside the car. If I hurt her, I didn't mean to. But going by the look on Lynn Anne's face, I might as well have been a serial killer. Her expression, locked in my memory forever, makes me feel like that moment more than any other truly sealed my fate.

What happened to me next was a perfect storm of bad choices, bad advice, and bad luck. Maybe my fate was sealed the moment I walked out of that meeting. Or maybe there was still a chance I could end up at Episcopal—if I made a real effort to get along with my family and stayed on my best behavior. But I just couldn't control my anger when it came to my parents. It was like I was allergic to my mom and dad.

Had I known what this would cost me, I'm sure I would have found an emotional antihistamine. But how was I to know? I couldn't avoid a place I didn't even know existed.

If my future was still undecided when I left the consultation, two incidents helped push it along. The first happened just a few weekends later. It was the spring formal and I was going with Steve, a friend's older brother.

Melanie came over the afternoon of the dance and we got ready together. I had a silk sweetheart-neck gown picked out for the occasion, long and navy blue. Melanie helped me tie my hair back into a sleek ponytail with two strands curled in the front to frame my face. My mom drove us to our friend Jenna's house, where everyone was posing for photos in the backyard. Steve put his arm around me and I smiled. But I was ready for the photo part of the evening to be over and for the drinking part to begin.

When the parents left we all piled into our rented limo and headed to a pre-dance dinner. We passed around water bottles filled with pilfered alcohol. The problem with this mode of underage drinking, stealthy as it might have been, was that it was impossible to keep track of how much we'd had to drink. We had pure vodka in the bottles and were mixing it with the glasses of orange juice we kept ordering at the restaurant. Which was a pretty suspicious beverage to pair with Italian food, especially as we were drinking glass after glass and signaling the waiter for more.

Now, I wasn't exactly a novice when it came to drinking. It wasn't uncommon for me to throw up on a Saturday night, and I'd blacked out once or twice. But this time was different. I either drank too fast or much more than I realized because pretty quickly I felt way too drunk. While everyone else ordered dessert, I escaped to the bathroom and became acquainted with the porcelain.

I know I was in the stall for a while. Someone must have checked on me, but I can't remember an interaction. I probably sent them away, slurring that I was fine. *Just give me a minute.* A minute that turned into ten and then, without thinking it through, I had called my mother.

"Mo-oom. I need you to come pick me up."

The same part of my brain that thought calling my mom was a good idea was dead-set on waiting for her outside. But standing up wasn't really an option, so I made a bed out of the stoop. When my mother arrived I was sprawled out on the concrete in my once-perfect silk dress and formerly sleek hair. My mom picked up my shoes and helped me to the car where I promptly passed out until the next morning.

It wasn't my finest hour. And the fact that my parents didn't scold me was probably an indication that they had already decided to send me away. Or, at the very least, they were discussing their options. They were probably just waiting for the school year to be over. And maybe, just maybe, I still could have turned things around if it hadn't been for the other thing.

The other thing was weed. Specifically, an eighth of it—which I had bought several weeks before. It cost me fifty dollars, plus an extra ten for a glass smoking bowl, and I didn't even smoke it. Not one single nugget. I don't even know why the hell I bought it. Probably to seem cool, to feel like I could hang with the older kids who actually liked weed. Some part of me probably just wanted to know if I could get away with it. I stashed the weed in a little pouch and hid it under the slats of my bed. It was kind of thrilling to have a secret, although I forgot all about it pretty quickly.

So when I came home one day to my father yelling that I was a pothead, my initial reaction was complete outrage like usual. It was the pee test all over again! As soon as he produced the pouch, the jig was up. There was no point in trying to explain that I hadn't smoked any of it. Even I knew how stupid that sounded. All I could do was accuse my parents of snooping around my room.

"You're grounded until further notice," my dad said. "School, sports, and church. That's it."

Chapter 4

SCHOOL, SPORTS, AND church, that's it. The terms of my grounding actually weren't all that bad. Finals were approaching, which meant a few weeks of studying, but then my freshman year would be over. As for sports, I'd begun checking out more and more. I was good enough that I could go through the motions without really trying. I could give it my half effort and get by.

I'd been going to church for many years, starting the day with Sunday school and then meeting up with my family for "Big Church." I never minded Sunday school. In fact, as a kid, I enjoyed the picture books that showed Jesus tending to his flock and the animals on Noah's ark. The Big Church service portion wasn't so bad either—even though my mom always made us sit up front. It was a little boring, and I was always starving by the time we got out, but I passed the time by doodling in the program.

It was mostly the people that I had a problem with; all that Southern hypocrisy. I had learned the lesson of false virtue a few years back. It was just another Sunday and everyone was dressed in the standard church uniform: Lilly Pulitzer printed dresses for the women and Vineyard Vines ties for men and boys. I was no exception and neither was my neighbor, a girl about my age who was a troublemaker like me. Her skirt was pressed, her hair was smooth, and one of her eyes was freshly black and blue.

A few days later I asked her how she got it. She told me without hesitation that her father hit her. I don't know if she told anyone else, and I have no idea if the rest of the congregation suspected abuse. But I do know that on that Sunday, most of the congregation pretended not to notice. Those who asked if she was okay accepted whatever bullshit lie her family offered and went on with their business.

It wasn't surprising. This was how the people in my town dealt with hard issues, especially if the families with the problems had some money and went to church. By the end of my freshman year, I was over church just like I was over everything else in my life. In spite of my feelings, my parents still made me go almost every Sunday.

So when they agreed to let me spend the night at Jenna's with the caveat that I be ready to go early Sunday morning, I didn't think twice. It sounded just like our regular routine. I didn't see the sleepover as the giant red flag that in retrospect it so obviously was.

My parents picked me up around nine. I could tell something was off the moment I got in the car, still wearing my pajamas. They seemed tense about something but were acting overly cheerful.

"Morning!" My mom's voice was even higher than usual. "Have fun?"

I nodded. I was hungry and wondered if there were pancakes at home. But we weren't going back to our house. My dad missed the turn onto our street and kept driving in the opposite direction.

"Where are we going?"

My parents said nothing. They shared a significant glance and I saw my dad's eyes flick to the rearview mirror. I turned around and looked in the back row of seats. I noticed my pink baby blanket and a pillow sitting on top of a tote bag.

"Where are you taking me?"

"To camp," my mom said. "Summer camp."

I used to love summer camp. Growing up, I went to some sort of outdoor sleepaway program pretty much every year. My favorite was an aviation-challenge camp in the woods where I got to play with flight simulators and completed a series of special-ops missions. That was all little-kid stuff. I'd explicitly told my parents I wanted to spend the summer at home with my friends, and now they were tricking me into going anyway.

It made me furious. I felt betrayed and hurt, like they were just trying to get rid of me.

"I don't want to go to camp," I said. "I told you that."

My mother turned around and smiled. "I know. But your dad and I think it'll be good for you to spend some time in a new environment."

"I don't need a new environment. I want to go home."

My parents were silent.

"Did you hear me?" I was screaming now. "I said, take me home!"

"Lower your voice," my father said.

"No. Not until you turn the car around."

My dad's face was getting red. I could see the rage in his eyes when he took his gaze off the road and looked directly at me.

"This isn't optional," my father said. "You're going to a camp like Outward Bound. You need some structure in your life, Elizabeth."

It was like an explosion had gone off. My dad and I began to scream at each other, using all the ammo we'd been stockpiling for years.

"You're just trying to get rid of me."

"We're trying to help you," my mom said.

"This isn't the kind of help I need."

We went back and forth like that for a while, a tennis match of anger. My mother looked mortified, trying in vain to referee.

"Okay," she said. "Everyone just calm down."

"I'll calm down if you turn the fucking car around and take me home."

"But you love camping."

"Why are you still pretending this is supposed to be fun for me? Why are you always pretending?"

My mom looked up helplessly at my dad. He shook his head.

"Absolutely not," he said. "We talked about this and she's going. No matter what manipulative shit she pulls."

I racked my brain for some manipulative shit to pull. I began calling every number I had saved in my flip phone, hoping someone would pick up. Melanie and Nick didn't answer, but I got Jenna on the second try.

"Jenna, you have to help me." I spoke as quickly as I could. "My parents have totally lost it. They're crazy liars and they're trying to take me to some Outward Bound bullshit."

My family was close with Jenna's family and I could see the effect the call was having on my mom. She looked horrified and when she turned to my father I thought she was about to take my side. But my dad seemed to anticipate this. He put his hand on her knee and shook his head. My mom nodded and said nothing.

This made me even more furious. Like usual, my mom was on everyone's side at once. She wanted to placate both me and my father, but that was impossible. So she did nothing. I felt trapped and decided I needed to get out of this car one way or another.

I looked out the window. The highway was relatively empty and I tried not to focus on the pavement rushing by. In one quick motion, I unbuckled my seat belt and reached for the door handle. I would have done it too. I really would have. I opened the door with every intention of jumping. But while I had played Air Force for a week at aviation camp, my dad had actually lived it. He had the instincts and the reflexes to anticipate my move. I was partly out the door when his hand gripped my arm and shoved me back into the car.

I heard my dad click the safety lock the same moment I saw red and blue lights flashing from behind.

"Oh, come on," he said. "You have to be kidding me."

He slowed down and glanced in the rearview mirror. There was a cop car right behind us. The officers must have seen the door swing open.

Kidnapping, trafficking. This is my chance.

As my father maneuvered to the shoulder I tried to think of the worst things I could claim. I needed to convince the cops that I had been stolen and was being taken away against my will. That actually described the situation pretty well. I just left out the part about being related to my parents.

It almost worked too. The officers came around to my door and addressed me directly.

"What's going on here? Miss, are you okay?"

I shook my head violently. "No! I need help. I'm being kidnapped."

"Officer," my father said, "she's our daughter."

"He's lying."

The officer peered through the window to get a better look. He had his hand on his waistband. He moved to the front of the car while his partner kept watch.

"I'm going to need you both to get out of the vehicle."

My mother seemed truly shaken, but my father was over being worried. He was just done with me and my bullshit.

The cops led my parents off to the side of the road where they had a brief conversation. It didn't last more than a minute, and I could see the officers shaking their heads. One of them escorted my mom and dad back to the car. The cop looked at me in the backseat.

"Have fun at summer camp," he said.

We drove off in silence. As upset as I was, I knew I'd been bested. My dad was seething with the quiet rage I knew so well. But something had shifted in my mother. It was all too much for her—the screaming, the cops, the fact that I was now crying. We hadn't gotten more than a few more miles down the road when she turned to my dad and sighed.

"Bill. Let's just take her home."

My dad inhaled sharply. He didn't say anything, he just veered off the highway and got back on going the other direction. I knew a huge fight was coming for my parents. As always, I was a source of friction.

When we got back, Jenna was waiting for me outside our house. I'd called her a second time to see if she could pick me up. I jumped out of the car and got straight into hers. I didn't ask my parents and they didn't try to stop me. I was so angry at what they'd try to do, but at least I didn't have to go to summer camp.

Except I was never actually going to summer camp. There was no plan to send me to Outward Bound. The place my parents picked out for me ended up being much crueler and more abusive than a so-called leadership program.

I would find that out a few short weeks later. For the first month of my summer break I went to parties and stayed over at Melanie's. I drank and spent time with Nick. I avoided my parents as much as possible. I wasn't even offended when my mom planned a vacation for my brother and sister without including me.

Little did I know the trip was about me, after all. With everyone out of the house it would be so much easier to have me kidnapped.

Chapter 5

I WONDERED IF Mrs. Winston was watching from her window the night I was taken away. The elderly woman next door never seemed to sleep, not since the incident with Dr. Winston. She spent all day and night sitting in her breakfast nook drinking cup after cup of coffee and staring out the window.

Did she see my captors arrive? Two hulking figures dressed in black, entering my house in the middle of the night. What did she think when they reemerged with their prisoner? The angry girl from next door who once upon a time pretended to be an Olympic gymnast in the backyard.

Did she think I was being kidnapped? Did it occur to her to call the cops?

I was the criminal. That was how I felt, at least, manhandled and forced into the back of the black SUV. The doors and windows were child-locked, but the female escort still insisted on sitting with me in the backseat. Apparently I was such a flight risk I couldn't even wear my shoes lest I kick through the glass, wriggle through the broken window, and disappear into oncoming traffic.

They must think I'm an action hero. An action hero in baby-blue pajama pants from the Limited Too.

Not that the thought of escape wasn't tempting. If the woman hadn't made a point of unzipping her duffel bag full of hand-cuffs and restraints, I might have gotten physical. Instead, I slid all the way up against the door, trying to get as far away as possible from her.

Will she actually use those handcuffs on me?

This is a nightmare. But I'll wake up any minute now. Then I'll head downstairs for chocolate chip pancakes and start my day.

I didn't wake up, because there was nothing to wake up from. I forced my eyes forward as the car pulled out. I didn't want to turn around and see my father's face. I also didn't want to turn around and *not* see my father's face. I was pretty sure he'd gone back inside the house. Maybe he was even in my room, relieved that his problem child was being taken away.

"And we're off," the man said. "Easy as pie."

Fuck you. I wanted to say the words out loud, but I didn't. I hated these people as much as I'd ever hated anyone, and I didn't even know their names. She was just a broad-shouldered, severe woman and he was a guy with a receding hairline and a self-satisfied expression.

Fuck you, fuck you, fuck you.

I watched my neighborhood recede from view. I had no idea then how much of my life was disappearing right alongside it. I couldn't have imagined the truth: that I'd never swim competitively or play soccer again. I wouldn't make another honor roll, wouldn't win another trophy. All the things I thought of as my life's achievements were becoming worthless and moot.

We turned the corner and Melanie's house came into view up ahead. I wanted to scream. I tried to scream so loud she'd wake up and come running to my rescue. I couldn't make a sound, though. I was paralyzed with shock, shrieking on the inside yet completely silent where it mattered. The familiar homes faded away and the SUV started racking up miles. I had no idea where we were going, but I wasn't about to ask. So I sat in silence, angry and confused.

I couldn't stop replaying the morning over and over in my head, wondering if there was any way I could have stopped it. But my father's expression was crystal clear. I saw him mouth the words *I'm sorry* again and again, practically shrugging. I knew his mind was totally made up.

Pretty soon there was no city left at all. Just the wide highway that split the greenery in half, a few scattered cows, and the occasional fast-food restaurant. We passed a sign letting me know we were no longer in South Carolina and something switched on inside me. The shock was waning and a plan began to form in its place.

If I could just get out of the car, I'd be able to run. I could head straight for the woods and hide out for a while, until it was safe to find a phone. These ogres might be bigger and stronger, but I was definitely faster. All I needed was a reason for them to pull over. A reason that would require them to give me back my shoes.

"I have to pee."

The man looked at me in the rearview mirror. He laughed.

"I said, I have to pee."

"She speaks," he said. "I was starting to think you'd turned into a mute."

"You're in luck," the woman said. "We have to stop for gas soon."

I continued scheming on the way to the next exit. The car pulled to a stop inside a grimy rest stop. *Perfect.* The woman walked around the car and opened my door, giving me very little room to maneuver.

"Can I have my shoes?"

She handed me my sneakers. After I slipped them on, the woman gripped me by the arm and led me through the gas station toward the stinking restrooms in the back. When we reached the door I tried to break free of the woman's grip.

"Hang on. You don't think you're going in there alone, do you?"

"I am not gonna pee in front of you."

"Fine. I'll wait out here and you can leave the door open." She smiled. "Don't worry, no one's going to look. I'll be right here the whole time."

I went into the bathroom, upset that my plan was a bust. Back in the car, I relinquished my shoes. Instead of getting back on the highway, we drove a little farther up the road, halting at a row of fast-food joints.

"You should eat."

"I'm not hungry," I said, realizing that I was really, really hungry.

"Hey, I don't care one way or the other. But this is the last real meal you're gonna get for a while. So maybe suck it up and get some Chick-fil-A?"

I crossed my arms, stewing. "Chicken biscuit, I guess."

Back on the highway, the view became increasingly sparse. We were traveling away from even the occasional cow, heading straight for the mountains. I took small bites of my sandwich, almost too anxious to chew. Soon we were crowded by dense clusters of oak trees in all directions.

If I had a map, I would have known we were in a southern region of the Appalachian Mountains. But all I had to orient myself was an endless stretch of identical dirt and trees, dappled in the afternoon light. Miles went by without any sign of human habitation before we finally reached a double-wide trailer plopped down right in the middle of nowhere.

My captors led me straight inside, where a middle-aged woman had clearly been waiting for my arrival. A plaque on a small desk spelled out an unremarkable name, Jill or Ann or Jan. She ran her icy eyes up and down before landing on my face.

"Elizabeth, I assume?"

"Don't bother," the male escort said. "She doesn't talk."

My captors signed the paperwork Jan handed them and turned to me.

"Well, this is good-bye," the man said. "Good luck, kid."

Just like that they were gone, leaving my life as abruptly as they'd swooped into it. I felt a pang of something like fear or regret. Stockholm syndrome had crept up on me and I was almost sad to see them go. Sure, they'd tormented me all day and not one minute had passed without me actively hating them, but they were the devils I knew. The fear of whatever was about to happen to me next sat in my gut in the shape of a massive knot. I wanted to run after them and beg them to kidnap me again.

"Don't you even think about it," Jan said. I realized I'd been looking longingly at the door. The woman eyed me suspiciously while she riffled through the folder with my name on it. I didn't know what was in there at the time, but I'd later learn that she was looking at a series of waivers. Apparently, my parents had signed quite a few of them. Documents that listed a series of risks that could befall your troubled teen should you decide to ship them off to the woods. Short-term injury, long-term injury, psychological damage, death.

We are not accountable for any bad shit that happens, basically. *Do you accept?*

Yes. My parents signed them all. *We accept.*

I don't believe they knew quite what they were signing off on, though. Because no one really did. It was a time before the internet could offer up ready feedback and quick access to real accounts. Before the take-downs circulated—exposés on the wilderness therapy industry. Programs like mine that operated from the most remote and unchecked places in the country. Where no one was watching and tragic things happened all the time.

Cause of death: Dehydration. Cause of death: Hyperthermia. Cause of death: Internal bleeding. Head trauma, spider bite, severed artery, suicide by hanging, suicide by pocketknife.

Cause of death: My first-ever strip search?

"Clothes off and arms up," Jan said. "Let's get this over with."

"I'm not taking my clothes off."

"Then we'll do it the hard way. And don't try anything stupid. Cops are a phone call away."

I could tell I didn't really have a choice. I stripped down until I was wearing only my underwear.

"'Clothes off' means clothes off. All of them."

Humiliated, I got completely naked.

"Spin around. Arms out."

This is insane.

"Three rotations."

How is this even legal?

"Squat and cough."

Squat? And COUGH?

I shut my eyes and waited for Jan to finish humiliating me.

"You're clear."

Yeah. I'm aware.

Instead of returning my T-shirt and pajama pants, Jan handed me my new uniform. It consisted of a giant T-shirt in bright, inmate orange and a pair of cargo pants. They had zippers at the knees, a pants/shorts two-for-one. I put on the clothes and a pair of stiff hiking boots while Jan fumbled around inside a cabinet.

She returned with a cup wrapped in plastic. "So, what are we gonna find?"

"Huh?"

"What drugs? Easier just to tell me now."

"I'm not on any drugs."

"Hey, you can lie to yourself all you want. It's your life to ruin."

"Why would I lie? You're literally about to drug-test me."

"Yeah, well." She handed me the cup. "Guess we'll know soon enough."

I walked into the bathroom. All day, I'd felt like I was sinking. It seemed impossible that I could go any lower.

"Door stays open," Jan said.

I unwrapped the cup. For the second time that afternoon, I peed while someone waited just a few feet away. Jan took my urine sample with a gloved hand and shoved a backpack in my direction. It was one of those giant hiking rucksacks, stuffed to the gills as though I were about to embark on a carefree summer of bumming around Europe.

The contents of the pack were anything but romantic. They included two plastic tarps, a sleeping bag, Crocs, a roll of toilet paper, some rope, and three pairs of unflattering underwear.

Jan clucked impatiently. "Time to go. Backpack on."

I hoisted the thing over my shoulders. It weighed almost as much as I did, and I stumbled out the door. An ancient, rusty truck idled by the trailer. The driver was a young guy named Nate, and to my horror, I found him extremely attractive. On any other day I probably would have enjoyed this. But it was this day, the worst day of my life, and I hated Nate just for being part of it.

The engine actually started right up, and Nate took off down the bumpy road. He drove without a map, navigating by memory. It was a blur of right and left turns until, finally, orange dots appeared in the fading light. We pulled up to a makeshift campsite, where a dozen or so teenage girls sat cross-legged in the dirt. They seemed to be eating, though I couldn't even begin to guess the contents of their bowls.

All I knew was that they looked absolutely miserable, even more miserable than I felt. With their dirty faces and greasy hair, they looked almost feral, transformed by the woods.

Panic set in and I turned my pleading eyes to Nate. "Please don't leave me here."

He chuckled, like he'd heard this plea a thousand times. He tossed my backpack from the truck and it nearly knocked me over. He grabbed my arm and marched me across the campsite. Away from the silent girls sitting on the dirt and toward the staff, six women talking in a circle of Crazy Creek chairs.

"Welcome to camp, Thirteen."

"I'm fifteen," I said.

"Not your age," Nate said. "Your number. You'll catch on."

The counselors didn't seem much older than me. They looked like college kids, in charge for the first time and reveling in their power.

"We use numbers a lot here," one of the women said. "Whenever you're away from the main camp or in your shelter. So anytime you're not right in front of us, you'd better be yelling out your number. Or we'll have to assume you're up to something. And this is the fourth group of campers out here, so collectively you're Group Four."

"I want to call my parents," I said.

"Oh, there's no making calls out here."

Another woman grinned like a Cheshire cat. "In fact, you're not even supposed to be talking to the other girls. Not while you're on Earth Phase."

Earth Phase. What the hell is that?

"Your mentor will explain everything tomorrow. For now, why don't you go find a spot away from the group and journal about your feelings."

Journal about my feelings? Are you kidding me?

There were no words for what I was feeling that day, only a mess of scribbled ink. I was experiencing every negative emotion at once: fear, anger, sadness, confusion. At the same time, I was completely numb from the shock of it all. I don't know how long I sat by myself in the eerie quiet of the woods. It could have been ten minutes or two hours. Eventually, a staffer retrieved me and my still-blank journal.

"It's time to set up your sleeping bag," she said. "You're with us tonight."

She walked me over to the large staff shelter and watched as I pulled out my sleeping bag. She had me roll it out in the tight space between two beds, so close we'd basically be sharing oxygen. I wanted to scream. All day, I'd been forced to give up more and more control. My life didn't belong to me anymore. I was a toy for these strangers to manipulate and taunt, and everyone's favorite game seemed to be taking away my shoes.

"Hand 'em over." The staffer snapped her fingers impatiently.

"Why?"

"Are you kidding? Try running off in Crocs and see how far you get. Your parents told us about the stunt you pulled on the highway."

I gave her my boots. My stupid, uncomfortable boots that I didn't want anyway. As I tried to get even slightly comfortable inside my sleeping bag I heard the other girls moving around outside.

"Group Four," a staffer yelled. "Time for bed."

A few minutes later, the footsteps stopped. And the numbers started.

"One."

"Two."

"Three."

Each voice was different. Most of them sounded bored and automatic, they knew the drill and were executing like good soldiers.

Ten. Eleven. Twelve. Then silence.

"Well?"

"Huh?"

"You aren't exempt." She folded her hands. "Like I said...if I don't hear you, I'll assume you're up to something. And then I'll be mad and you'll be in trouble."

"THIRTEEN." I yelled it at the top of my lungs.

"Atta girl."

Thirteen. That was my identity. I wasn't Elizabeth, the soccer player from South Carolina with a soft spot for pancakes and action movies. Because she no longer existed. I was a number, just another girl in an orange T-shirt, that was totally interchangeable. If one of the T-shirts left, I'd become Twelve. Then I'd become Eleven. The role of Thirteen would be played by someone new, the next troubled teen to arrive, pleading, in a rusty pickup truck.

Chapter 6

IF I SLEPT at all that first night, it was only for minutes at a time. Whenever I turned or shifted, if I even breathed a little too loudly, I'd be blinded by a flashlight shining directly in my eyes. They called it "run watch," and it felt like a great excuse to get in a little psychological torture. Zipped in my sleeping bag, surrounded by staffers on every side, how could I possibly have tried to escape? I didn't even have my shoes. Until suddenly I did, when they were hitting me on the shoulder like an aggravating alarm clock. Waking me from ten or twenty minutes of sleep.

"Time to get up."

I blinked in the obnoxious face of a staffer.

"Pick up the pace. This isn't a hotel."

"No shit," I said under my breath.

"What was that?"

"Nothing."

Outside, the sun was just starting to rise. The chill was gone from the air, but it wasn't yet hot. Birds were chirping and everyone else stayed mercifully silent. If I hadn't been so angry, if the atmosphere had been less Cell Block D, I might have even said it was a beautiful morning.

Instead, I fumed my way through the encampment. I found a tree off to the side and sat down in the dirt, arms crossed. I wasn't yet welcome to join the group, which was perfectly fine by me. I was so pissed off I could barely even hear my own thoughts above the monologue running in my head. *I'm so fucking mad. I'm so fucking mad. No one talk to me, I'm too fucking mad.*

The other girls were eating breakfast. Somewhere between mush and paste, the cuisine was a scoop of dried oats soaked in filtered water from the creek. *No way am I eating that, not a chance in hell.* Yesterday's chicken biscuit would have to sustain me for a little longer. I was fantasizing about the hunger strike I'd go on when a staffer named Kendra appeared with my backpack.

"How come you aren't eating, Thirteen?"

Kendra looked even younger than the other counselors, but she had a bitterness in her that should have taken a lifetime to acquire. She was one of the counselors I slept next to and she wielded her flashlight like a weapon.

"Not hungry," I said.

"Impossible. You haven't eaten since you got here."

"I haven't been hungry. Maybe I'll never be hungry."

"Go ahead," Kendra said. "Starve yourself to death."

I shrugged. *Fine.*

"Here's the deal, though." She was enjoying herself. "You don't eat, you don't get off Earth Phase. You don't get off Earth Phase? That means more escorts and another long car ride. To somewhere much, much worse."

Worse than this boondock prison? Yeah, I'll take my chances.

Something told me I wasn't going to win this battle. That my opponent had gone through this routine before, probably with more than a few of these other girls.

"Your choice, though. I'm not gonna force you or anything."

She knew she'd won. Already she was pulling things out of my backpack. A tin bowl, shiny and new, a spoon, and a ziplock bag containing one carefully rationed serving of dry oatmeal. *Et voilà,* breakfast was served.

I added water to the bowl and waited for the oats to soften into paste. She rattled off a list of rules. I was to eat my full ration of oats. I must drink exactly four bottles of water a day. No funny business and no getting sneaky about hydration. I would have to show her the contents of my water bottle several times a day.

"Full, half full, and empty," she said, pointing to lines in the plastic. "Can't have you dying of dehydration."

No hunger strike, no thirst strike? I could still protest in my own way. I began to hoover the oatmeal, barely chewing before it was down my throat. Bite after bite, I kept my expression blank and made myself swallow. Kendra looked down and smirked. A fly was getting cozy in my bowl, excreting all over my breakfast. But I didn't let it faze me. I swatted it away and ate even faster, forcing down the chalky sludge, insect shit and all. I finished my full ration, by some miracle of God, and started chugging from my water bottle. I made eye contact with Kendra and gulped without pause until I reached the halfway point.

She was silent for a moment. Then she rolled her eyes. "Go wash your bowl."

I felt a twinge of satisfaction and a rising wave of nausea. I got up slowly, determined to keep the contents of my stomach in check. The other girls were bent over with their water jugs, washing up. I watched them for a moment and a thin, light-haired girl caught my attention. She was holding her bowl out in front of her, peering into it. Checking her reflection.

I watched her for a moment. Then I rinsed my bowl and held it just as she'd done, trying to find myself inside this sad, inverted mirror. I was blurry and faded, hardly even there. In other words, I looked exactly the way I felt. I glanced back at the girl and wondered if she was experiencing the same thing.

How long has she been here? Does she do this every day? How many times has she seen her own reflection as some warped, shapeless thing?

But I was reading too much into things. The girl wasn't soul-searching,

I realized when I saw her pinch her face. She was using the bowl as a mirror in a desperate attempt to pluck her eyebrows.

"Are you Elizabeth?"

Another girl popped up next to me, smiling. She seemed far too peppy for the situation we were in, and I briefly wondered if some girls came here by choice.

"I'm Polly. Your Earth Phase mentor."

It was maybe the tenth time someone had used that term without explaining what the hell it meant. Part of me was curious, but I mostly didn't even want to know.

"It's okay for us to talk," Polly said. "Since I'm showing you around. But normally we're not supposed to. Unless we're in earshot of the staff."

I nodded.

"And don't forget to call out your number," she said. "Even if you're just going to the bathroom. Or they come after you."

"Got it."

"You got here last night?"

"Yep," I said.

"Brutal. The first couple days are the worst."

"Yeah."

"But it'll get easier. After a week or two. Three at the most."

"Oh, I'm not staying that long," I said. And at the moment I was confident it was the truth.

"You're gonna try and run?" Polly said. "I wouldn't. They'll catch you. They'll sic the cops on you, whatever it takes. They always do."

"Then I'll figure something else out." I was stammering. "I mean, I shouldn't even be here. Someone screwed up or . . . I don't know."

Polly gave me another cheerful smile, but this time it was laced with pity. Her attitude was starting to get under my skin. She was so positive, like a helpful tour guide rattling off rules as we walked around the camp. She explained where to sleep, how close to stay at night. Something I didn't quite catch about bears. We were heading deeper into the woods.

"Hey, Polly," I said. "Why are you here?"

Polly turned. "I'm your mentor!"

"I mean, like why are you here in the woods? What did you do?"

She shrugged. "I had sex with too many boys."

"How many boys?"

Ten? Twenty? What has Polly been up to?

"Three. *Promiscuous* was the word my parents used."

"Oh." I raised my eyebrows.

"They were right, obviously." Polly smiled. "How many people have *you* had sex with?" Polly said.

"Technically none."

"*None?* Come on. Lying doesn't work here."

"I'm not lying," I said. And I really wasn't. Technically, I hadn't slept with a single boy.

"Drugs?" Polly said. "It has to be drugs."

I shrugged. "I've smoked weed a couple times. Tried Molly. Drank."

"Seriously?" She laughed. "You're telling me you're a virgin who's smoked weed a *couple times?*"

"Exactly. I'm not supposed to be here."

Polly seemed annoyed. "Well, you must have done something."

"I don't know. I just hate my parents, I guess. And they kind of hate me too."

Polly stopped abruptly and I pulled up beside her. A stench had been wafting through the air the whole time we'd been walking. Suddenly, it was an assault. I looked at a depression in the ground, covered thinly in dirt, and realized what it was.

A shithole.

"Here's the latrine."

A literal shithole.

"We dig a new one at every campsite."

I felt my oatmeal rising once again.

"And you have to do it a certain way." Polly seemed totally undaunted.

"Six inches wide, five inches long, twelve deep. Are you paying attention? You need to know this, for when it's your turn."

I wanted to laugh, it was so absurd. Here was this girl, this troubled teen, trying so hard to be a model student. Going on about the dimensions of a hole filled with feces like it was calculus? I didn't get it. But Polly misinterpreted my confusion.

"You'll have a ten-inch shovel," she said. "That's how you measure."

"Yeah, I'm not doing this. Not digging it, not using it."

"Not an option. If you lay a surface turd and the staff finds out? You're screwed."

"A *surface turd*?" She made it sound so technical.

"Whatever. You've got to shit in the hole, okay?"

I shook my head.

"You can pee wherever you want, though, like you've been doing."

Polly led us back to camp, running through more rules and regulations. Water should be boiled, on account of the bacteria. Stay close, but yell out your number if you have to walk away. No showers, just sad billy baths using cans of creek water and a bandanna.

"A bandanna?" I said. "Is that my washcloth or my towel?"

"Both."

Of course that was the answer. I exhaled my frustration.

"How long do people stay here?" I said.

"Depends. On what your ed consultant thinks, what the staff tells your parents. Your behavior definitely plays a part."

"My behavior? Great."

She nodded sagely. Like I was still in denial but I would learn. And then I'd be just like her.

"How long have *you* been here?"

"Five weeks. And I'm almost done."

She said it like it was an achievement she was proud of. Which worried me, to say the least.

"And that's . . . normal?"

"It's super fast, actually. Carolina? You'll meet her. She's been here for three months."

"*Three months?*"

"Yeah. But they like to keep the druggies longer."

There were no words for what I was feeling. Nothing was making any sense. So I tuned her out, pretended we were speaking different languages. I didn't trust this girl one bit, someone so completely fine with a situation that was clearly insane.

She's an ass-kisser. A fake. She's a surface turd of a human being.

We got back to camp just in time for group therapy. The girls formed a circle and sat cross-legged in the dirt. They looked like kindergartners at story time. Kindergartners who did hard drugs and had sex with *three boys.*

Polly joined the circle, but I was told to watch from outside. After a moment of strange silence, a freckled staffer held up a stick. With each ceremony, she broke it in half signifying the start of group, and the floodgates opened. One by one, the girls were asked to "check in" with themselves and assess their current feelings.

"I feel sad. I feel this way because I miss my parents."

"I miss my parents too. Also, I missed prom."

"I feel lonely. I feel this way because my best friend overdosed."

"I feel angry."

"Why do you feel angry?"

"Because I don't want to fucking be here. But I've *fucking been here…* for three fucking months."

I looked up and examined the speaker. Dyed black hair half grown out, face filthy and narrowed. *Carolina,* I thought.

"Anger is a secondary emotion," the freckled staffer said. It was a phrase I'd come to hear a lot.

I saw Polly nod in agreement.

"It's what's underneath the anger that matters. What's underneath your anger, Carolina?"

"More anger."

I wanted to laugh, but I held it in. The girls were asked to list alternative feelings. Primary feelings, whatever that meant. *Hurt. Scared. Helpless.*

The ever-present *sad.*

I quit listening and instead tuned in to the frequency of the birds. The trees became palm trees, sheltering me from the sun. The dirt became sand. *I'm on a beach in South Carolina—wait, Hawaii!—and I don't have a care in the world, because I'm young and I'm small. No one has ever hurt me and maybe they never will. I can spend all day in the sand. I can still feel happy. Happy is a primary emotion.*

The sound of sobbing snapped me back to attention. It was Twelve who was crying, the second-newest girl and, not surprisingly, the second-cleanest.

"What feelings are behind those tears?"

"Confused," the girl said. "I feel confused."

"Why do you feel confused?"

"Because I don't think I'm supposed to be here. I'm pretty sure my parents made a mistake."

Dammit. That was my line.

"You keep saying that." The staffer shook her head. "But there weren't any mistakes. Your parents want you right where you are."

Twelve started crying even harder.

"Girls," the staffer said, "can anyone enlighten our new recruit on what might be behind her confusion?"

"Maybe she feels betrayed? Abandoned by her parents?"

"The same thing happened to me." A filthy redhead leaned toward the crying girl. "I don't know why my family sent me away either."

"Danielle, you failed a drug test the day you got here."

"Yeah," Danielle said. "Because someone spiked the church wine."

"Spiked it with what?" Polly weighed in. "It's alcohol."

"With *drugs.*"

"What kind of drugs?"

"I don't know, asshole. The kind that shows up in a piss test."

After the session ended, Kendra sat down with me. The time had come for me to finally learn all about the mysterious Earth Phase. Which really wasn't all that mystifying, after all. There were four "phases" in total: Earth, Fire, Water, and Air. Each came with a new set of privileges, like a flashlight or a knife. Or the ability to have a conversation with another human being.

"You get off Earth Phase when your life story is accepted," Kendra said.

"My life story?"

"Yep. It's exactly as it sounds. You'll write about your life, what went wrong. Everything that led to your parents giving up on you . . . and sending you to us."

Can't wait.

"How long does it have to be?" I said.

"Long. As long as it needs to be. No skimping on details. I want you to list every bad thing you've ever done. Every lie, every drug. Every blow job."

"It's gonna be pretty short then," I said under my breath.

I pulled out my notebook and a pen and was sent on my way. I sat down under a tree and got to work immediately, not recounting the sordid details of my life but writing a letter to my parents. It was a desperate appeal begging them to please, please let me come home.

From my tree I could see the other girls preparing dinner—a glorious feast of dry beans and boxed rice. A few of them struggled with a crude wooden device that seemed related to the process. Meanwhile, the staff clustered around a fancy camping stove that sizzled with bacon and grilled cheese sandwiches.

"How's it going?" Kendra said.

"Okay."

She peered over my shoulder. When I tried to hide my notebook she grabbed it.

Dear Mom and Dad,

I know you'd never want to hurt me. Which is why I'm sure there's been a mistake. This place is so horrible. It's not like summer camp at all. Will you please come get me? I promise I'll be better from now on.

Kendra started laughing. She gave me back the notebook.

"Don't waste your time," she said. "You hungry?"

I shrugged and looked at the girls. "What's that wooden thing?"

"Bow drill. They're trying to bust a fire. If they can't, they eat cold tonight."

Dry beans from a bag. And uncooked Minute Rice. Even better.

Meanwhile, my mouth watered from the smell of bacon. I was relieved when one of the girls finally got a flame to spark, even though that girl was Polly. Naturally, I assumed it meant I'd be eating my beans hot. I should have known better than to expect such a luxury. Kendra informed me that as long as I was still on Earth Phase all of my meals would be uncooked.

I could barely force myself to swallow my dehydrated beans and rice. At the same time, I was starving. I plugged my nose and ate as quickly as I could, the first and last time I'd use that technique. Within minutes I was in excruciating pain. My stomach tightened up like a clenched fist and I felt like I was going to throw up. It was my first experience with something I'd later learn was called gut bomb. Some version of it hit me every time I had to eat uncooked rice and beans in the woods. The clenching feeling was from the rice hydrating itself by sucking up moisture from my stomach.

After dinner, the girls cleaned up while I watched from my spot on the ground, holding my belly. They stomped on the fire and rinsed the pots. They gathered the remaining food and tied it together with rope. Then they took turns tossing the bundle up into a tree until it finally caught a branch and stuck. I realized with horror that this must be what Polly had been trying to tell me when she rambled on about bears.

"You're sleeping with us again, Thirteen."

The staff was still gathered around their fire, munching grilled cheese.

"Amazing," I said, mumbling below my breath.

I handed over my boots and went into the staff tent. I could tell which sleeping bag was mine because it was a good two inches lower than the others. The staff all had thick foam pads beneath their bags while I was given the equivalent of a yoga mat to buffer myself from the hard ground. As I lay there trying to get comfortable, I could hear them talking and laughing just outside.

They were talking about us. Talking shit, to be precise.

"Did you hear Rebecca in group today? Trying to deny that she's ever done coke?"

"She's a party girl if I've ever seen one."

"Am I wrong or are these kids way worse than when we were here?"

Everything suddenly clicked into place. A lot of the staff were former campers themselves. Yesterday's troubled teens, returned to repeat the cycle of abuse.

Hey, maybe I'll be back one day. Or maybe I'll never even leave.

"What do you think about the new girl?"

I recognized Kendra's voice. Ice ran through my veins.

"The angry blonde? She's not leaving anytime soon."

"I'll bet she's a two-monther."

"Easily." Kendra laughed. "I bet you she's here for three."

Bitches. Who does that? Making bets about the worst thing that's ever happened in my life?

I was in a rage. My fists were balled and I could barely contain myself from walking right out and using them on Kendra's smug face. I forced myself to relax. I took deep breaths and imagined a white light. The white light of my childhood, a heavenly glow I learned about in Sunday school. But while I had my doubts about heaven, I was pretty certain that hell was real. It sure felt like I was in it.

Chapter 7

My Life Story:

My memories start when I was about four years old. That's when my family was living in California. After my dad came back from Desert Storm. I was so young I didn't know who he was at first. He was just some man who was hugging me and seemed happy to see me. We were living on the Navy base. One day my dad took me to watch the planes fly in and out and it became my favorite thing. I wanted to do it every day. And I was obsessed with movies like Top Gun and Con Air. Looking back, it seems I had been trying to impress my father before I could even read.

For the second time, I was woken by the slap of hiking boots hitting my sleeping bag. I emerged from the staff tent and saw the other girls packing up. They folded tarps and stuffed sleeping bags into backpacks like they'd done it a million times before. It was mindless and automatic, and that was terrifying.

"Fifteen minutes," a staffer yelled. "Then we're moving out."

The girls divided up the communal gear and added it to their load. They took turns helping one another with their packs. One girl had to sit on the ground to secure the snap around her waist, while two others lifted her to her feet.

I bet I don't need help.

I didn't. I felt a tiny amount of pride as I hoisted my pack onto my shoulders. It weighed almost as much as I did, and I wasn't exactly putting on extra oatmeal and ramen weight. I was glad I didn't need to ask for help, and I figured a lifetime of athleticism had given me an advantage. But maybe I was wrong. Maybe that girl had started out just like me, capable and strong-willed. Before true exhaustion set in. Before the woods wore her down. I knew I'd get there eventually, and the thought of that alone made me tired.

"Girls!" the staffer was yelling. "Let's get a move on."

We filed out of the campsite. Watching it recede, I found myself shocked at how pristine the area looked. It appeared totally untouched, with absolutely no sign of human habitation. Thirteen teenage girls and their guards disappeared into the wilderness without a trace.

Am I even here at all? Do I still exist? What if I'm just a phantom, some half-alive version of myself?

My pack was definitely real. Already it was burning blisters into my shoulders. I had a whole day of hiking ahead of me and many more days after that. It was an activity I'd know very well by the end of my time in the woods. Hiking just to hike, going nowhere in particular. Sometimes it felt like we were just walking in circles, and honestly, we probably were.

"Thirteen, stay in back."

We marched out single file. Three girls in a row, then a counselor, then another three girls. Since I was on Earth Phase, I brought up the rear with a staffer right behind me. I hated the feeling of being watched, especially in the ever-increasing brightness.

The heat bore down without reprieve. By early afternoon I'd found myself in a predicament, a wardrobe-related dilemma. I had unzipped my cargo pants off at the knees and my legs felt so much cooler in shorts. But the trade-off meant walking through brush and thickets with my legs bared to the world. By the time we were done for the day I was covered in scratches and bug bites. It was like I was a kid again.

If only that kid could see herself now.

For a moment I felt impossibly sad.

Eh, I bet she'd be too busy climbing trees to care.

We arrived at our next campsite, which seemed just as random as the first one. In fact, besides a few small differences in terrain, it could have been the same place. One perk of being a lowly Earth Phaser was that I didn't have to set up. No latrine digging for me. I was sent off to "reflect" and to get back to work on my life story.

I was five the first time I tried to run away. It seemed like a fun thing to do, even though I had nowhere to go. We were living on another base in Oakland where I had a best friend named Chloe. One day, the two of us plotted our escape. But we only made it as far as the guard gate. Once we moved to South Carolina I got a lot better at it. I would sneak out in the middle of the night and meet my friends at the tennis court. Or I'd try to spend the night at Melanie's because her dad never cared what we did.

"Hey, Thirteen, guess what?"

Kendra was standing over me.

"I'm going home?" Maybe if I said it out loud, it would be true.

"Nope," she said. "But you're out of the staff tent. And off run watch."

"Great," I said. "What does that mean?"

Kendra's eyes glinted. "It means you get to sleep all by yourself tonight."

As relieved as I was to be out of the staff tent, I might have been even more terrified by the thought of spending the night alone.

"Go set up your shelter," Kendra said.

"How do I do that?"

"Ask your mentor."

I wandered the campsite until I found Polly. The sun had slipped past the horizon and twilight was coming. I shivered, more from the thought of darkness than the cold. My mentor was tying up her remaining food when I found her. She slipped right back into docent mode.

"First, we have to find you a good site," she said, leading me to the outskirts of the camp.

"What makes a site good?"

"Trees. Spaced about eight feet apart. But you obviously don't want their roots sticking out."

We walked the area. It seemed like all the good spots were already taken. I pointed to a cluster of trees that seemed like they might work.

"Too close to Carolina." Polly shook her head. "We need to be fifteen feet apart from each other, at least."

That's a lot of space. What if a bear comes? Or an ax murderer?

I was beginning to realize just how alone I was going to be and how dark it would get. It almost made me wish I was back in the staff tent.

"Here!"

Polly had found me a suitable site, fifteen yards away from every other tent. I dropped my backpack and listened to her instructions.

"It's pretty simple," she said. "Basically, you have a ground tarp and a roof tarp. Ground tarp goes under your sleeping bag. Roof tarp, you tie from one tree to the other."

"Got it," I said.

"Want me to wait with you? I mean, it's pretty self-explanatory, but I totally will if you need help."

"I think I can manage."

I started unpacking. My tarps had that new plastic smell, so out of place in the wilderness. Polly waved and walked away, smiling.

She's always fucking smiling. It's like she's posing for the brochure. She's the "after" and I'm the "before."

I smoothed the ground and put down one of my tarps. I tried to get my roof set up, but the knots I was tying wouldn't hold. As soon as I got one side up the other would come loose. The rope was too slippery, the trees wouldn't cooperate. Stubbornly, I kept trying. No way was I about to admit defeat. Not if it meant running to Polly for help.

She did this on purpose. She knew I wouldn't get it on the first try. I bet she's dying to come over here and show off her perfect tarp-hanging skills. God, what a bitch.

"Psst." A whisper interrupted my brooding.

I turned around and saw a girl with dyed-red hair holding on to one end of my tarp.

"Do it like this." The girl demonstrated an easy but sturdy knot. It was simple if you knew it, but of course I didn't. "Try the other side."

She pantomimed the knot as I tied it. The tarp held.

"Thanks," I said. "That was getting annoying."

"It's supposed to be. They're really into control around here. If you hadn't noticed."

I laughed. "No kidding."

"I'm Marissa."

"Elizabeth."

I liked Marissa instantly. Something about her no-bullshit demeanor was comforting. Familiar. I saw a version of myself in this girl.

"Where are you from?" she asked.

"South Carolina."

"I'm from Texas," Marissa said. "It sucks. But this place sucks more."

"I feel like I'm in hell or something."

"It gets easier. Just keep your head down and give them what they want. And I'll keep looking for a way out of this shithole."

"Let me know what you find," I said. "I want to go with you."

We both turned at the sound of footsteps. Polly was back and she didn't look happy. My new friend rolled her eyes in my direction. She winked as she walked away.

"Just checking her work," Marissa said, passing my mentor.

"Wow," Polly said. "How generous of you."

"I'm a saint," Marissa said. "Looks good, by the way."

Polly gave Marissa her fakest smile. She was circling my structure, looking for flaws. But the tarp was still secured and it hung tautly across the branches.

"I guess that will work," Polly said. "Sleep tight."

Sleep tight. Sure, no problem.

I settled into my sleeping bag. Beams of light swooped over the campsite as staffers went girl to girl, checking in, maintaining control. I knew that soon the flashlights would be off and I would be alone in total darkness.

My lifelong fear.

"Boots."

Kendra shone her flashlight right in my eyes. I handed her my shoes and she smiled.

"Sleep tight, Thirteen."

Soon the boots were all collected and we did a final countdown. The flashlights faded away and the blackness started to consume me. I pushed my head out from behind my tarp as if gasping for air. There was a distant campfire glow by the staff tent and a few pinpricks of light in the sky. I couldn't even see the moon. I held my hand out in front of my face and tried to bring it into focus. When I couldn't, I grabbed the tarp and ran my fingers along its crinkly surface. It was the only way I could orient myself to this planet.

Just breathe. Deep breaths, think of something happy. Or at least something not terrible.

I had never felt so scared in my entire life. Every tiny sound was heightened as though an amplifier had been placed directly outside my tent. Crackling leaves and popping sticks. My heart caught each time. It could have been the wind or it could have been a bear. A serial killer or a figment of my imagination. In the distance, I heard one of the girls begin to cry. Soft at first, it soon turned into outright sobbing. It was a human sound and it was actually a relief.

Wait. But what if she's crying because she's getting murdered?

The idea of running away suddenly seemed hilarious. I was too scared to even move. There was so much fear coursing through my body there wasn't any room for anger. Just the terror of the night and a million worst-case scenarios playing out inside my head.

Dismemberment. Rape. Rabies. Ghosts.

I had been praying out of habit for so long that it surprised me to feel a genuine urge to share some real words with God. I usually repeated the same list of names, the people I hoped would stay safe and protected—then added in a prayer for the poor and war-broken for good measure. But suddenly I was scared and confused and didn't have anyone else I could turn to.

Dear God,

Am I in hell? Because that's what this feels like. I don't even know if I believe in you anymore. If you're supposed to protect me, then why am I here?

God, if you're real, please, please just help me make it through the night. And please get me out of this place. Just tell me what to do and I'll make it right.

I prayed myself into a night of fitful sleep. In the morning, I woke up with a stiff neck, but the rest of my body parts were still intact. Another day of hiking led to another uneasy night. Pretty soon, it was Sunday. And in the woods, we had a different kind of church on Sundays. Each week, a psychotherapist named Rick would drive out to the sticks and hold court from a folding chair. One by one, we'd meet with him for an individual session. He'd ask questions and nod like he was listening to the responses, but mostly he liked to talk. Which made him more like a preacher than a therapist. But really, he might as well have been God. Rick had more control over our lives than anyone.

"You're up last, Elizabeth." The staffer smiled. "Number Thirteen."

"Fine by me," I said.

"Why don't you get back to your life story?"

Sometimes we smoked weed but usually we just had beer. Or tequila if someone managed to siphon some from a bottle in their parents' liquor cabinet. The one time I took Molly, I'm not even sure if I felt it. I was scared to drink too much water because I heard you could die, drown your body. Someone said if you drink orange juice you feel it better, but I don't know if that's true. We were at Bethany's dad's house. Mostly we jumped on the trampoline. I remember feeling like I couldn't stop laughing, even though nothing was funny.

In another sense, Sundays were also a day of rest. Not the kind of rest I was used to, of course (sports, TV, hours on the phone gabbing about nothing). At least there was no hiking.

Because so much of our fate was in Rick's hands, everyone was on their best behavior around him. Even the staff seemed less vicious than usual. I later learned groups of counselors would rotate in and out on a weekly basis. Kendra and the rest of them were headed straight for a week of freedom.

It wasn't exactly shore leave, but I actually felt a little bit relaxed. No one was breathing down my neck, and the sounds of the woods were much more cheerful in the light of day. We were even given a little cocoa powder to mix in with our oats during breakfast.

It was late afternoon by the time I was summoned for my appointment with Rick. I walked out to the clearing where my new therapist was stretching his legs. He was about my dad's age, dressed in a flannel shirt and hiking boots. He introduced himself and sat down in his fold-up chair. I sat down facing him, cross-legged in the dirt.

"So," Rick said. "How are you adjusting?"

How am I adjusting? I'd say pretty fucking horribly!

I shrugged. "Um. I don't really know."

Rick folded his hands in his lap. He seemed to be studying me.

"All right then," he said. "I hear you're having a little trouble getting your life story finished."

"I'm not sure what I'm supposed to say."

"About your life?"

"Yeah," I said. "I mean, I don't really see the point."

"Well." Rick leaned forward. "It's all part of the process, Elizabeth."

"What *process*?"

"Don't you want to work through your troubles?"

"I guess?" I didn't really mean it, but I tried to play along.

Rick laughed. A good-natured chuckle.

"I'm afraid you don't have a choice. Not if you want to get through the program and go home."

GO HOME? Did he really say those magical words?

If only I'd known then that "the program" was going to last until I was seventeen.

My whole body suddenly felt tingly. I was actually alive, I realized, for the first time in days. I squeezed my eyes shut and sent a thank-you up to God, just in case he was responsible for my shifting fate.

"You're totally right," I said. "The process is super important."

"Glad we're on the same page." He smiled. "Can I see what you've written so far?"

I passed my notebook to Rick and looked at my hands. They were empty, so I wound my fingers around in circles. It was my big nervous habit, constantly needing something to shred or pull apart. I was definitely nervous watching the therapist read my work.

I'm not sure when I became incapable of feeling other people's love. I used to wish I was one of my dad's patients because he's so nice and happy around them. But when he gets home he's always agitated and tired. My dad and my brother fight a lot and then my brother takes it out on me. We used to get physical, pushing each other around. Maybe that's just normal sibling fighting, I don't really know. I don't really know how I got this way at all.

"Elizabeth!"

I looked up. My cuticle was bleeding.

"This is really good work," Rick said. "I don't know what you're so worried about."

"Really?"

"Absolutely. In fact, I'd say you're nearly done."

"Man," I said. "I was not expecting that."

"What were you expecting?"

Rick shifted forward in his chair. It was obviously a practiced gesture, warm and inviting, but it worked. I began to open up about how hard the last few days had been. How shocking it was to leave my home in the middle of the night and how darkness was my biggest fear. He was understanding and kind, even as I started to cry. He seemed encouraged by my vulnerability and I realized what I needed to do.

I needed to drink the Kool-Aid.

"I'm just so sorry about everything," I said, sniffling. "All my anger. And the sneaking out. It wasn't okay and I finally see that. I understand why my parents needed to send me here."

Rick seemed satisfied. My heart pounded against my rib cage, inflated by hope.

"That's a great first step, Elizabeth."

First step? No, no, no.

"I get it now." I wiped my eyes. I wasn't giving up just yet. "I mean, it's crazy, you know? But I feel like I actually learned my lesson."

Rick smiled. He handed back my notebook and stood up from his chair. "We'll get into that more next week."

I was disappointed but not discouraged. I knew it couldn't have been that easy. It would take one more week; a week of obedience and contrition. A week of becoming Polly's clone. And then he'd see that I was ready to go home.

I shook Rick's hand and walked back to the campsite. My spirits were about as high as they could be for a girl with a metal bowl and three pairs of underwear to her name. The rest of the group seemed to be on the same wavelength. Rick had brought provisions from the outside world, and along with another week's supply of food and clothes were a few pairs of cheap plastic sunglasses and some disposable cameras our parents had sent.

"Psst! Hey, Elizabeth."

Marissa was grinning. She tossed me a pair of sunglasses. I put them on and posed like Maverick from *Top Gun*. She aimed her camera and pressed down on the shutter. I heard a click and felt for a moment like I still existed. Like I hadn't vanished after all. There was proof right there in that plastic Kodak camera.

Chapter 8

AFTER ABOUT A week on Earth Phase, I was supposed to ask permission to join the group. No one actually told me this, however, and it was my impression that asking for things was generally frowned upon in the woods. So it took a few hints and leading conversations before I finally got the gist.

"Can I join the group now?"

"Do you think you're ready?"

"Sure."

"We agree. Congratulations. And welcome."

The next morning, I was led out to a clearing a short walk from camp. The rest of the girls were already there, sitting cross-legged in the dirt. Apparently they were waiting for *me* to arrive.

What the fuck am I getting into?

There was something creepy about the scene laid out before me. Dozens of stones and pebbles formed a crooked circle on the ground. Inside the ring, the word *FIRE* had been spelled out, an all-caps arrangement of sticks and leaves. Instinctively, I wanted to turn around and run.

Instead, I was pulled into the middle of the circle. Polly stood up, beaming. She held a daisy chain in both hands and placed it on my head like a crown. It was all so cultish, like a spooky pagan ritual. I was suddenly worried about being a virgin. Was I about to be I sacrificed to the god of troubled teens?

"Welcome to Fire Phase, Elizabeth."

Nicole, one of the new staffers, broke a stick in half. I sat down in the circle and hugged my knees to my chest.

"Fire Phase is all about transformation," she said. "It's about learning from life's obstacles and overcoming them. So your true potential can emerge like a flame."

Oh god. Never mind the virgin thing and the blood. Are they about to burn me at the stake?

"First, can you tell us something Earth Phase taught you?"

"Um." I fidgeted. "I guess I learned that I'm okay being alone."

"That's an important lesson."

Nicole turned to the girls and asked them to share what I could expect to learn from Fire Phase. More than half the girls never got past this second stage, which made the whole system feel pretty arbitrary.

"I learned that I can't control everything," Polly said. "So it's important to make the most of the things that *are* in my control."

"I learned not to give up," someone else said.

"I learned that it's better to work smart than to work hard."

"Sometimes life tests you just so it can make you stronger."

"I learned how to drain a blister," Carolina said.

The other girls laughed. After a few more inspirational clichés, the ceremony was coming to an end. Nicole asked Polly to stand.

"Do you have a gift for Elizabeth?"

My mentor nodded. She presented me with a block of wood, cradling the thing like it was more precious than gold.

"It's a gift from the earth," Polly said. "So you can carve your very own spoon!"

A wooden spoon. We skipped right over that in cotillion class, and I did a whole year.

In addition to crafting utensils under the watchful eye of a staffer, I was given the task of literally making fire. Just like they did in the time of cavemen, using wood and rocks and a can-do attitude. Specifically, I needed to make my very own bow drill, a primitive tool that had almost holy status in the woods.

Bow drilling is a slightly more sophisticated version of rubbing two sticks together. By spinning one piece of wood rapidly against another, the idea was to create heat through friction. First there'd be smoke, then a few sparks, and eventually the tiniest ember would begin to glow. That ember, precious as a newborn, would be carefully transferred to a prearranged stack of dried kindling. Then you'd have to blow on it, slowly and with just the right amount of force, until actual flames emerged. When the kindling was strong enough it would go into the fire pit at the center of camp. With enough stoking and the right nurturing environment, it would grow into a healthy, fully developed fire.

Did the cavemen invent the metaphor too?

After my first Fire Phase breakfast, a staffer named Lisa took me aside. She explained the ancient art of bow drilling as though it were some great rite of passage.

"This isn't about throwing some twigs together and calling it a day," she said. "You're building a tool for yourself. A tool that will serve you for a lifetime. Long after you've left this place behind."

That sounds great and all. But when do I get to the "leave this place behind" part?

Lisa ignored the skeptical look on my face and continued her presentation. First, I needed to gather my materials. A rock from the stream nearby and several pieces of wood.

"Don't skimp on your materials. Spend the time now and it will save you a lot of grief later."

I nodded.

"And be on the lookout for cedar trees. That's the best wood. Poplar's fine too."

I nodded.

"Any questions?"

"Nope. Sounds good."

"Good luck," Lisa said. "I believe in you, Elizabeth. You just have to believe in yourself."

There are four components to a bow drill. There's the base (called a fireboard), the spindle, the bow, and the top rock. The fireboard and the spindle are both made from dead, dry wood—the drier, the better. The bow, on the other hand, should come from a more flexible piece of wood, one roughly the length of your forearm. The top rock needs to fit nicely in your palm, with bonus points for smoothness.

I wandered the forest, picking up sticks and tossing most of them aside. The whole time I yelled my number on an endless loop.

"Thirteen... Thirteen... Thirteen."

What the fuck does a poplar tree look like?

"Thirteen."

And why didn't I bother to ask?

"Thirteen."

This might be the stupidest thing I've ever done.

Hey, maybe I'll get lucky and find a book of matches.

"Thirteen."

I can't wait to be Twelve. Only one syllable. That's like half the effort.

It was late morning when I returned to camp. I had two different rock options and a stack of wood that Lisa deemed acceptable. It wasn't all grade A cedar. But for a caveman tool, it would do.

"The fireboard is the base," Lisa said. "The foundation of the whole tool."

My materials were laid out on the ground in front of me. Lisa was explaining how to take these sticks and rocks and turn them into a bow drill. Mostly this involved carving, but metaphors were an important part of the process too.

"What are your foundations?" She handed me my fireboard. "What structures formed the backbone of Elizabeth?"

"Maybe the Navy?" I shrugged. "Or church?"

"Those are strong foundations. Explains why you're so chaste and obedient."

I looked up, ready for the next insult, but Lisa only winked. I wondered if she was one of the staffers who'd been on the other side. A former troubled teen, pissed off and aloof, mumbling sarcastic comments as she wandered in search of poplar trees.

"Okay, time to carve," she said. "Can I trust you to be careful with my knife?"

But no, Lisa didn't fit the bill. Not enough of an asshole.

"Yep," I said. "No stabbing or slashing, promise."

Lisa handed me her knife and watched as I carved a V-shaped notch into the fireboard. Then I got to work on the spindle, whittling it down to a point on one side. The spindle, I was told, represented the friction in my life. *My parents.* That one was easy.

"Now the bow." Lisa picked up my curved piece of wood. "Maybe the most important piece. This is the driving force behind everything else. What drives you?"

I shrugged. "Anger?"

"Hmm. That's a secondary emotion. Try something else."

"I guess I like winning. Being the best at something."

Lisa nodded. "What are you the best at?"

"I'm an athlete," I said. *Was an athlete.*

"Then you should pick this up in no time."

Lisa had given me a piece of string. I tied it to each end of the bow, twisted the spindle into the middle of the string, and placed the spindle in the hole of my fireboard. The pointed piece of wood fit nicely inside the notch I'd carved. Really, my bow drill didn't look half bad.

"You're just about there," Lisa said. "One last thing."

She handed me a tangled mass of shredded twigs and dried grass.

"What is this?"

"Your nesting. A little bundle of safety and nurturing. I really want you to dig deep for this one, okay?" Lisa smiled. "Think about your own nesting. It can be a person or a place. A time when you felt safe and loved."

Instinctively, my mind went back to the beach in South Carolina. I loved it there when I was a kid, before things got bad. When my mom and I would stroll along the shore collecting shark teeth. We'd walk until we couldn't take another step. And then we'd collapse on the sand and count our teeth like it was a competition.

Sometimes my dad would wake up really early and take me out to see the sea turtles. The beach rangers would show us nests of unhatched eggs. We'd help them rope off each one and affix signs that banned digging in the area. Since I had trouble falling asleep, my dad came home from work one night with a CD of ocean sounds. I listened to that thing every night for years, letting the whales and the dolphins sing to me as I drifted off.

"What are you thinking?" Lisa asked.

I was trying to remember our relationship as it was back then. But all I could see was his face the night I was kidnapped. Those cold eyes and blank expression.

"The beach in South Carolina," I said, shrugging off the memories. "I've always loved swimming in the ocean."

The Atlantic had never been more enticing than it was in that moment. I felt the grime of the woods all over me. Dirt and sweat, bug bites and scrapes. Not to mention all the blisters I was about to acquire from my first attempt at bow drilling.

Goddammit. This is gonna be impossible.

I wanted to scream. To build up enough friction for a spark, I'd need to move the bow back and forth dozens, if not hundreds, of times. But I couldn't get the spindle to stay in place for more than a few seconds at a time. The moment I started to build any momentum at all, I'd lean too far over the board or lose my footing. Inevitably, the spindle would slip out of its groove and I'd have to start all over again. After an hour, I was white-hot with rage and frustration again. I figured I had a better chance of spontaneously combusting and starting a fire that way.

It was getting close to sunset. I'd already been told I couldn't eat hot until I busted my first fire, but the staff decided to up the ante. If I couldn't get an ember going by dinnertime, the entire group would have to eat cold.

I heard someone groan. It was Isabelle, the Australian girl with alopecia.

"This is crap," she said.

"What did you say, Isabelle?"

"I said, it's crap." She faced the staffer head-on. "It's completely unfair. And I don't want to eat cold tonight."

"Very encouraging," the staffer said. "What a great message to send Elizabeth."

Isabelle looked at me. I leaned over my kit, determined to make it work. I got maybe three full seconds of friction before the spindle slipped.

"She's not gonna get it. No offense. No one busts a fire the first time."

So I'd been set up to fail. Knowing that didn't make me feel any better, nor did it gain me any sympathy from the other girls. I hadn't even spoken to most of them. Now they'd hate me before I even got a chance. I wanted to snap my drill in half and just give up. But I couldn't let the staff see me acting out of anger. Not when I felt so close to convincing everyone I'd learned my lesson and was ready to go home.

So I kept putting the spindle back in the groove and trying one more time. And one more time after that, until my fingers bled and my whole body ached. Eventually I was forced to stop and join the other girls for a dinner of cold, dehydrated ramen.

I was frustrated that I didn't have a single spark to show for all my blisters. But for the sake of my image, I was glad I hadn't given up. I genuinely still thought I'd be going home soon. It was a beautiful delusion, a small balloon of hope tied around my wrist. But it wouldn't last long. The next afternoon, my precious balloon popped.

Group therapy was a totally different experience in Fire Phase. As strange as it was to sit outside the circle, forced to watch but not allowed to talk, it sure beat actual participation. For the first two days I tried to stay under the radar. I admitted to feeling sad and confused and gave simple explanations for my emotions. I was sad because I missed home, I was confused because everything felt so unfamiliar. They were obvious answers, impossible to pick apart, so no one tried.

Everything changed once I had to participate. As soon as the ceremonial stick broke in half, I was asked to start. Greta, my least favorite of the new cycle of staffers, handed me an envelope. It was already opened, and inside was a faxed letter from my parents. The first contact I'd had with them since getting to the woods.

"Your impact letter came," Greta said, as if those words made perfect sense.

"My what?"

"Letter from home. Explaining the effect your bad behavior had on your family."

Great. This should be a nice, light read.

I nodded and put the faxed letter in my cargo pocket.

"Hang on," Greta said. "You've got to read it."

"Now?"

"Out loud."

I shook my head. *No way.*

"Elizabeth, you have to confront the truth. That's the only way you're ever gonna change."

A knot formed in my throat. Everyone was staring at me. I fought back tears and removed the envelope from my pocket. My hands shook as I unfolded the letter and held it up to my face. Too close, so I wouldn't be able to look at anyone else.

"'Dear Elizabeth,'" I read. "'First we want to tell you how much we love you. How much we have always loved you even when you've tried to fight it. We only want what's best for you. You may not realize it yet but we've put you in this program for your own good. We had to save your life, sweetheart.'"

"Sweetheart"? I hate when she calls me that.

"'Your anger had gotten out of control. It was destroying our family. Your outbursts, the way you'd scream at me, "I HATE YOU."'"

I bit the inside of my cheek to keep from crying. I kept my eyes trained on the letter and tried to ignore the circle of faces staring up at me. My voice shook as I continued to read.

"'Your father and I, we just want to help you. And all you've ever done is push us away. All that rage inside of you. I don't know where it comes from. But I do know it isn't healthy. And frankly, it's upsetting to be around you when you get like that.

"'Elizabeth, do you realize your little sister is afraid of you?'"

Where do you think I got my temper? It's not like I'm the only problem. And anyway, Emily loves being the favorite child. The good daughter, who'd never even dream of calling her mother a fucking bitch. She is, after all, only ten.

"'And then there were the public fits. You had no problem screaming at me in front of other people.'"

What about all the times my brother yelled at me? Called me a bitch, told me I was a slut. Sure, just skip all that, no biggie.

"'And honey, did it occur to you that those older boys were using you? None of them really cared about you, not in the way you deserve to be cared about.'"

No, Mom, it did not occur to me. You don't even know them, so you have no idea what you're talking about.

"'It's the job of a parent to protect their child. And in your case that means protecting you from yourself. All the sneaking out and the drinking. It was like you were incapable of telling the truth. You even lied about the car accident. What were you thinking? Because you refused to deal with the consequences of that night, the burden fell on your father and me.'"

Wow. Sounds a lot like being a parent.

"'It felt like a cry for help. But you wouldn't accept our help, or our love. You turned on us again and again until we had no choice but to intervene. For the sake of our family, we couldn't let you continue to take your anger out on us. Even worse, on yourself. It was like you were dying inside. When Lynn Anne offered us this solution, it was like a lifeline. I only pray that in time you'll come to see it the same way.'"

You saw me dying inside and thought the best way to deal with that was to throw me out? What about weekly therapy? Or some after-school program? Instead it was just good-bye, you're too difficult for us.

My paralyzing fear had turned to paralyzing outrage. It felt like my family was making me the scapegoat for a lot of our problems: the anger that belonged to my dad and brother just as much as it belonged to me; the drinking that was somehow perfectly fine when my brother did it; the lack of real communication.

Maybe scapegoating me made it easier for them to deal with the guilt of sending their child away. Or maybe they really did believe I was the root of the problem. Either way, the letter did not go over well with the staff. They had read my life story and found it at odds with my mom's account. Of course, they were going to believe her version over mine, the one where I was a raging monster, torturing my family and on the verge of self-destruction.

"So you're a liar, huh?"

Greta's eyes narrowed, her stare burning right through me.

"I didn't lie," I said.

Not technically, at least.

"You sugarcoated. Made yourself the victim."

"Manipulative, this one," another staffer piled on. "Had us thinking the worst she did was sneak out a couple times because her parents were too strict."

Greta nodded. "Never mentioned that whole psychotic rage part. *How convenient, you stopped at blow jobs.* You can't honestly expect us to believe you've never had sex with all the drinking you were doing."

I had been willing away tears the whole time, but the floodgates wouldn't hold. I put my head in my hands and cried for the rest of the session. It was so unfair. Instinctively I knew that any attempt to defend myself would only make things much worse. I'd never wanted to leave a place so badly in my life.

But where would I even go? Back home, to ruin my family's lives some more? Only to be evicted once again.

That night felt like the worst one yet. I kept my head down during dinner and did my cleaning in a quiet fog. I got into my sleeping bag, hardly even caring about the dark. I could feel my spirit fading. I was becoming a ghost of myself. I could either embrace it or turn into something much worse. *A Polly.*

"Psst."

I had just closed my eyes when I heard a whisper outside my shelter. I jumped in my sleeping bag, prepared for the worst. But it was Marissa, sneaking over to me in her Crocs. She put her hand over my mouth. *We have to be quiet.*

"Hey," she whispered. "You okay?"

I shook my head. "I hate everyone."

"Me too," Marissa said. "Let's kill them in their sleep."

"Okay," I said. "But we need a plan."

"Poison?"

"Could work." I was actually smiling. "I say we sneak over to the staff tent, steal their flashlights, and see what we can find."

There was a rustle nearby. We both froze and let it pass.

"I gotta get back," Marissa said. "But listen. Don't worry about what happened in group. They do that shit with everyone. It's another one of their games."

She disappeared into the darkness, heading back to her shelter. I felt a little better knowing I hadn't been singled out, but I was still pissed off. At the staff for manipulating me like that. At my parents for putting all the blame on my shoulders. Even though I thought they were probably coached on exactly what to write, it still made me furious to think about. When the sobbing girl started up her nightly routine I found myself crying silently along with her. Tears soaked my filthy cheeks. I burrowed deeper in my sleeping bag and tried to fall asleep. I just wanted the day to be over.

"Storm drill! This is a storm drill!"

I blinked against the darkness.

"Everybody up, grab your packs!" The voice was so, so loud. "Hurry. Lightning doesn't strike on your timetable."

I scrambled out of my sleeping bag in a panic. Someone threw my shoes, hitting me square in the back. I threw on my pack and traced the beam of a staffer's flashlight.

What the hell is happening? Are we being attacked?

I ran outside, surging with fear and adrenaline. A moment later, I spotted the other girls walking away from camp. They were moving quickly but with little urgency. Whatever the disaster was, it hardly seemed to faze them.

I followed the others to an open clearing, a gap between two sections of tall trees. They spread out in a line, calculating distance with robotic precision. Marissa noticed my confusion and grabbed my arm.

"Take fifteen steps and stop."

"What the fuck is happening?" I said.

"Ugh, storm drill . . . it's the worst," she said. "Just watch what I do."

Storm drill. The words hadn't registered at first, but now they seemed pretty self-explanatory. Like everything else, this was an amusement. They'd managed to gamify a safety drill.

I counted out fifteen paces and stopped. I mimicked Marissa's movements, widening my stance and lowering my body into a crouch. For the next hour, we were forced to remain like that, yelling our numbers over and over.

I'm so sick of being Unlucky Thirteen.

Chapter 9

I WOKE UP exhausted and deflated. I was sore from crouching all night, and my head pounded like I had some kind of emotional hangover. To make matters worse, I was told to prepare for a full day of hiking. We packed up our stuff and cleaned the campsite.

"Remember," the staff kept saying, "leave no trace."

Once again, we were out of there before the sun was up. It was especially hot out, and my cargo pants didn't stay pants for long. Sweat pooled and soaked my T-shirt, and I could feel my throat going dry. But I didn't want to drink too much water. If I finished my bottle now, I'd have nothing for later. So I trudged forward in a dehydrated daze, just putting one foot in front of the other. I tried not to think about how tired I was. Or how thirsty I was, or how upset. Basically, I was trying not to think about anything at all.

The screaming began like a domino effect. One girl after another, shrieking in order, all the way down the row. I barely had time to register what was happening before I felt the pain all over.

"Fuck! Get it away! Get them away!"

We were all hopping around and trying to escape. Bees swarmed like a buzzing black cloud. I'd never seen so many goddamn bees in my life.

"They're gonna kill us," someone said.

"Just keep moving. Go!"

Half of us were still screaming as we ran. The other half had switched over to crying. We kept on running long after we were out of immediate danger, convinced the bees were following us like tiny drones. Finally, we collapsed to the ground to catch our breath and assess the situation.

Apparently we had stepped on a "ground nest," which is something I hadn't even known existed. As long as they aren't disturbed, ground nests are usually pretty harmless. Unfortunately, being stomped on by thick-soled hiking boots counts as a disturbance.

The staff, impossibly, was completely fine. None of them suffered even a single bee sting. It was insane enough that for a moment I felt like a conspiracy theorist.

The bees were an inside job.

The rest of us all had multiple wounds. I counted five right away. Three of them were on my legs and I cursed myself for having unzipped my cargo pants. My blisters had just started to pop and now I had to deal with bee stings. Isabelle had it worst of all. She'd been near the front of the group and the stings were swelling up all over her pale, hairless skin. Polly, who still had her pants zipped at the knee, was stung only once.

Still, a bee sting is a bee sting. One, five, or however many were on poor Isabelle, we were all in a lot of pain. But that didn't mean we could stop hiking. The staff checked in with us one by one, not to actually help but to make sure we weren't allergic, and remarkably, none of us were. Not even Allison, a dramatic girl from Tennessee, who was playing up her reaction so intensely I thought she was going to faint.

Hmmm. More evidence for my conspiracy theory.

"Okay, girls," Nicole said. "Let's walk it off."

"But it hurts," Allison said through gasps. "It really, really hurts."

"Are you gonna die?"

"No."

"Do you need an EpiPen?"

She shook her head.

"Then there's no reason we can't keep on moving."

Slowly we got back up. We continued our hike, limping and grumbling. Eventually the pain became less immediate, turning into a dull soreness that would last the rest of the day. But nightfall was still several hours and even more miles away. The heat bore down. Our tears dried and sweat dripped into our wounds.

"Civilians!"

The staffer at the head of the line halted.

"Civilians up ahead."

Each staff member repeated the warning so it traveled down the line. I'd been briefed on the rules for encountering so-called civilians in the wild. But this was my first time actually coming across people from the outside world. I'd forgotten that T-shirts could exist in colors other than orange.

"Eyes down, Elizabeth."

I averted my eyes and got into position. The protocol for civilian encounters was to stop walking immediately, turn in a uniform direction, and look straight down. Eye contact was strictly forbidden, which meant there was no way to gauge the hikers' reactions. Though I imagine they were probably strong ones, especially that afternoon. On any other day, we'd be a group of sullen, filthy teenage girls in matching outfits. But on this day, we were also covered in bee stings, clearly miserable and unable to hide it.

Maybe they'll stop for us. Maybe they'll call the cops.

I tried to look as pathetic as possible.

Yes, Officer. Thirteen teenage girls. Filthy and covered in bee stings. One of them didn't have any hair.

But the footsteps didn't let up. If the hikers were alarmed, they didn't show it. I made a mental note to write a letter as soon as possible. *Help. I've been taken hostage.* I could hide it in my pocket and slip it to the next civilian I encountered. It was a solid plan, a perfect plan, just as long as the staff didn't catch me first.

There were many ways our counselors maintained control in the woods. Things like taking our shoes at night and making us recite numbers were the practical measures. Sometimes they'd threaten to call the police. But the thing that really terrorized us into submission was the threat of lockdown.

There were facilities in and out of the United States that could hold a kid until she turned twenty-one. Basically, these were private detention centers with no federal regulations and nonexistent state oversight. All it would take to end up there was a staffer convincing our parents that more extensive measures were needed to handle our behavior. Would it work? Who knows. Most of us never imagined our parents would send us off to live in the woods.

Nothing seemed impossible anymore. The idea that it could actually get worse, that we could lose even *more* freedom, was usually enough to deter us from any really terrible behavior.

"In lockdown you can't even brush your teeth without someone watching over your shoulder."

"Ever seen a straitjacket? That's because you've never been in lockdown."

"You're complaining about a hike? Try a week in solitary confinement."

"Or a dog cage."

"There are electric fences in lockdown."

Rick, my therapist, was the first person to threaten me with lockdown directly. I'd left our first meeting with the impression that he was a kind man, my only ally, but I couldn't have been more wrong. He was a master game player, doling out kindness just so he could rip it away. Which he promptly did the following Sunday.

"You're lying, Elizabeth. You're only hurting yourself."

Rick had been hounding me for my life story since our session began. I tried explaining that I'd been confused about the assignment, then I tried apologizing. But none of it mattered. He was determined to make me feel as terrible as possible—and it was working.

"I don't know how I didn't see all that anger in you," he said. "It's like you wear a mask."

"I don't. I'm just ... me."

"It's chilling. And I'm a professional."

"It's not like I'm angry all the time."

"Sure sounds like your parents think you are." Rick shook his head. "You're a danger to every other person here. Really, I should send you straight to lockdown. I don't think you understand the gravity of this situation, Elizabeth, what exactly it is we do here. We are observing you so we can decide what program we feel is the best fit for you. The good little girls and boys go to the good therapeutic programs, the bad little girls and boys go to the lockdowns. You don't want to go there, trust me when I tell you that."

I started to cry.

Can he do that? Just snap his fingers and send me to an institution?

"Luckily for you, I believe in second chances."

"Thank you," I said. I wasn't above groveling.

"You're gonna write a letter of accountability. Owning up to every single thing you've ever done. Every sin, every indiscretion. Every little secret you thought you could keep hidden. None of this faux-innocent crap. If you hide anything else from us or sugarcoat the truth, it's not going to be pretty. You got it?"

I nodded, but I could see trouble up ahead. Maybe I hadn't quite owned up to my anger, but the rest of it was true. I *had* admitted all my indiscretions. Clearly, they weren't good—or bad—enough.

"Thank you for the second chance," I said. "I won't let you down."

The threat of lockdown loomed over me like a black cloud. I had no idea how I was going to write an accountability letter that would meet whatever impossible standards Rick had set. To make things worse, I was separated from the group once again so I could work on my letter without distraction.

I sat down in the shade and took out my journal. There were a few disclosures I could offer, things I hadn't wanted to share before. Like how the first blow job I gave fell into a gray area of consent. There had been no kissing, no buildup. We were sitting on my bed, my pink bed in my pink room, and he unzipped his pants. I knew what I was supposed to do and he guided me. He pushed my head up and down, hard, until my eyes watered. Half from the force of it, half because I wanted him to love me. Even though I hated every second of it, and even though he knew that, this was as close to love as I was going to get.

There was one good thing about Rick's Sunday visits. On his way out to whatever cluster of trees we were stationed by that week, he stopped at the intake trailer to pick up a new round of provisions. Along with the usual rations we were each given a sausage link and a block of American cheese. This was our Sunday dinner. It felt like a treat, but it wasn't meant to be. We ate cheese and sausage on Sundays simply because they were the most perishable items. If we didn't get to them right away, they'd spoil in the heat.

After subsisting on congealed beans and soggy oatmeal all week, meat and cheese was practically fine dining. It was the first meal I didn't have to force myself to swallow, and I daresay I even enjoyed it. Unfortunately, my digestive system had grown used to the beans and oatmeal. I felt the effects of these new rich foods immediately. Just as soon as they arrived the cheese and sausage were ready to exit my body.

I grabbed a few squares of toilet paper and asked to use the bathroom.

"I'll be listening for your number."

We'd been at the campsite for a few days and the latrine was especially disgusting. The smell was unbearable, like a rancid version of the food I'd just eaten. I started gagging when I was still ten yards away. By the time I reached the latrine, I was fighting back vomit, my body ready to expel its contents by any means.

"Fuck you," I yelled into the hole.

I retched, spitting out half-digested sausage.

"Thirteen," I yelled back toward camp.

I can't do it. I won't do it.

"I fucking hate you."

I meant the hole. I meant Rick. My parents. Lynn Anne Moore. Even the bees were getting a piece of my wrath. *Fuck this.* I turned away from the smell and ventured a little deeper into the woods. There, I found a bush and turned it into my own personal latrine.

"Thirteen!"

I walked back to camp with newfound confidence. Like a dog marking his territory, I'd just laid my first surface turd. It was a tiny act of rebellion, but it felt a lot bigger. I was letting the world know it hadn't beaten me yet.

The feeling lasted until bedtime. That was all I got, an hour's reprieve from dread and sadness. Zipped into my sleeping bag in the all-consuming darkness, a familiar terror crept back in. There was an eerie sound track that played in the woods each night. In the background, owls hooted and wind swept through the trees. Up close, leaves rustled and twigs snapped under the foot of some creature. It was probably a squirrel or a raccoon. But in my mind, it could have been anyone or anything.

I shivered. I craved my baby blanket more than ever. It was unfair, even cruel, that I couldn't have this one tiny comfort. I wanted to disappear into the pink-and-white knitting and stay safely inside forever.

"Weed. Pot. Mary Jane. Reefer. Every generation calls it something different." A staffer named Taylor had begun the following day's group session with a lecture. "But they all say the same thing. *It doesn't count. It's not a real drug.*"

She looked around the circle. Because of my unofficial demotion back to Earth Phase, I sat outside the circle once again.

"You're thinking exactly that right now, aren't you?"

A few of the girls stifled nervous laughter.

"Thinking that I don't get it," Taylor said. "Because it's natural. It's medicinal. It isn't a big deal. But your brains? They're still developing.

And you'd better believe weed gets in the way of that. And it leads to other things, doesn't it?"

Not for me. Nothing bad happened to me because of weed.

"Carolina," Taylor said, "what was the first drug you tried?"

"Reefer," Carolina said.

"And how old were you when you switched to hard drugs, Isabelle?"

"Fifteen," Isabelle said.

"Wow, I bet there's a story there," Taylor said. "What happened that made you start so young?"

"Nothing. It was just...around."

Taylor raised her eyebrows. *Around?*

"Not my parents or anything," Isabelle said. "I have an older brother."

Taylor flashed a look at the staffer sitting across from her.

"And he did drugs?" the staffer said.

"Him and his friends, yeah. They were always just in the house. Getting high."

"And they offered it to you?" Taylor leaned forward. "Or did you ask for it?"

Isabelle shrugged, like she didn't remember.

"You asked for it, didn't you?"

"I guess."

"And they let you do it with them, didn't they?"

Isabelle nodded.

"But not without getting something in return."

She looked confused.

"Oh, come on," Taylor said. "Don't act all naive."

"I don't know what you mean."

"Isabelle, this game with you is getting really old, and if you don't start getting honest with yourself, we are just going to keep you here longer."

Isabelle looked as scared as I felt, stuck with no way out.

"Was it a hand job? Blow job? Both?"

"No," she said. "I don't know." The tears started slowly, leaking from Isabelle's lashless eyes.

"This is a safe space, Isabelle."

She continued to cry. Her eyes were wide, terrified.

"Was it . . . more?"

Isabelle was sobbing now. She buried her face in her hands.

"Oh no," Taylor said. "You poor thing. So young. And such a violation." She looked proud. Like she'd cracked the case. A major breakthrough. "Well, it really explains a lot, don't you think?"

Taylor called an end to the meeting. As the rest of us walked away, she took Isabelle aside.

"I'm proud of you," she said. "We really broke through today. This is going to be great for your progress."

As the rest of the group split off to journal, Marissa came up to me. "I bet they make her write a letter," she whispered.

"To the guys?"

"Maybe. Or her parents. They do stuff like that all the time."

I thought about it all night. Isabelle hadn't actually admitted to anything. In fact, she tried to tell Taylor that she was wrong about her brother's friends. Taylor kept pushing, though, unwilling to accept anything but the darkest version of the story. The trauma that would explain everything and prove that the brutal tactics of the woods were saving us, after all.

I realized this was exactly what Greta had been trying to do to me when she accused me of lying about being a virgin. After seeing the way Isabelle was basically forced to admit to a false story, I wondered if I'd have to do the same. Taylor seemed to think Isabelle's tears proved something—a dark secret, finally exposed. I don't think they were about that at all. Isabelle was frustrated and scared. She was worried she'd never get out of the woods. Or worse, that lockdown was in her future.

Something else crossed my mind then. What if I did write about the blow job I didn't actually want to give? Would that information make its way home? I imagined my father pounding on the door of my class-mates' houses. And my brother, vindicated in his rage. How could I ever go back to school after something like that got out? I'd be an outcast, a pariah. That is, if people actually believed me. It was equally possible I'd be accused of lying. The crazy girl with the crazy stories. It was a lose-lose situation any way I looked at it.

I was going to have to make something up.

As soon as I had the thought I knew I was stuck with it. I was scared for my life and didn't know if my limited traumas would even suffice. I figured saying what they wanted to hear was my best shot at surviving. One road led to lockdown and the other to a social catastrophe in my hometown. This was a middle way. I would compromise the truth to keep myself safe. It didn't feel great, but it was the only solution I could think of. I opened my journal and started writing, and I felt sick to my stomach the moment I did.

I knew this was the worst possible thing I could have lied about, but it was the only way. Lying was a lot better than lockdown until I was twenty-one years old.

It's the first week of summer. I've just finished my freshman year and my whole class is at the beach. We'll be there for five days, staying in rental houses, two or three to a room. I'm with Jenna and her mom is our house's chaperone. Jenna's mom is cool. She lets us stay out late and throw parties in the backyard.

There's a group of guys in the house next door. They're older, probably sixteen or seventeen. Maybe even college aged. The night I meet them I'm drunk on Jägermeister. Jenna's mom had gone to bed and we're trying to be quiet. But I get so drunk I step on a broken bottle in my bare feet. My foot starts gushing blood. One of the guys is a lifeguard. He gets his first-aid kit and bandages my wound. Jenna's mom never has to know.

We have a big party on our last night. The guys from next door come over and they bring vodka. I mix it with orange juice and take big sips. I drink a lot of vodka and orange juice. Then the lifeguard is there and he's asking me about my foot. He's asking to check my wound. He says he has a Porsche and do I want to see it?

I say yes. I'm so drunk I can barely walk straight. He shows me the car. And suddenly I'm in it and we're kissing. There's nothing I can do. I have no control over my body so I leave it. My vodka-soaked mind is miles away and my body belongs to someone else. The lifeguard assaults me and when it's over, I pretend I'm asleep. That way I don't have to think about it. I don't have to admit that I let it happen, not to myself or anyone else.

I don't know what I would have done if my lie got any pushback. The staff could have questioned my story or probed me for more details. Maybe I would have taken it all back, but the more likely scenario was that I would have doubled down on my lie—leaving me feeling twice as guilty and sick to my stomach. But no one questioned me. The staff seemed pleased to have another example of success with one of their campers. My parents now had an explanation for the dark moods that overtook me, a justification for why I was this way. Never mind that I had been angry for years before that summer at the beach. At least for that moment I was no longer a candidate for lockdown, I had finally done real work. I could go to one of the therapeutic schools where they can only keep you until you are eighteen.

The craziest part was, I never really had to talk about the incident again. I was let back into the group like nothing had happened. Even Rick didn't get into specifics. At our next meeting, he simply asked if I felt better after letting people in. I was grateful I didn't have to wallow in my lie, but it did seem questionable from a therapeutic standpoint. What kind of counselor doesn't work through the emotions surrounding a confession like that?

I wondered how many other girls had made things up. I asked myself that question many times.

All of them, probably.

The longer I stayed in the woods, the more affirmed I felt in my decision. Manipulating the truth was just survival. It was a tool, a psychological bow drill we could use to keep ourselves safe. Unspoken but not uncommon. But it still felt like I was entering dangerous territory.

What happens now? Am I going to be defined by this one night, a horrific incident that didn't even happen? Will I have to go over my story again and again, rehashing the details so many times I actually start to believe them?

It felt like the lie was stuck to my soul, had become a part of my identity. I wanted to scrub it off. If I could have, I would have taken the hottest, longest shower of my whole life. Of course that wasn't an option. So I took a sponge bath, the cold creek water and bandanna a poor substitute for the total scouring I craved. I wanted new skin, untouched by cruelty and manipulation. Without the residue left by all the Ricks and the Kendras and the Lynn Annes of the world. But the best I'd get was a fresh pair of underwear and a T-shirt I hadn't been wearing for three days straight.

Chapter 10

THE NEWS FINALLY arrived that Polly was getting out. Like an inmate released early for good behavior, Number Five had jumped the line. She got the official word during an afternoon session. Her parents had written a letter, a saccharine missive heaped with annoying praise that she read aloud.

"We're so proud of you. You're a shining star. Our good girl was in there all along."

Polly read all this with a placid smile. But when she got to the next paragraph she let out a shriek.

"I'm going to Oakley!"

I knew about Oakley, but only because Polly talked about it all the time. It was one of the many overpriced therapeutic boarding schools most kids attended straight from the woods. To hear her sing its praises, you'd have thought it was an Ivy League college and not a school for rich fuckups in the middle of nowhere.

"At Oakley you get to ski," Polly had told me half a dozen times. "And there's white-water rafting in the summer."

Thrilling. To be honest, I didn't pay much attention to the chatter about schools at first. I was convinced that if I could just make it through my time in the woods without getting sent to lockdown, I'd get to go home.

The odds were against me, but I refused to accept them. So I took in the rumors as a passive listener.

Good to know, but that doesn't really concern me.

I had managed to glean that there was something of a hierarchy in the world of therapeutic boarding schools, and Oakley was apparently one of the better ones. Meaning: more expensive and less strict. A place for medium-troubled teens. Not as rough as the lockdowns or the military institutions. More outdoorsy than Carlbrook, less austere than Mount Bachelor. Nothing at all like Montana Academy, which seemed to be entirely focused on ranchhanding.

"I leave in three days," Polly said, practically squealing. "Oh my god, and my parents are coming to pick me up!"

"Yep," a staffer said. "They're really proud of you, Polly. You should be proud of yourself."

Polly's comic grin expanded, then morphed into a frown.

"Oh wow," she said, looking around the circle. "Only three days. I'm gonna miss you all so much."

We mumbled in response. No one seemed particularly upset about Polly's departure, not even the girls with numbers lower than hers. The ones who'd been here longer but hadn't "progressed" with the same speed and enthusiasm as my ass-kissing mentor. It was a relief that she was leaving, although I had no doubt she'd be extra peppy until then, reminding me every day that she was leaving while I was still stuck in the woods.

For the next two days, Polly talked incessantly about Oakley. The school, she explained, was basically a ski resort in the mountains of Utah. There was a rock-climbing gym and a pottery studio, and resident dogs roamed freely. Marissa had heard a rumor that Oakley was basically a halfway house for kids fresh out of lockdown, but if Polly knew that, she was in total denial.

"I feel like the luckiest girl in the world," she said, her fake grin now permanent.

I woke the morning of Polly's departure to find a note outside my dwelling.

DON'T GIVE UP.

Thanks. That's just soooo helpful.

All day, she was like a backwoods Santa Claus, gifting pieces of her bow drill set and uneaten food. Polly had made it to Water Phase, the third stage, which meant she had a flashlight in her possession. I'd coveted that light on many a dark night, but Polly wasn't allowed to pass it along to me or anyone else. The only way to earn a flashlight—or a Crazy Creek chair, should one make it all the way to Air Phase—was to kiss a lot of staffer ass.

So I ended up with Polly's trail mix.

"I didn't even eat the M&M's," she said.

In the afternoon we gathered for her graduation ceremony. The setup was similar to the one I found waiting for me the day I joined Fire Phase. We had arranged pebbles in a circle, where Polly's name was spelled out in flower petals, letters alternating between pink and blue. It was supposed to represent transformation—the blossoming of a new, better Polly—but it looked more like a grave marker. In a way, I guess it sort of was.

"I can't believe this is actually happening!"

She stepped into the circle, beaming. Her parents were there, beaming right back. When Kendra broke the ceremonial stick in half, I fantasized about grabbing it out of her hand and thrusting the pointed edge toward Polly. I could hold her hostage, like some sort of pirate, and force her parents to drive me out of here.

"Today we celebrate a special girl," Kendra said, "and acknowledge all the hard work and growth that's led up to this point. Polly, you're proof that with the right tools and a good attitude, anything can be accomplished. I'm proud to send you off on the next leg of your journey."

"Oh my god, thank you so much."

Polly's parents clasped hands. They both wore khaki slacks and lace-up loafers in some prim approximation of camping attire. Neither looked like they'd spent much time in the wilderness. They had a WASP-y, repressed vibe, and I pictured the moment they found out about their daughter's sexual exploits: *Three boys! How could you do that to us?*

Now they were working hard to seem warm and loving. Good parents who would never send their daughter away unless it was a last resort. They had to save her from herself.

And look how well it worked. She's not even a real person anymore.

Polly's mother sat forward. "Sweetheart, we are so proud of you. You've turned your whole life around."

Her father nodded. "You're becoming exactly the kind of young woman we've tried to raise."

"It was a hard decision to bring you out here." Polly's mom blinked away tears. "And we didn't come to it lightly. But it was the right one. This place has exceeded our expectations."

"Thank you, Mama," Polly said, nodding. "Thank you for saving me."

Mentally, I rolled my eyes.

Polly's mom turned toward the circle. She looked from girl to girl, but she clearly wasn't really seeing any of us. She wasn't taking in the sunken eyes and the scowling lips. The layers of caked-on dirt that made us appear more mud than flesh. She was seeing only her own daughter, her wayward child who had beaten the odds and was going to be okay.

For a little while, maybe. On the outside, at least.

"You know what?" Polly's mom said. "I wish I could call every one of your parents and tell them how great you're all doing."

The ceremony ended, and we moved on to Polly's good-bye dinner. It was still just rice and beans, but at least we ate hot. Not only that, but the staff actually started a fire for us, showing off their superior bow-drilling skills. Nevertheless, the sight of gelatinous beans sliming across half-cooked lumps of rice didn't exactly have Polly's parents salivating.

"You're welcome to join us," a staffer said. "There's plenty to go around."

"Oh, that's so nice of you."

Suddenly the couple was tight-lipped and stuttering, cutting one another off in a desperate attempt to avoid eating this crap.

"If only we'd known."

"Such a shame."

"But we have reservations in town."

Waffle House takes reservations now? I remembered all the fast-food joints from the drive up and wanted to laugh.

Polly's parents seemed ready to go. After all the speeches about how wonderful the program was, they couldn't wait to leave the woods. They urged their daughter along, helping her load her pack into Nate's truck.

My blood boiled as she climbed into the front seat. I wanted to run over and jump in. Maybe I could hide in the truck bed, escape somewhere between Appalachia and Utah. Instead, I ate raw ramen noodles, biting right off the block, and ignored the hand frantically waving goodbye out the window.

Turns out Polly wasn't all the way gone just yet.

I was boiling the head of my toothbrush, as per our nightly ritual to avoid a painful death by listeria, when the staff called us over. Kendra's face was expressionless, and she wielded her flashlight like a weapon.

"Everyone follow me. Stay close."

"Where are we going?"

"You'll see. No talking, Allison."

We'll see what? A bear? A dead body. Maybe it's one of us.

We did a quick count of the girls. Out of habit, I expected thirteen, but there were only twelve of us now. Once again, I felt like a ghost.

There is no Thirteen. Now I'm Twelve.

Kendra marched us through a dense thicket of trees. Up ahead, another staffer stood with her flashlight pointed downward. The spot she marked was small, too small for a body.

That is, a body left intact.

"Circle up," Kendra said. "Everyone in."

We clustered together and peered into the beam of light. For a moment

I had no idea what we were even looking at. As my eyes adjusted, something else started happening to my nose.

It's poop.

We all seemed to realize the same thing at once.

It's human poop.

I wanted to laugh. And I could tell a few of the girls were right there with me. The whole thing was so absurd. Fourteen people standing around in the darkened woods, gazing at a mound of human feces.

"Ladies," Kendra said, "this is a surface turd."

No shit. Wait. Literally, yes shit.

"Surface turds, as we all know, are not allowed."

Once again, I stifled a laugh. Either from gagging or giggling, most of us were covering our mouths.

"Someone," Kendra said, "needs to claim it."

Claim it? Claim the pile of shit? This might be a new low.

"This isn't a joke," the other staffer said. "We're going to stand right here until someone owns up."

Kendra moved her flashlight off the turd and directed it toward our faces, interrogation-style. One by one, she started calling people out.

"Allison? Is this your way of trying to exert some control?"

"Ew," Allison said. "No way. That does not belong to me."

"Carolina? Seems like your style."

"It isn't," Carolina said.

"She's right," Isabelle chimed in. "Arson? Totally."

"Or vandalism," Marissa said. "But not this."

"Elizabeth?"

I was caught in a grin.

"Maybe you got lost on your way to the latrine?"

"No, ma'am," I said. "Wasn't me."

Not this time, at least.

"Well, it was one of you." The other staffer was losing patience. "So we can drag this out all night, or you can just speak up."

"What if it was Polly?" Allison said.

"It wasn't," Kendra said. "Don't try and weasel out of this."

"But how do you know?"

"Come on, girls. Don't try to pass the blame. Polly wouldn't do that, not on her last day."

"I mean, isn't that exactly when she'd do it?" I said.

Marissa laughed. "That's when I'd do it."

"Nice try," Kendra said.

She dismissed our absurd line of reasoning, not that I blamed her. But the longer we stood there, the more it began to feel like it probably *was* Polly. Minutes ticked by and the turd remained unclaimed. None of the other girls even seemed guilty, and these were some generally guilty-seeming girls.

Even the staff seemed to come around to the idea. Not that they admitted it or anything. It was late and a person can stand around staring at a piece of shit for only so long. The interrogation moved from casting blame to fixing the problem.

"Well, *someone's* gonna have to clean this up. We aren't leaving it here."

"You want us to clean up Polly's shit?" Carolina said.

"No," Kendra said. "For that snide remark, I want *you* to clean up Polly's shit. Or whoever's shit it is."

"That's disgusting."

"Find a stick. No arguing or we'll be here all night. The rest of you can run pack drills."

"In the dark?" Isabelle said.

"Yes, in the dark. Let's hope there are no more surprises lying around."

Oh god. Anything but fucking pack drills.

I absolutely hated pack drills. We all did. They were pointless and hard, a mix of physical exertion and anal-retentive folding. Basically, we had to run from Point A to Point B, drop to the ground, empty our knapsacks, then immediately put everything *back inside*. We had five minutes to complete the task, get up, and do it all over again. I couldn't figure out what it could possibly be a "drill" for. Except maybe some obscure Japanese game show.

DON'T GIVE UP.

I arrived sweaty and exhausted at the foot of my shelter, where Polly's message sat glittery and annoying in the silver moonlight.

Fuck you, Polly.

I lifted my boot and stomped down hard, right on the word *DON'T*.

Now it's more realistic. All I want is to give up. To go to sleep and stay asleep until this whole thing is over.

I threw my boots outside my shelter for pickup and lay down. As tired as I was, I couldn't fall asleep—not even for a minute, much less eternity. There was something off about the night. Something different I just couldn't put my finger on.

The crying. It's gone.

I'd gotten so used to falling asleep to distant sobbing that I'd stopped even registering it as strange. It was my new songs of the sea CD— ambient noise, the same every night. Its sudden absence was jarring. It could also mean only one thing.

Polly was the sobbing girl. She cried at night to make up for smiling all day.

It really had been an act, and it worked like a charm.

Turns out Polly was kind of a badass the whole time.

Chapter 11

Eleven

I began losing track of time. All the days blended together and I could no longer remember how many of them I'd spent in the woods. After Polly left I became Twelve and soon enough I was Eleven. Summer began to fade as fall approached. At first it was a relief to hike without the sun beating down so harshly, but the overcast days brought their own kind of dreary fatigue.

I had just become Ten when the nights got so cold I started sleeping in all my clothes.

Ten

As miserable as I was, I had to put things in perspective when a new girl named Stephanie arrived. There was something off about Stephanie. Her body worked differently, her eyes and tongue and even the way she walked. But these physical anomalies were nothing compared to her behavior, which was aggressive and insolent from the start. If I arrived angry, Stephanie was enraged. She stomped around, kicking up dirt and yelling, from the moment she got out of Nate's truck.

Stephanie was neurodiverse. She was defiant not just because she was angry, but because she was completely overwhelmed. I couldn't believe her parents would send her off to a place like this. Or that the staff seemed to show no sympathy for this girl with special needs. I wanted to give her a hug and tell her things would get easier, but I knew it was against the rules. I knew for someone like Stephanie, there was no reason to think it *would* get any easier.

In fact, it got harder. Stephanie's first few days were excruciating to watch. Her first hike was a shorter one and she got through it all right. But the second time we set out to wander across the woods, Stephanie wasn't having it. We'd been out for only an hour or two when Stephanie decided she'd had enough. She threw a full-on tantrum, screaming and kicking. It only escalated from there until, eventually, she plopped down on the ground and flat-out refused to move.

"Get on your feet right now," a staffer said. "Or you're seriously in trouble."

But she shook her head and held her ground. The staffer tried to physically lift Stephanie to her feet.

"You're on a path straight to lockdown. Is that what you want? The way you're going, there's a straitjacket in your future."

Stephanie didn't even respond. She just balled her fists and stayed seated. It was kind of heroic, really. The rest of us had never seen anyone stand up to the staff like this. If it got us out of hiking, we'd practically name a holiday in her honor. Clearly, Stephanie wasn't going to back down and the staff would have no choice but to call it a day. It was either that, or leave a vulnerable minor all by herself in the middle of the Appalachian woods.

Wouldn't you know it, they did just that. Two staffers stayed behind and the rest of us marched on.

When we finally arrived at our new campsite the staff huddled together around a two-way radio. For the next fifteen or twenty minutes they were so preoccupied with the Stephanie situation, not to mention being down two counselors, that they barely even noticed the rest of us. After weeks of constant surveillance, when every movement was tracked and every word policed, this little bit of freedom had a dizzying effect.

At first we just talked a little more than usual. Then we started quietly sharing "war stories," relating anecdotes from home just to see what we could get away with. Sitting with Marissa and Allison, it occurred to me that if there was ever a time to run away, this was it.

"Think we could pull it off?" I said.

"Maybe for a night," Marissa said. "But they'd find us for sure come daylight."

"We need to pull a Stephanie," Allison said. "Make it so they don't know what else to do with us."

Allison grinned and stood up. She climbed the branches of the nearest tree and jumped, trying to land on one foot. She ended up on her ass instead and we all started laughing.

"What are you doing?" Marissa said. "Are you trying to break your leg?"

"Nah. Just sprain it."

I was halfway up the tree by then. I tried to mimic Allison's move, but my instincts took over and my other foot came down at the last second.

"Dammit!"

"Guys, there's no point." Marissa grabbed the back of Allison's shirt to keep her from the tree.

"We can totally make this work," I said. "Maybe a higher tree?"

"There's no point," she repeated. "Best-case scenario, you'll get x-rays and a real doctor. Worst case, some guy in town who thinks he knows how to set a bone."

"Or Nate," I said. "He seems like the type."

Marissa shrugged. "Either way you're only gonna end up right back here. Hiking in a fucking cast."

"At least you'd get to sleep in a real bed for a while," Allison said. "Oh god, and take a shower."

"Hardly." Marissa shook her head. She craned her neck to make sure the staff was still clustered around the radio. "Wanna hear about the time I got West Nile?"

Marissa launched into her story. Really, it was about the time she *didn't* get West Nile, but that's just getting technical. It was only her second week in the woods when the illness hit. Fever, rash, swollen glands. At first the staff accused her of faking her symptoms. They made her hike with a fever and wouldn't let her eat hot. Marissa kept getting sicker and sicker and the other girls were convinced she had West Nile virus. Finally, the staff decided to take her into town where a doctor let them know she actually had a kidney infection.

"The worst case he'd ever seen," Marissa said. "Said that out loud and everything."

The doctor ordered a week of bed rest. The staff gave her forty-eight hours to recover. She spent two days in a run-down motel with a counselor on constant guard. She put cardboard over the windows and covered the bathroom mirror.

"And after all that, they wouldn't even let me take a fucking shower."

"Holy shit," I said. "That's insane."

It *was* insane. And it really killed the mood. By the time the staff called us over, we'd lost all sense of excitement. Things didn't get any better when we heard Stephanie's fate.

Kendra cleared her throat. "Stephanie will no longer be a part of our group. She'll remain in the woods with two dedicated staff members, but she won't have the privilege of remaining a part of this unit."

It was a serious consequence. It reminded me how high the stakes really were. Maybe Stephanie really did remain in the woods. But we never saw her again. More likely she ended up in lockdown.

Nine

Nine felt right. Familiar. It was the number on all my old soccer jerseys, Mia Hamm's number. She was wearing nine when her team won the World Cup, when they secured Olympic gold. It's right there on the poster taped to my bedroom wall, the one I placed directly at my eye line so I'd see it first thing every morning.

I really thought I could be just like her one day. I thought I could be like all the women on my wall. Tara Lipinski. Dominique Dawes. Brandi Chastain. But I was nothing like those women and I never would be. I was suddenly embarrassed to yell out that I was Nine.

I didn't deserve it. I was no Mia Hamm.

Eight

"Packs unzipped, right now," a staffer yelled. "Don't make me say it twice."

All six counselors stared us down, pacing the area on high alert. They were like detectives, hot on the trail of a missing knife. It had been in the staff tent and now it wasn't—stolen, they were convinced, by one of us.

"No one moves until we find it."

They went through our packs one by one. All of our things, folded just so, were dumped straight out onto the ground. At first, the thought that one of the other girls had stolen a knife was kind of exciting.

Maybe we can stage a mutiny. Or hold the staff hostage while we eat all their bacon.

But as they searched the piles over and over again I started getting restless. I hopped from one foot to the other to keep my legs from cramping. Sitting down, of course, was out of the question.

"It's obviously not here." I kept my voice low so only Marissa could hear me.

My friend nodded. "Probably buried out by the latrine or something."

"Who do you think it was?"

"No idea. Carolina?"

"Maybe. Or one of the new girls."

"Oh my god." Marissa's eyes went wide. "What if it was Stephanie?"

"Yeah," I said. "And that's why she disappeared. She tried to stab her guardians."

But the two staffers who'd remained with Stephanie had been back for days. They were there right in front of us, taking apart bear bags and turning sleeping bags inside out. And they both seemed completely unstabbed.

"Holy shit."

Marissa and I had the thought at the exact same time. We tried to keep from laughing.

"*What if they stabbed Stephanie?*"

The knife never turned up. Who knew if it was ever even missing at all? It was possible the whole thing was another game, a way for the staff to mess with our heads and maintain control.

Seven

I've always hated green peppers. As a kid, I refused to eat them. After many dinner table standoffs, I finally wised up and started hiding them in my napkin. Even in the woods, half-starving and deficient in every vitamin not found in ramen, green peppers were the one vegetable I couldn't stand to eat.

At first it didn't matter much. Most weeks our veggie was a cucumber, or maybe a few pieces of cauliflower. But as the season turned, the ever-durable bell pepper entered heavy rotation. I would hide my weekly ration and bury it as soon as I could sneak away. Which was a fine strategy until the random pack searches started in the aftermath of the missing knife.

"What is this?"

Kendra held up my bear bag like it was contraband. Inside, a week's worth of uneaten peppers had gone limp and wrinkled.

"I don't like raw peppers," I said.

"And I don't care. You should have eaten them by now."

I nodded, hoping that if I seemed sorry enough Kendra would move on. As if Kendra ever moved on from anything without doling out some sort of humiliation.

"Would have been a whole lot easier for you," she said, "if you'd eaten them with your meals. Instead of all at once."

"There's no way I could possibly do that."

"Better figure it out. Until you finish every last bite, no one can start hiking. Don't make me have to tell Rick you are being difficult again."

Just the thought of all those peppers made my stomach churn. But Kendra meant what she said, and I didn't want to be the reason everyone else got stuck with a night hike. So I sat down with a jug of water and began to eat. It was that or maybe I'd end up like Stephanie.

I figured the quicker, the better. The more water, the better. I felt like throwing up after the first bite and I just wanted it to be done. So I chewed and swallowed and chugged. The food rose back up and I forced it down. I'd eaten almost all the peppers along with half a gallon of water when it finally became too much. I leaned forward and vomited up a bright green concoction. My half-chewed pepper bile sat in a neat pile on the ground.

At least that's the end of it.

But it wasn't. Kendra examined the mess.

"You did that on purpose. You didn't even chew."

"Yes I did," I said.

She shrugged. "Eat your vegetables, Elizabeth. No one hikes until you do."

She looked at the ground. It took me a moment to realize what she meant. She wanted me to eat my own vomit, right off the ground.

This has to be my low point. No way it gets worse than this.

Six

"What are *Separates?*"

It was one of the new girls talking. She was fresh off Earth Phase and overly enthusiastic about being allowed to speak. The girl still had the shine of shampoo in her hair and her face wasn't filthy, and her legs were shaved. Stubbly, but shaved. It was something I hadn't even thought about for ages.

"Pretty much what it sounds like," Kendra said. "For the next three days each of you will be confined to a plot of land. We will bring your meals directly to you. There will be no speaking, not even to staff."

"What if we have an emergency?" the new girl said.

"Unless it's a matter of life or death, *no speaking.* Any thoughts you have, write them down in your journal. You may read. You may write. I recommend you do both. This is a time for silent contemplation. It's an opportunity to reflect on the choices you've made thus far and the choices you plan to make going forward."

The new girl groaned. But Separates sounded more like a gift than a punishment to me. Three days without the staff hovering over my shoulder? Three days off from hiking? It was practically a dream come true.

"Any questions?" Kendra said. "Well, write them down in your notebook."

I was taken to my section of the woods. I set up my shelter and looked around. None of the other girls were close enough to identify by sight, but I could see their orange T-shirts peeking out from behind the trees. It was nice to be alone, and my setup actually felt a little cozy. Immediately, I thought about how nice it would be to fall asleep with the warm sun on my face. But napping didn't qualify as self-reflection and was thus forbidden. Given how frequently they checked up on us, there was no point trying to get away with it.

We definitely couldn't run. They had taken our boots, leaving us with just those Crocs. I had my journal and the book we'd all been given:

Man's Search for Meaning, Viktor Frankl's account of surviving a World War II concentration camp.

I didn't feel like bullshitting deep thoughts in the pages of my notebook—I had a feeling anything I wrote would travel straight from my pencil to the staff and possibly even to Rick. My initial bliss was beginning to curdle. It was too much solitude with nothing to do but throw rocks at the trees.

Bull's-eye. That makes six games for Elizabeth and four for the tree.

Once I'd mastered tree darts there was nothing left to do but read. So I finally cracked open *Man's Search for Meaning*. It was, to my great surprise, an incredibly inspiring book. I kept reading even as the sun was going down and my eyes had to strain to make out the words. The fact that these people had survived under such terrible and cruel conditions almost made me angry at myself. As bad as the woods may have been, it wasn't a Nazi concentration camp. Not even close.

I still have choices. I still have some control.

As I read on, I realized that Frankl was actually making the point that survival is relative. That even in the darkest situations, an individual's attitude has a real effect on whether or not they make it through. The message really spoke to me. I couldn't control my circumstances, but I could control my own reactions. I could choose to let my rage fizzle out instead of exploding every time I was provoked. I knew the staff expected me to be angry. That it was part of the reason I was still in the woods with no end in sight. They were looking for the girl who had nearly jumped out of my parents' car into oncoming traffic, the girl my escorts thought they'd have to restrain.

The anger hadn't gone anywhere. It was still simmering inside me, always threatening to boil over. But all of a sudden, it felt like fuel. It meant that I was strong, that part of me still wanted to survive. I didn't write any of this in my journal, of course, but I thought about it all night.

Five

The weather took another turn when the sky got cloudy and stayed that way for a long time. Late summer had transformed into early fall. *Appalachian monsoon season. This is what all the storm drills were for.* Every time the sky cracked open we'd all gather in an open field to sit on our packs, feet planted on the ground in case lightning struck. We'd stay like that for hours until the rains finally stopped and we could go off and eat our dinner or bundle up inside our sleeping bags. Coziness, I was learning, was a relative concept.

It often rained for days on end before a reprieve came in the form of a sunny morning. Dry weather was a double-edged sword. It meant longer hikes even though the days themselves were getting shorter. Sometimes we wouldn't reach our new campsite until sunset and we'd rush to set up our shelters in the dwindling light.

One night I climbed into my hastily arranged sleeping bag without bothering to look around. I was exhausted and cold, ready for sleep's numbing embrace. I turned onto my side, expecting my head to touch down in dreamland. Instead it landed on something slimy and wet, something that squished. I sat up immediately.

That was an alien. I just touched an alien.

It was much worse. It was a slug. A long, fat slug that left a trail of mucus on my sleeping bag.

Another bedtime disaster came after a week of clear skies, so cloudless I convinced myself the stormy season must be over. A routine day of hiking brought us to yet another identical campsite. A seasoned veteran when it came to finding the best sleeping areas by now, I was particularly excited whenever I came across a ditch or a crevice between two trees. The right trench could make you feel almost like you were sleeping in a hammock, or on colder nights, nestled inside a cocoon. It was a bonus that on this particular evening the perfect crevice happened to be right next to where Marissa was setting up her own tent. That meant we'd be able to talk a little before bed without staff overhearing and chastising us for telling "war stories."

These nighttime chats had become as important as food. As brief and infrequent as they were, they sustained me. With Marissa, I could actually speak my mind. I was a regular fifteen-year-old having a normal conversation with her friend. Not a prisoner or a flight risk, not the girl with limited access to her own shoes. Sometimes I was even able to forget, to step outside the nightmare and just exist. For a few moments at a time, the woods receded and I remembered what it was like to feel free.

That night the woods asserted itself with extra force. It was like a punishment. Reality's revenge because I had dared, even briefly, to escape it. I was nestled inside my cocoon, protected from the cold and as comfortable as I'd been in months. My eyelids grew heavy and I felt sleep coming toward me. The next thing I knew, I was drowning.

It took a moment to realize what had happened. I registered the water and my instincts kicked in. I leapt out of my shelter and found myself under a sudden, torrential downpour. The sky had cracked wide open, and the rain had turned my perfect, cozy crevice into a river. Everything was soaking wet. My sleeping bag and my extra clothes were completely drenched. I was soaked from head to toe.

"Come on, girls." The staff was rushing around with flashlights. It had started storming. "This is what we've been drilling for."

I shivered violently as I ran toward the road with the other girls. I put down my pack and hunkered down to wait out the thunder and lightning.

For the next three days I hiked in wet clothes. For the next three nights I slept inside a trash bag. On breaks from hiking I hung my sleeping bag in the sunniest spot I could find, hoping it would just hurry up and dry before I caught pneumonia. There was no sympathy from the counselors, who refused to let me wear the dry clothes Marissa was offering. It was my fault for picking the ditch, they said. I should have known better.

I didn't argue and I didn't complain. Not even once. I was beginning to control the way I reacted and it felt a little like power.

Four

But the staff didn't like power. They didn't like that it was getting harder to provoke me. Not that it kept them from trying anyway.

One night after a full, hard day of hiking, I was called out to handle the bear bags. I'd done it before, the nightly ritual of tossing a rope over a tree branch for our food to hang. Usually any branch taller than a bear was acceptable but not tonight. I was told to reach a specific branch, one way up the trunk of the oak tree.

"That's too high," I said. "I don't think I can reach it."

The staffer smiled. "Oh, I think you can."

I spent almost an hour trying to toss the rope over the branch. Until I got it right, no one was allowed to go to bed. So I flung it over and over, even as my arms got weaker and each toss was lower than the last.

They're trying to provoke you. They want you to snap.

Eventually it was clear that I wasn't going to lose my temper and I most definitely was not going to reach that tree branch. So I was relieved of my duty and another girl was brought in. She flung the rope a few times. It caught on a much lower limb, and we all went to bed.

Three

I had been dreading life in the woods without Marissa. It felt like she was my only friend in the world, and once she graduated I'd really, truly, be all alone. At the same time, I was happy she was finally getting the fuck out of this place. She was sent off to a military school in Florida, some second-tier place I'd never heard of before and would likely never hear about again, but she seemed happy.

I still think about her sometimes and hope things turned out okay for Marissa. But I never spoke to her again.

Two

Eventually, even Carolina had to graduate. She'd been there for so long, always one tiny misstep away from lockdown, and the fact that she avoided it seemed like an achievement. A pair of escorts loaded up Nate's truck and Carolina slid into the back with barely so much as a good-bye. When the sputtering engine finally caught, Nate stepped on the gas and headed down the mountain.

I felt like I'd been in the woods for an eternity. Like whole lifetimes had gone by while I'd been hiking the same endless circle. Even still, the realization that I'd been there longer than anyone was startling. It was so hard to wrap my head around, and yet it was the truth.

One

I said it out loud just to hear what it would sound like.

One. One. One.

Then I yelled it at the top of my lungs.

Chapter 12

I LOOK AT my time in the woods as a string of bad days, spooling out one after another. Some days were really bad, and some felt more like a dull ache. The longer I was there, the harder it was to imagine ever getting out of the woods. I learned how to smile even when I wanted to cry; I learned how to laugh when I wanted to yell. There were moments of levity, too, of course. My late-night chats with Marissa and the time, midhike, when someone starting humming "Wonderwall." One by one, we all joined in. For whatever reason the staff didn't intervene and we belted out the whole song as we trekked, a choir of girls in filthy orange tees.

It was a routine, like anything else. Old girls left and new girls came; our rations of ramen and oats were replenished; we hiked; we met with Rick on Sundays. I became neither Polly nor Carolina. I wasn't a rebel and I wasn't a Girl Scout. I just got through each day as best I could, not stirring the pot for good or for bad, trying to remember what real life was like.

But I still had moments of hope when I was optimistic about my fate.

My life isn't gone, it's just on pause. If I can only get through the next day, and the day after that, this hell will be over.

Then my grandmother died. As per usual, I got the news in a letter.

My grandma was old, but her death was unexpected and I had to read the words twice before they sank in. I was close with my grammy, my father's mother, who lived nearby. I'd spend weekends at her house, picking flowers and painting rocks. She taught me how to cross-stitch and took me on trips to visit old Civil War battlefields. The thought of never seeing her again made me genuinely sad.

Did she think I was really away at summer camp? Off having fun instead of visiting her when she got sick? What did my parents tell her? I hope she didn't think I was just blowing her off.

Maybe it was wishful thinking, but I assumed the letter meant I'd be going home. My parents were probably already on their way to pick me up. I knew I wasn't supposed to leave the woods until I graduated, but surely an exception could be made. It was my grandmother's funeral, after all. My only chance to say good-bye.

"You can write her a letter if you want," the staffer named Greta said.

"A *letter*? Are you serious? And then what, mail it off to heaven?"

"Your father, actually, has offered to read it out loud."

"At the funeral?" I said.

Greta nodded. "Everyone agrees. Staff and your parents. It's important you stay on track out here."

I couldn't believe it. If the funeral of a person I loved wasn't enough to get me home, then nothing ever would be. I had been teary-eyed all day, but now I was really sobbing. I grabbed my journal and went off to sulk under the shade of a nearby tree. I was furious and more miserable than ever. The worst part was that I had no idea where my unhappiness was actually coming from. Was I really so grief-stricken over the loss of my grandmother? Or was I just upset that I didn't get to leave the woods?

After all, Grammy was as much of a hologram as anyone else by then. I hadn't seen my family for months. My friends were moving on with their lives. While I was stuck in Fire Phase, so disconnected from the world that I no longer knew what was real.

Dear Grammy, I'm sorry I'm not able to attend your funeral. It doesn't seem fair that I can't be there today, but I want you to know how much I'll miss you. You taught me how to sew and took me on so many trips. I loved hunting Easter eggs at your house and going to parades. You always had cherry cough drops in your pocket, and you'd sneak them to me like they were candy.

I can't believe you're gone. It saddens me to think of this as a good-bye, but I know life is everlasting. You'll be watching over me for now until we meet again someday.

I love you.

"For God so loved the world that he gave his only begotten son that whosoever believeth in him should not perish, but have everlasting life."—John 3:16

Good-bye, Grammy.

I wrote it again.

Good-bye.

The first one was for her and the second for me. I was saying good-bye to my old life. Because I finally understood that I was never going home again. Not really. The home in my mind was no longer a real place. It was a memory of a dead thing, nothing more, and I held a funeral in my mind right there beneath that oak tree.

Everything changed yet nothing changed. My future was uncertain, but my present was very much the same dull routine. Another hike, another fire, another hole in the ground. I handed over my boots at night and got them back each morning. Time lost its meaning and I'd given up counting the days long before I got to a hundred.

"Congratulations, Elizabeth."

Kendra said it like it was a good thing. She smiled at me and the rest of the group clapped.

"Thanks," I said, playing along.

A hundred days.

"How does it feel?"

I have no idea.

In one sense, it was an accomplishment. A testament to my strength. I'd actually survived in the woods for a hundred days. I'd slept a hundred nights on the hard ground, feeling completely alone, surrounded by darkness. And I hadn't given up.

"It feels pretty good," I said.

At the same time, a hundred days is a lot of fucking days. I'm not sure exactly what was keeping me in the woods so long. Maybe it didn't seem like I was doing enough emotional work or becoming a full-on Polly. I suspected the real thorn in my side was my reputation as the girl who'd tried to jump from her parents' car. I wondered if the staff might be trying to keep me around long enough for that troublemaker to reveal herself, for all that anger to come rushing out.

I never let it happen, though. And yet there I was, watching girls leave who'd arrived after me, still yelling out "One" every time I had to pee.

They couldn't keep me there forever. My time was almost up. It just had to be. Even Kendra seemed to know we were just going through the motions. Her friendliness was so unsettling I almost wished she'd go back to being bitchy.

"Lucky you," she said. "Have you picked a meal?"

"Chocolate chip pancakes," I said without missing a beat.

I'd had awhile to think about my answer. I'd seen a few other girls reach the hundred-day mark, and they were rewarded with a food item of their choice. The rest of us would fantasize about our own picks, and I always came back to the pancakes I used to have on Sunday mornings. I never expected I'd be stuck in the woods long enough to actually ask for them.

I got my reward during my next one-on-one session with Rick.

"Have a seat," he said. "How are you this week?"

"Good. I feel good."

"You seem good."

I nodded. *Just going through the motions.*

"Tell me," Rick said. "Do you feel as though you've been making progress?"

"Definitely. I'm so happy I was able to open up to you guys about my past. I feel like now I can put that all behind me and work on becoming a better person."

"That's wonderful news. We've noticed the same thing."

"Thank you." I forced a smile. "Thank you for helping me."

Rick seemed satisfied with the interaction. He pulled a plate wrapped in tinfoil from beneath his seat.

"As promised, chocolate chip pancakes."

He handed me the plate and I sat back. Maybe it was a power move or some weird perversion, but he was actually going to watch me eat. I wouldn't let that stop me, though. I'd been fantasizing about this moment for days.

I unwrapped the tinfoil, expecting to see warm, gooey chocolate chips bursting out of a thin, fluffy cake. But these pancakes were cold and dense. They were soggy with syrup poured hours before. I took a few bites and felt my stomach churn. After months of subsisting on little more than rice and air, the rich batter sat like a rock in my gut.

"Enjoying?"

A serpentine smile crept across Rick's face. So that was why he wanted to watch. He'd known all along that the pancakes would be too rich for me. I took one more bite to spite him, but that's all I could manage. The last thing I wanted was to spend the rest of the day hovering over the latrine. It just wasn't worth it.

I left the rest of the food with Rick and made my way back to camp. Nate's truck was parked by the creek, and I saw him passing off a brand-new girl. She looked like a fighter, just like I'd been once. Nate and I crossed paths on his way back to the pickup.

"You're looking skinny, Elizabeth."

No shit. It was like he and Rick had conspired to taunt me.

"Too skinny."

I shrugged. "I think I'm about the same."

But in reality, I suspected I'd been losing weight. I hadn't looked in a mirror for more than three months, but I had stretch marks on my thighs that definitely hadn't been there before I got to the woods.

"If you lose any more weight," Nate said, "I'm going to have to take you to get checked out."

Then give me some fucking real food. Not soggy pancakes and dry ramen. What the hell do you expect?

As much as I wanted to unleash an angry tirade at Nate, it just wasn't worth it. I needed to keep my head down. Avoid the bait. I couldn't give them one single reason to justify keeping me in the woods any longer. Either way, they'd win. I wanted the version where I'd be gone before they could take a victory lap.

"I won't," I said.

A week later, the letter I'd been waiting for finally came. It was handed to me during group and I nervously scanned the page, knowing I'd have to read it out loud.

"'Dear Elizabeth. The weather report says you've been getting rain. I hope you're managing to stay dry.'"

My heart raced as I began to share my father's words.

"'My last call with Rick was very positive. He says you're making great progress. Your mother and I are proud you've been able to accept that you're ultimately to blame for your own anger. We love you and have forgiven you.'"

"That's nice," one of the counselors said.

"'I know you want to come back to South Carolina,'" I continued reading. "'But Mom and I don't think that's going to help you. Even if we sent you to a Christian school, your wild friends would still find you. We feel that a boarding school would help your self-esteem so you won't need fulfillment with beer, pot, and parties. And we think we've found the perfect place for you.

"'Carlbrook School, in Virginia! It has a beautiful campus with lots of great kids. In fact, there are several from South Carolina. And, guess what? They're building tennis courts as we speak!

"'Please trust us. We're not doing this to be mean, we're doing it out of love. We just want you to get better so you'll be happy and safe for the rest of your life.'"

I read the rest of the letter in a daze. Right up until that moment, some part of me had still been praying for a miracle. Hoping that maybe I'd be the exception, the one kid who actually got to go home. But no, I was headed to a boarding school just like everyone else.

My graduation was scheduled for the end of the week. My parents, no big shock, would not be attending. After not getting to attend my grandmother's funeral, the pain and disappointment just felt like par for the course. Instead, they invited my old pals, the kidnappers, to pick me up and transport me to a place called Halifax, Virginia.

Carlbrook. That's one of the fancy schools.

It wasn't home. At least it wasn't lockdown, though, and I was finally getting out of the woods after three miserable months.

Compared to all that, how bad could this other place be?

122

PART II

Chapter 13

ONCE I KNEW I was leaving the woods, time passed more quickly. It was easier to hike all day when it felt like I was heading toward some destination. I made it through my graduation ceremony and gave away all my decent possessions to the other girls. I had just handed off my trail mix when I heard Nate's truck sputtering down the road.

"God," I whispered, "if you exist, thank you for getting me out of here."

I got into the truck and looked around at the other girls.

"So," I said. "I guess, um, good-bye."

"See you."

I got into the truck and Nate pulled out. My last impression of the woods was of waving hands and sad, dirty faces. *Fuck you for getting to leave,* they all seemed to say. But I didn't blame them. I'd thought the same thing every time I watched the truck drive away with a girl who wasn't me.

It took about fifteen minutes to get to base camp. My escorts were waiting by the intake trailer. Once again, they were dressed in identical black. The man grinned when I stepped out of the car.

"We meet again," he said.

Intake Jan called me into the trailer. She handed me a thin, frayed towel and a sample-size bar of soap.

"There's a shower on the other side of the door," she said.

A shower. An actual, real shower. Sort of.

It wasn't exactly a spa. The shower was tiny and caked in the grime of the thousand kids who'd come through before me. I could almost feel them there with me as I stepped inside, waiting for the water to turn as hot as I could possibly get it. Two thousand arms scrubbing and scrubbing, a thousand bars of soap dissolved into slivers. We couldn't possibly get clean enough. It was the most thorough shower I'd ever taken, and still, dirt and sweat clung to me like a layer of skin. I had scraped myself raw, but I hadn't managed to wash away the last three months.

And somehow I still smell like the fucking woods.

The scent was trapped in the fibers of the T-shirt my parents had sent to base camp. I smelled the tartness of the woods even as I sat inside the SUV, even after we'd left the Appalachian Mountains behind.

If I closed my eyes and tried really hard to forget, I could almost pretend my escorts were chauffeurs. They were hired drivers, after all. They had dropped me off and now they were picking me up. The same two people in the same black SUV, paid to ferry me around. Chauffeurs. Just as long as you ignored that three-and-a-half-month gap in the middle.

The drive went much better this time too. In fact, my escorts and I were even getting along. They talked about the night they grabbed me from my bed. Apparently, I was one of the angriest kids they'd ever met, pure rage and spitting venom. But now I was subdued, glad just to be back in the civilized world.

"Chick-fil-A, right?" the woman asked.

"Yep," I said.

I was almost touched that they'd remembered my fast-food preference, even if it was only from a truck stop with three options. I ordered three chicken biscuits this time, because the fact that I even could was almost too good to believe. I scarfed the first one down right away and got to work on the second. I didn't care about gut bomb or my last biscuit going cold. I was going to eat every last bite out of principle, even if it took the whole drive.

I looked through the window and watched the trees go by behind glass.

I sniffed the glorious stale air, a mix of chicken, the man's aftershave, and the cheap, filmy soap I'd just used to shower. I had actually made it out of there. I'd managed to survive hell for more than a hundred days. And while I wasn't exactly thrilled about my next destination, the fact that I was heading somewhere else, anywhere else, had me almost delirious with relief.

I unwrapped my last biscuit and asked the escorts to turn up the radio. It was a country station, not my favorite, but I hadn't heard music in so long I would have been happy with polka.

Pretty soon, we crossed over into Virginia. My nerves spiked. I tried to prepare for whatever was coming.

"Get ready, kid," the male escort said. "We're there in about five."

I looked out the window. We were in a town that had been worn down and neglected, just like everything else along our path since we'd veered off the highway. My view was all crumbling barns and abandoned houses, cars left to rust. There was no way this setting was five minutes away from an expensive boarding school, the place that had been described, essentially, as *the place where all the fancy fuckups go.*

"Where are we?" I asked.

"Right about the middle of nowhere."

I turned back to the window. Already, the landscape was changing. There were fewer and fewer houses and eventually there were none. For several miles all I saw was green, just tall trees and lush grass. Then a glimpse of stone in the distance.

"Is that it?" I asked, even though I already knew the answer.

It was like driving through an oil painting. A long stretch of white fence ran from the side of the road up to an old and elegant stone mansion. The lawn was perfectly manicured, the trees freshly pruned. A sign read "Carlbrook School: Visitors by Appointment Only."

The SUV pulled onto the sprawling grounds. Up ahead, I saw the huge stone mansion I'd spotted from the road. Everything was so quaint, with cobblestone paths and Victorian streetlamps. We stopped in front of a carriage house, smaller than the mansion but still old and stately.

My escorts walked me to the door. Only this time, they didn't grip my arms or jostle me around. I guess I'd actually earned their trust or something.

Oh my god, I have Stockholm syndrome for the second time.

I wasn't prepared to start something new already. I hadn't even begun to process everything that had happened in the woods. So when they tried to send me through the doors of the carriage house, I wouldn't budge.

"Okay. This is where we leave you."

"Wait."

The escorts stared at me. "Yes?"

"Nothing," I said quietly. "I just don't want to stay here."

"You'll be all right," the woman said. "At least you're out of the woods, right?"

I forced a smile.

"Good luck, Elizabeth."

I was the school's concern now. My escorts had shuffled me off to a woman in her thirties who introduced herself as Cynthia—although she might as well have said Lynn Anne Moore. She had the pastel cardigan and the loafers, the light Southern accent and the false smile. Cynthia even had the same hair as Lynn Anne: a shoulder-length bob, undoubtedly curled by foam rollers. They could have been relatives or clones, different models of the same "education expert" robot.

Wherever she came from, this Lynn/Cynthia, she was leading me through the front door.

The carriage house was small, a few closed rooms, a small library. She led me to her office where two girls sat waiting.

"This is Maggie." She nodded toward one of the girls. "She'll be your big sister."

"Hi," Maggie said. "Nice to meet you."

She was small and unassuming, with brown hair tied up neatly in a ponytail. She had a tomboy vibe like me and seemed friendly enough.

"You too," I said.

The second girl, however, would be a whole different story. She stood up and shook my hand before Cynthia even introduced her.

"And this is Beatrice. She's part of the Friends Committee."

"Welcome to Carlbrook, Elizabeth." Beatrice gripped my palm and gave it a firm shake. "It's going to be so nice to have you here."

"Sure," I said, trying to free my hand.

"Okay, let's get you through intake," Cynthia said.

I joined the others on the couch and looked around Cynthia's office. It was neat and well-appointed, just like her. It was Lynn Anne's office and it was my mother's house. A very specific Southern brand of perfect.

Cynthia had a black three-ring binder on her desk. I saw my name printed on the spine. It was basically empty, but it would fill up quickly with all kinds of notes about my behavior and descriptions of my deepest, darkest secrets.

"So, I assume you know the drill. The whole *clothes off, spin three times* routine?"

"Again?"

Cynthia nodded.

"But I came straight from the woods. Where I was stuck for three months. How could I even get my hands on something illegal?"

"It's protocol, you know?" She shrugged. "Come on, up. The sooner you do it, the sooner it's over."

I stood and looked down at the couch where the other girls still sat.

"In front of them?"

Maggie, at least, had the decency to look away, but Beatrice was smiling like some sort of diplomat. An ambassador for the school, or maybe its mascot.

It's a weird lesson to have already learned by fifteen. How to be strip-searched with dignity. Or, at least, how to make it seem on the outside like you aren't dying on the inside. Like your self-respect isn't shriveling with each rotation. I had been a varsity athlete when I was still in middle school. Now my most impressive feat was to cough and squat after spinning around three times.

I don't know whether to take a bow or collect tips.

Cynthia cleared me and I got dressed as quickly as I could. When I crouched to tie my shoes, Beatrice began chattering in my ear about the wonders of the school. "It's really opened up my whole soul, you know?"

Nope, not really. Good for your soul, though.

"If you're all set," Cynthia said, "the girls will take you over to the sleeping mods."

We left the carriage house and started walking across the campus.

I assumed my parents had visited the school. I wondered if Beatrice had performed her ambassadorial duties for them too. As soon as we started walking across the campus, I understood exactly why they'd chosen Carlbrook.

It was beautiful, just as stately and picturesque as Episcopal. There were Corinthian facades on the stone-crafted buildings. The grass was lush and perfectly maintained, the trees were tall and leafy. A lake bisecting the grounds was dotted with geese—enough to be scenic but not so many they might become annoying. It was like walking around inside a snow globe, quaint but also very insulated. Like there really was a barrier between Carlbrook and the outside world.

I'd later find out the dark history of these grounds. The property had been a tobacco plantation in the pre–Civil War era. It was a place where enslaved people toiled, and learning that made the serene beauty of Carlbrook even more insidious.

"Just a little farther," Beatrice said, "and we'll hit the sleeping mods."

"We're roommates." Maggie smiled at me. "It's you, me, Brittany, and Kristen."

Four people? In one room?

Panic rushed my brain, a flurry of white static like snow. Very quickly, the picturesque scene began to fall away. We reached the edge of the grass and veered toward the woods. This was nonbrochure territory. A row of double-wide trailers fanned out across the edge of the woods, mobile homes pretending to be dorms. And one of them was mine to share with a group of other girls.

At least it's shelter, right? At least it's not the woods.

Beatrice gave me a hug good-bye while Maggie opened the front door to our sleeping mod. We walked in and ended up looking right at the communal bathroom. Inside were three showers and three stalls. A single small mirror hung over the sink. At least there was a door, though, a luxury that did not extend to my new bedroom.

There were eight bedrooms in the trailer. My new home was small, especially for a space I would be sharing with three other people. There were two bunk beds, two dressers, and two flimsy IKEA closets. We each got two drawers and half a closet for all of our things. Since the other beds were already taken I knew I wouldn't be getting that top bunk spot that every former camp kid covets.

"You're right below me," Maggie said, pointing to a lower cot.

Hey, at least it's a bed. Under an actual roof. That you don't even have to set up or anything.

By all accounts I should have been relieved. The truth was, after sleeping in the open air for so long, the trailer felt suffocating. It suddenly occurred to me that I'd never shared a room before. I'd always had my own space, even if that space was a shelter. Now I had not one roommate, but three.

"We're in luck," Maggie said. "It's a good room. No one snores or anything."

It wasn't long before my other two roommates walked in. The non-snoring Brittany and Kristen.

"Welcome to hell," Brittany said, laughing.

"Bans, Brittany," Maggie said.

"Sorry. Stupid bans. I always forget."

I looked around to see if anyone was going to explain what the hell they were talking about. *Nope.*

"What are bans?" I said.

"Basically it means, like, you're banned from stuff," Brittany said.

"For now it means you can't speak to anyone else who's new," Maggie said. "Or gesture, like, nonverbally. Actually try to avoid eye contact altogether."

"Seriously?"

This was somehow even stricter than the woods.

"For like the next month," Brittany said. "Just while you're pre-Integ."

"Pre-what?"

"It's the name of a workshop," Maggie said. "Integritas. I think it's Latin or something."

Brittany nodded. "This place is obsessed with workshops. Integritas, Amicitia, Animus . . ."

Huh? What is it with these places and weird, made-up names? Fire Phase was bad enough, but Integritas? That's just ridiculous.

Maggie must have noticed my confusion. She cut Brittany off before she could finish her stream of Latin.

"It'll make more sense when you're here longer."

"Actually, though?" Kristen, the third roommate, said. "It really won't."

It was the first thing she spoke to me, and her only contribution to the conversation. But it made me like her immediately.

"Okay," Maggie said. "Let's get you unpacked. Your parents sent a box of clothes. Let's make sure everything's within standard."

Within standard? Seriously? Who talks like this?

"We'll start with the jeans you're wearing," she said. "We can only wear jeans on weekends, as long as they're in standard. And those are not."

I looked down at my pants. They seemed pretty normal to me.

"What's wrong with my jeans?"

"I can see your ass," Brittany said.

I was confused. Was she trying to suggest my jeans were too tight? They actually felt a little loose.

"What do you mean?"

132

"The outline," Maggie said. "Jeans can't cling like that here."

"Are you serious? That's, like, all I own."

"Well, let's have a look."

There was a big cardboard box on the floor. My name was written in the neat, flowery handwriting I recognized immediately as my mother's. I could see her in my room, packing up the box, and it made me want to scream.

Earlier in the day my escorts told me about a little trick they used to tell how much trouble to expect from a kid. Apparently, the state of their room was a near-perfect indication of the state of their psyche. The messier the bedroom, the more trouble to expect. As Maggie rooted through the box, pulling out one neatly folded item after another, I had the urge to push the whole box to the floor. Nothing about my mental state felt tidy and clean.

"Here," Maggie said, holding out a pair of corduroy pants. "Try these."

I put them on. Once again, there I was, stripping in front of people I'd just met. Really, what kind of a future did this school have in mind for me?

"Close. But they're a little frayed at the bottom," Maggie said. "Let's keep going."

I tried on outfits for my roommates. Another pair of jeans, a graphic shirt, a tank top, denim shorts. All rejected outright.

"I used to wear stuff like that," Brittany said. "And now I get to dress like my dad's secretary."

A pair of loose pants were deemed unacceptable because they were embellished. An Abercrombie & Fitch polo was nixed for its logo. Pretty much everything I owned went into the "no" pile.

Too tight, too short, too long, too colorful.

The "yes" pile contained one pair of loose pants, a single oxford shirt, and a few sweaters. I was also allowed to keep a few things as weekend wear, but all the tees my mother had packed were old soccer or swim shirts. It seemed almost cruel to have to look at them, these relics of my old life. I should have kept one of my orange shirts from the woods. I'd rather wear a reminder of the nightmare I'd survived than the dreams I'd given up on.

"Look," Maggie said, "I know what you're thinking. 'Fuck these rules, I'll wear what I want.' Right?"

Well. Now that you mention it.

"Maybe," I said.

"I get it. We all do. But don't let them call you out for stupid stuff like clothes, okay? It's just not worth it."

I felt my stomach sink. I was out of the woods, sure, but maybe I wasn't yet out of the inferno.

Maggie smiled at me. "It's not actually all that bad here. I'm just saying, you'll have an easier time if you blend in where you can."

She handed me a J.Crew catalog. On the cover, a young blonde modeled khakis from a sailboat. She looked calm and happy. She looked a little like I used to look, back when I still knew how to fake it.

"Circle what you want." Maggie passed me a pen. "And we'll have your parents order it ASAP."

"Ooh," Brittany said. "Let's get matching sweater sets!"

"Brittany . . ."

"Elizabeth, what's your favorite color?"

"Um—"

"You have two choices." Brittany cut me off. "Gray and brown."

"Bans!" Maggie said. "You two aren't supposed to be talking."

Chapter 14

I'VE THOUGHT A lot about the advice Maggie gave me that first day at Carlbrook. That I should blend in and not make waves, keep my head down and just get through each day as best I could. It was exactly what she seemed to be doing. She wasn't performative like Polly; she didn't have to be the best or the most enthusiastic. She just had to be part of the line marching forward, navigating from the middle of the crowd. Maggie's graduation was on the horizon when I met her, and her attitude of quiet submission kept her on a steady path. She'd have to tolerate the dumb rules and fake Latin just a little longer and then she'd be free.

It was good advice, a helpful tip to her school-assigned little sister, offered in good faith. *Try to blend in where you can. Just take the indignities, the unfairness, and look the other way.* So why didn't I listen? Why didn't I model myself after Maggie, shuffling forward in my baggy jeans along the path of least resistance? I don't know. But it's a question I think about a lot.

I circled items in the J.Crew catalog almost at random. Half of the stuff in there was already on the three other girls in the room, so what did it matter? I handed the catalog back to Maggie, and she helped me put away the few items I was allowed to keep. A single pair of pants hung in the closet and the tops went into the drawer.

"Make sure you fold everything really neatly," Maggie said. "And your shoes need to be lined up along the bottom of your closet."

I refolded the sweater in my hands. "Got it."

"Dorm heads check your spaces every morning, so it's important you don't forget. Clothes must be put away, always. Beds made, with no wrinkles and all the corners tucked. Here, I'll show you."

She went back to the box and pulled out the bedding my mom had sent. There was a new duvet and crisp, white sheets. Everything looked perfectly nice and comfortable. It was standard, ordinary bedding, and that was what made it so strange. I could hardly even picture these things in my mother's shopping cart. There were no intricate details, color-coordinated to match the curtains that accented the wallpaper, and they certainly weren't monogrammed.

Nope, not a single E.L.G. in sight.

I guess there wasn't much of a point to making everything look nice when no one would see it. The perfect things were for the house, after all, and the imperfect stuff got shipped away.

"Well, this looks like it's been well loved."

Maggie was laughing. There was one more thing inside the cardboard box, folded and tucked away in the corner.

My baby blanket!

I grabbed it from Maggie. It had been months since I'd been able to wind my fingers through its knit loops, knowing it was there to keep me safe. I felt better the instant I had it back. For a moment I forgot about the soccer shirts and the plain duvet, just grateful my mom had remembered to pack my blanket.

"I can keep it here, right?"

"Just make sure it's tucked away neatly, okay?" She smiled. "If you remember. I mean, I'm the one who does the morning check."

I was glad to have my baby blanket. I folded it up and stashed it under the unwrinkled duvet. My corners were tucked, my pillows were fluffed. And my blanket would be there waiting for me at the end of the long day.

"Looks good, cadet," Brittany said. "Now, stand and give me twenty."

"Drop and give me twenty," I corrected.

"What? Oh, yeah. No time anyway, we have to get to dinner."

The "dining mod" was directly across from where we slept. A massive stone dining hall was under construction across campus, but for now we took our meals in another double-wide. This one had been turned into a single room filled with foldout tables and stools. Dinner was served buffet-style from tin catering platters: dry chicken, watery green beans. There was also a salad bar stocked with only the most fattening varieties of dressing.

It was better than dry ramen, though. I made a salad, still full from the trio of chicken biscuits I'd gorged on earlier. I brought my tray back to the table where my roommates were sitting.

"Remember," Maggie whispered, "you're on bans."

I nodded.

Right, bans. No talking, no eye contact.

For that reason, my first dinner was pretty uneventful. I ate my salad slowly and in between bites, I watched the vinaigrette congeal around the stale croutons.

I met exactly one new person who actually made an impression. Her name was Charlotte and she wore a black cashmere sweater and a giant black Gucci belt. She walked directly up to me and shook my hand.

"Hi. You're new." She had a hint of an accent, something European. "Welcome to the Carlbrook School for Spirited Underachievers."

I laughed without realizing that Charlotte had just recited the school's actual motto. Maggie shot her a warning look. I watched her as she walked back to her table, already certain she was someone special. She was a high-society rebel who would be put on bans with the color black and designer labels not long after this interaction. They wanted her to blend into the J.Crew catalog just like the rest of us.

When we were done eating, Maggie led me out of the trailer.

"Are we going back to the room?" I said.

"Not yet. It's time for Last Light."

"What's that?"

"Well." Maggie smiled nervously. "You'll see."

We headed toward the main building, the big stone mansion I'd seen from the road, known as the commons. It was just as beautiful on the inside, with floor-to-ceiling windows and a crystal chandelier. Portraits of past students hung on the walls. I paused in front of the first series. There were eight kids, seven teenage boys and a teenage girl.

"That's the first graduating class," Maggie said. "Two thousand two."

I looked more closely. "There was only one girl?"

"I know. Can you imagine?" Maggie turned to me. "Hey, you're from South Carolina, right?"

"Yep," I said.

"I'm pretty sure that's the same place as her."

It was a strange coincidence, but I hardly gave the girl in the portrait a second thought that night. It wasn't until a few weeks later, after I'd met several other students from my town, that I began to suspect something more than random chance was at play.

"Ready?" Maggie said as we walked down the hall. "This might seem a little intense at first."

Intense? That's an understatement.

We entered the commons area, where Last Light was getting under-way. All of the furniture had been removed from the center of the room, pushed and stacked against the wall. This was to make space for what I can describe only as *human furniture,* a tangled mess of bodies stretched out across on the floor.

How about we go with horrifying?

Every head was in a lap. Every lap held a head There were teenagers and adults. Girls with girls and boys with boys.

(Holy shit! I forgot about boys!)

It was nightmarish, like some medieval depiction of hell. All Hydras and rat kings and tangled bodies.

"What the fuck are they doing?"

"Smooshing," Maggie said.

"*Smooshing?*" I said. "I am never, ever, smooshing."

"Don't worry about that yet. No one expects you to do it on your first night."

Maggie led me to the corner of the room where a few of the saner kids sat in chairs.

Thank God.

My relief lasted all of five seconds. When we got a little closer I realized that a lot of the chair kids were still doing some form of smooshing. They were rubbing shoulders or scratching heads. As someone who makes a point of avoiding all unnecessary affection, I was truly disturbed.

I scanned the area. I was relieved to see both Brittany and Kristen outside of the smooshing. Beatrice, on the other hand, was smack-dab in the middle of the pile. She didn't have just one head in her lap. No, Beatrice had two.

I'm sure the staff took note. Smooshing was a nightly occurrence, and I'd later learn that reluctance to participate meant that *cuddling* would become a therapeutic assignment.

"It's a beautiful night, isn't it, guys?"

The voice preceded the man coming into the room.

"We're so lucky to be alive."

This was Alan. The lead counselor of Carlbrook. He was late into middle age, chubby and pasty. He wore khaki pants, a button-up shirt, and a vest.

"Let's take a moment to feel all the love in this room. To feel how blessed we are to be here with all these beautiful people."

Is this a church? Or a seminar? What, exactly, am I about to become a part of?

"Take a beat," Alan said. "And say to yourself: *I am so lucky. I am so blessed.*"

I saw Beatrice close her eyes. Alan walked to the stereo at the head of the room. A moment later, Tracy Chapman's "Fast Car" began playing.

"Listen up, everyone," he said. "We have a new student. Just arrived this afternoon."

I could feel my face go red with the realization that he was talking about me. I dropped my eyes and stared directly at the floor.

"Why don't you stand up and tell everyone a little bit about yourself? We're so happy to have you here."

If I can't see him, he can't see me. Right? Isn't that how it works?

Maggie nudged me, and I had no choice but to stand. I felt naked all over again and had to remind myself not to spin around and squat.

"Hi. I'm Elizabeth. I'm from South Carolina."

I sat right back down as fast as I could but it didn't matter; everyone's eyes were on me now. The new girl, fresh meat. I assumed they were all wondering what I'd done to get here. Was I a slut? An addict? Some sort of psychopath? All the same things I'd thought every time a new girl arrived at the woods.

"Elizabeth is pre-Integ," Alan said. "So she's on bans with some of you newbies. But the rest of you should introduce yourselves and make her feel at home."

Home? Yeah, right. I don't know what this place is, but it sure isn't my home.

I tuned out the rest of the meeting and waited for my embarrassment to fade. I peeled my eyes off the floor and looked around at my new classmates, the smooshers, the nonsmooshers. A group of guys (nonsmooshers) caught my eye. They looked like guys I would have been friends with back at home. One of them stood out more than the others, a cute athletic type I later learned was named Luke. I brought my gaze back to Luke a few times, until I caught him looking back at me.

It had been months since I'd seen a member of the male sex my own age. Even the prospect of a crush was suddenly exciting. Maggie must have noticed because she gave me some advice on our walk back to the sleeping mods.

"I know it's no fun," she said, "but you should avoid boys if you can. At least the ones you think could be more than friends."

I nodded but didn't say anything.

"It'll just make things so much easier. Trust me."

Trust me.

As much as anyone else, at least. I had no reason not to trust Maggie. She was nice to me in those early days at Carlbrook. She was patient and helpful when I knew she didn't have to be. She wasn't fake like Polly, she didn't use me as a tool for proving her own greatness. She was just a normal girl at a fucked-up school who'd figured out a way to make it through.

So why didn't I listen when she told me not to spend time with Luke? To take the little things on the chin? To try to blend in?

I don't know. I have no answer. I just keep coming back to the other question, the one that still plagues me.

What would have happened if I had?

Maggie killed herself less than a year after graduation. She overdosed alone in her car, and by the time anyone found her it was too late. No one saw it coming, least of all me. Maggie seemed normal. Maggie seemed fine. Maggie seemed like she had things figured out.

Chapter 15

ONE OF MY classmates ended up at Carlbrook because his mom thought he was playing too many video games. Another girl was offered a deal: Complete the program and you can have your trust fund. (You know, like finishing school!) There were a few students who'd experimented with serious drugs and a couple who'd gotten into trouble with the law. But mostly, we were all in some version of the middle. Somewhere between heroin and *Call of Duty*. In fact, pretty much everyone was sent away for one (or two) of the following reasons:

1. Substances

Drugs and alcohol *was* a big category. But within this group was a whole spectrum of severity. There were certainly kids who had done hard drugs, those who swiped pain pills from grandparents' cabinets, and did lines of coke on the weekends. It was most common to see potheads and drinkers. Then there were those lucky kids among us whose parents overreacted to a missing bottle of vodka or found an eighth of marijuana hidden beneath the slats of a bed frame.

Overall, regardless of how serious a kid's drug of choice might be, no one with a true addiction problem was admitted to Carlbrook. It wasn't a detox center or a rehab, although it often felt like the intensity of a student's drug use was amplified by the staff to justify their continued stay at the school.

2. Academics

ADHD. Learning disabilities. Skipping class, failing out, or doing just okay in school when you came from a family that demanded greatness at all costs. These kids were fuckups but in a minor way; they played fast and loose with their futures. In other words, they were teenagers.

3. Sexual Activity

This category included approximately 50 percent of the female students and exactly 0 percent of the males. "Girls are promiscuous, and boys will be boys" seemed to be a sort of unofficial motto at Carlbrook. There, "daddy issues" was considered a psychiatric diagnosis.

Just like the drugs-and-alcohol category, there was a lot of variance in what was considered problematic sexuality. Some of the girls afflicted with the defect of promiscuity were actually just dealing with a religious or conservative household. Which is to say: There were definitely some slutty virgins at Carlbrook.

4. Mental Health

If a girl hadn't been sent to Carlbrook because she was too sexual, there was a good chance she had an eating disorder. Anorexics, bulimics, binge eaters, purgers. It was easy to recognize these cases because any visible change in weight meant they would soon have a bathroom buddy trailing behind them.

A lot of students were depressed or anxious, even suicidal. Some kids arrived with a clinical diagnosis: oppositional defiant disorder, OCD, mood disorders. Some of us were just difficult. We were sad or angry in a way our parents didn't want to deal with.

There was one issue that even Carlbrook considered too much of a liability. Serious cutters weren't supposed to be accepted. I don't mean those of us who occasionally cut or burned ourselves somewhere secret. I mean the dangerous cutters, the ones with scars like latticework on their arms. Mostly the school stuck to their rule, but there was one cutter who arrived a few months after me. Her name was Alice and her mom was famous.

Surely, there couldn't be a connection. Fame and special treatment, when has that ever happened before?

5. Trauma

A number of Carlbrook students had been through trauma. Abuse and sexual assault were common, and a few students had been deeply affected by the death of a friend or relative.

For some, the traumatic experience itself was the reason that person landed at the school. More often than not, it was the problematic behavior that developed in the wake of the trauma that made a Carlbrook kid. (See categories one through four.) There were kids whose trauma was home-based, like divorce or having been adopted.

There was overlap between categories, of course. Some of us could claim a little from Group A and a little from Group B, just enough from each to send us across some imaginary line. It often came down to a weird kind of math.

Joint + blow job + curfew violation.

Moodiness + bad grades + adopted at birth.

Maybe gay + definitely angry × a factor of Christianity.

Equals: a months-long tour of the woods followed by one to two years in Halifax, Virginia.

Ultimately, though, it didn't much matter whether it was a specific issue that landed a kid at Carlbrook or a general trend of troubled teen behavior. Whatever someone's path to Halifax may have been, once they were there, it could have been anything. The therapeutic curriculum was exactly the same for all of us. A one-size-fits-all treatment plan for opioid addiction, sexual assault, clinical depression, and spending too much time online.

In the eyes of the Carlbrook staff there was only one way to do things. A model was firmly in place, a cure-all for deviance, anger, and sadness alike. And where did this magical treatment plan come from?

The short answer is: a cult called Synanon.

And what the hell is that?

From one angle, Synanon is one of the strangest and most violent cults in American history. From another, it's the world's first therapeutic community and the model for America's rehab industry. For a brief time, it was also a religion—but that was more of a tax thing than a spiritual thing. From a pop culture perspective, the most well-known thing about Synanon might be an attempted murder case from the late 1970s. The intended victim was a lawyer named Paul Morantz and the murder weapon was a rattlesnake hidden in his mailbox.

If none of that rings a bell, you're probably still familiar with Synanon's most famous catchphrase.

"Today is the first day of the rest of your life."

The story of Synanon begins in 1958 in the city of Los Angeles. That's the year a man named Charles E. Dederich started holding small gatherings in his squalid Santa Monica apartment. It was just an informal group at first, some friends from a local chapter of Alcoholics Anonymous.

Chuck, as he was known, had been a desperate alcoholic for most of his life. He was a college dropout heading for his second divorce when he discovered the only thing he liked more than booze: AA. Specifically the part where he got to speak in front of a captive audience. He was a smart guy and a gifted orator, and soon he was going to several meetings a day just to hold court.

When Chuck spoke, people listened. Sometimes a few of them would head over to his apartment for a more informal discussion free from the rigid format of AA. Chuck would expound on his theories of addiction, throwing psychological and philosophical ideas into the mix. He quoted Emerson and Thoreau regularly and encouraged his friends to read books like *The Prophet* by Khalil Gibran.

The group started calling themselves the Tender Loving Care Club. Members talked up their meetings to other alcoholics struggling in the rooms of Los Angeles, and more and more of them joined. A turning point came when a heroin addict showed up at Chuck's doorstep in the throes of withdrawal. Alcoholics Anonymous considers drug users to be a different type of addict and therefore they are not allowed to attend member meetings unless they also have a drinking problem. Chuck Dederich took this guy in and set him up on his couch, where he sweated out his withdrawal.

Chuck took them all in. Suddenly the Tender Loving Care Club was Synanon, a name shrouded in mystery—not quite scientific, not quite religious, but somehow vaguely metaphysical.

This was, after all, Los Angeles at the dawn of the New Age. It was the beginning of the Human Potential Movement. Theories of self-actualization and newfangled spirituality were bubbling up at places like the Esalen Institute and the "church" of Scientology. At any other time and place, Charles Dederich's experiment might have stopped there. But Synanon dealt in self-help, and self-help was about to be huge. They had something none of the other groups had, something called the Game.

The Game was an attack circle, an experiment in radical honesty and saying all the things polite society would never allow. Members would split up into small groups and confront one another for hours, revealing dark truths and shameful secrets that the rest of the circle would then viciously criticize. When it came to the Game, anything was allowed as long as it wasn't physical violence. Members were actually encouraged to lie and cajole. It was all in the interest of self-actualization.

The Game wasn't only for addicts. It soon caught on with "squares," as they were called, nondruggies interested in experimentation. People began inviting Chuck to hold parties in their homes, specifically centered around playing the Game. Once the Hollywood set caught on, all bets were off. Celebrities like Natalie Wood and Leonard Nimoy were Synanon dabblers. Membership skyrocketed, and Dederich soon found himself running a multimillion-dollar operation. Historically, that has only ever gone one way.

The next decade of Charles Dederich's life was one of paranoia in full swing. Synanon went the way of many cults, which is to say, things got batshit insane. Those years were pockmarked by incidents of forced sterilization, spouse swapping, the creation of a paramilitary group with its own special type of martial arts (called Syn-do, of course), and the aforementioned rattlesnake attack. It all ended for Chuck Dederich in 1978, when he was arrested for attempted murder after a manhunt that found him drunk and despondent in a seedy motel.

But this story takes a sharp left turn before any of that went down. Back in 1967, when Synanon was still a media darling with nary a rattlesnake in sight, a man named Mel Wasserman had an idea. Mel was very much a square. In fact, he was a furniture salesman from Palm Springs— and by all accounts, a very good one. He had all kinds of qualifications when it came to pricing armchairs. He had absolutely zero qualifications when it came to any of the following:

Addiction, mental health, education, child care.

Wasserman saw an opportunity and decided to take the Synanon model of "treating" addiction and apply it to adolescents. Like Chuck Dederich, he started small, holding Game-like sessions in his home for local teenagers caught up in the psychedelic sixties. Only he called them "raps," probably as slang meant to appeal to teens.

Soon, Wasserman branched out. He bought property in Running

Springs, California, and opened up a school. He called it CEDU—the current explanation is that it was named for the school's motto: "See yourself as you are and do something about it."

It wasn't, though. CEDU was actually intended to be an acronym for Charles E. Dederich University, but Wasserman distanced himself after the whole spousal swap / forced vasectomy / rattlesnake thing. He did, however, pull the first CEDU staff almost entirely from Synanon. Wasserman didn't pay much attention to formal qualifications. Instead, he prided himself on the fact that they had real-life experience on the streets and on the withdrawal couch. Plus, they knew how to play the Game.

At first CEDU got most of its young addicts from the state. They were juvenile delinquents and small-time drug offenders, and their treatment was subsidized by taxpayer money. That is, until Wasserman saw a real opportunity to expand. According to his right-hand man, Bill Lane, an ex–heroin addict from Synanon, Mel was looking for a "softer" type of kid.

Meaning there was a lot more money in opening up his services to troubled teens of all sorts, not just the ones who happened to be addicted to drugs. He didn't amend his program or anything. Wasserman kept the same framework in place. One thing that continued to change, however, was his definition of "troubled."

To recap: A system for drug-addicted adults became a program for drug-addicted teenagers, which became a system for any teenagers at all.

CEDU began to expand. First came Rocky Mountain Academy in Colorado, then a CEDU middle school. A man named Michael Allgood, who'd known Mel since he was a troubled kid in Palm Springs, was sent off to open Cascade in Whitmore, California.

And how does this get all the way to Carlbrook School in Virginia? Rather directly, as it turns out. Randall Moore, the founder of the school, went to Cascade in the early eighties. His experience had been a horrific one, abusive and traumatizing, and he thought they could do it better. His intention was to create a different, better emotional-growth school.

Why, then, did he hire Alan?

Alan, our head counselor, was a CEDU man through and through. He began working at the school in 1980 and eventually worked his way all the way up the ladder. He also ran Rocky Mountain Academy for a time and was headmaster of another CEDU offshoot, a place called Mount Bachelor Academy that would eventually close, years after he left, because of allegations of child abuse. Among other things, the school was accused of making a female student put on a miniskirt and perform lap dances for male students and staff.

Thankfully, they didn't do that at Carlbrook, but the similarities of the programs are undeniable. Sometimes the terminology changed and sometimes it kept its original CEDU-rendered form. Here are some examples.

Request groups: Synanon's "Game" became CEDU's "raps" became "request groups" at Carlbrook. The term may sound innocuous, but the structure was exactly the same. We met every Monday and Friday for sessions that typically lasted about two hours. Groups were made up of fifteen to twenty students, grouped together according to "requests."

We were expected to call one another out during these sessions, and that meant requesting specific classmates we wanted to address for whatever reason. Maybe they'd broken a rule. Maybe you wanted to check in on their progress. Maybe you were just hoping to keep the spotlight off yourself. That was such a huge aspect of Carlbrook, constantly finding things to call out in other people as a form of self-preservation.

Lists were posted at lunch. If my name was listed along with several of my friends', or if it was directly under someone I had conflict with, a knot would form in my stomach and I'd spend all day with a sense of dread, knowing I was going to be called out.

Running anger: Group therapy was designed to push us to the point of total collapse. In the majority of these sessions, at least one student would experience a complete, almost primal breakdown. Walk into any room at Carlbrook on a Monday or Friday afternoon, and it was likely you'd see a kid with his head between his legs, screaming at the floor while snot and tears flowed and blood vessels threatened to burst.

The term for this was "running anger." I dreaded the moment I'd be forced to run my own anger for the first time more than anything else during my early months at Carlbrook.

Peer class: Here, we were grouped according to the time we arrived at Carlbrook. Peer classes took their names from the Greek alphabet. Each was a cluster of twelve or so kids, bound together by a single letter. Chi, Tau, Xi. It was kind of like being in a fraternity or sorority where every week was Hell Week.

I was in peer class Pi along with a dozen other students. These were the kids I became closest to as we went through the whole program together. Charlotte, Brittany, and Maya were all in my peer class.

Teams: If your peer class was your group of friends, your team was like your family. We met once a week, every Wednesday, for another group session lasting two hours. Running anger was a common occurrence on these afternoons as well.

Each team of ten or so students was led by an adviser. My first team leader was a woman named Catherine. She was the person responsible for my progress and also the one who disciplined me. In addition, she had weekly phone calls to share updates with my parents.

Standards and agreements: In Carlbrook-speak, this meant the rules. Some of them were normal, like "Students will respect the property of the school and other people." Some were harsher, like "Students will refrain from sexual or intimate activities with others." Others were just weird. Like "Students will recognize when a lady or gentleman is present."

Honor list: Consider this Carlbrook's version of a written confession. Before each workshop or program, we were required to make a list of anything and everything we'd done that was out of standard. We also had to list anything we knew *someone else* had done. Writing an honor list was a lose-lose situation. If you hadn't done anything wrong, no one believed you—and that in and of itself meant you were out of standard. It meant you were a liar and that you'd be punished accordingly.

It takes one to know one, though. The Troubled Teen Industry became the billion-dollar enterprise it is today by trading in deception. Every branch of this tough-love business is a twisted limb that somehow winds its way right back to CEDU.

In 1992, the ex-Synanonite Bill Lane formed a teen transport company to capitalize on the work he was already doing for CEDU. Decades later, escorting is an entire subindustry in its own right. If not for Lane, thousands of kids like me would never have known the joy of being abducted by strangers in the middle of the night.

Then there's the field of educational consulting. The domain of Lynn Anne Moore. Ed consultants, often without so much as a degree in matchmaking, charge parents at a premium to find the "right fit" for each problem child. The ties between prominent ed consultants and CEDU offshoots run deep, a network of hidden connections that lead certain advisers to recommend particular schools again and again.

For Lynn Anne, that school was Carlbrook. Technically, her consulting firm catered to parents seeking various forms of alternative education for their children. While I'm sure some of her work did involve matching gifted or artistic kids with traditional boarding schools, her specialty had always been troubled teens. Worried parents passed her name around when they didn't know what to do about their kids, and a lot of them ended up in Halifax, Virginia.

Her association with my alma mater wasn't exactly a well-hidden secret. She was personally acquainted with its founder. Knew him rather well, in fact. Randall Moore, the Cascade graduate who dreamed of creating a more humane version of a therapeutic boarding school, was Lynn Anne's son.

I learned this bit of information a few weeks into my time in Virginia. I'm sure I would have connected the dots eventually, but I didn't need to—my adviser, Catherine, blurted it right out. I'd begun that week's meeting by listing all the reasons why I didn't need to be at Carlbrook, another futile attempt at convincing someone to let me go home. She let me go on for a minute or two, indulging me, before she cut me off.

"Elizabeth, you're lucky to be here."

"It doesn't feel like that."

"Well, it should," she said. "If I were you, I'd be grateful for Lynn Anne Moore. She could have sent you somewhere so much worse than Carlbrook. It's your good fortune she saw you as a candidate for her son's school."

Her son's school? What the fuck? How is that legal?

It was shocking enough to stop me in my tracks, but only for a moment. The pieces fell into place pretty quickly. It suddenly made sense why there were so many students from South Carolina. It wasn't a coincidence that the first girl to graduate from Carlbrook came from my hometown. Nor was it merely by chance that I'd recognized the name of a kid in the peer class ahead of mine.

We all were there for one reason: Our parents had taken us to see a prominent ed consultant who worked nearby. She showed us inkblots and had us answer invasive questions. Then Lynn Anne Moore sent us straight down the Troubled Teen pipeline, where we landed on the quaint, manicured doorstep of her son's expensive school.

Chapter 16

MY FIRST REQUEST group was on a Monday afternoon. During lunch, Maggie directed me to the list of names posted in the commons. I was assigned to a group run by a guy named David and instantly began to dread whatever was coming next.

I walked into the room to find fifteen or so chairs arranged in a circle. About half of them were already taken, mostly by kids I was seeing for the first time. I did recognize one person from my dorm, a tiny, sweet-faced girl named Maya. I thought about taking the seat next to her, but I wasn't sure if that was allowed, as we were both on pre-Integritas bans.

I hovered awkwardly outside the circle, wishing I could sprint away or make myself disappear. I felt a hand on my shoulder and looked up to see floppy hair and a big, goofy grin.

"Hey, I'm Trevor," the boy said. "This your first group?"

I nodded.

"Come on, you can sit next to me."

We took two empty seats and waited for the rest of the students to file in. Once everyone was seated, a man strolled into the room. I figured this must be David. He seemed to be in his midforties. With his wispy goatee, combed-back hair, and khaki pants, he was basically another Alan-in-training.

He took the remaining chair and started speaking: "Who wants to start?"

A girl I'd never seen before raised her hand.

"Levi," she said, "I requested you because I know you had a hard phone call this week. Do you want to talk about that?"

"It was my brother's birthday." Levi shrugged. "And it just sucked I couldn't be there."

"Talk more about that," David said.

"He had a big party. And I'm stuck here, you know? It isn't fair. I just don't want to be here."

"You're still settling in," David said. "You're about to go through your first workshop. Let's check after you do Integritas."

Levi nodded.

"Who's next?"

Trevor raised his hand. He turned to face Kyle.

"Hey, Kyle. How's your program going? I wanted to check in because I miss you, man."

Kyle shrugged. "It's fine."

"Fine?" David said. "All you have to say is *it's fine*?"

"I don't know. I mean, it's a program."

"Come on." David's voice was getting louder. "How are you still so apathetic?"

The kid looked down at the floor.

"Do you just not care about anything?" David said. "Jesus, Kyle. You're sucking all the goddamn air out of the room. If you don't want to be alive, then you don't deserve to be. Why don't you just go through with it next time?"

"Fuck you," Kyle said.

"What was that?"

"Fuck you. FUCK YOU. I CARE, OKAY?"

"Do you really?" David crossed his arms. "That's not the kind of message a razor blade sends."

"I DO. I FUCKING CARE AND I WANT TO LIVE."

"There we go," David said. "Let it all out."

This was my introduction to running anger. Kyle cracked open completely. He put his head between his legs and began screaming at the floor. Soon his face was a fountain of tears. The sheer volume of the bodily fluids flowing from his face seemed impossible, like he was pumping them out from some deep reserve. Snot poured from his nose and wadded-up tissues piled up on the floor like a stack of origami ghosts.

"I hate myself. I fucking hate myself so much."

Trevor switched chairs so he was sitting next to Kyle. He leaned over his friend and tried to comfort him, rubbing his back as he spoke softly into Kyle's ear.

"I didn't deserve it." Kyle was wailing. "I was just a kid and I didn't deserve it."

It was excruciating to watch. This boy appeared to be in so much pain, the opposite of someone screaming life-affirming statements. Whatever was happening seemed far too personal, too intimate, for me to sit there watching.

His face reminded me of another face. Three faces, actually. They were a family, a group of strangers at the beach. I was just a little kid, but I remember those anguished expressions as clearly as if they were in front of me. It was a level of pain, so raw and acute, that I'd never encountered before. And I didn't see anything like it again until the day I saw Kyle run anger.

The family had just lost a young boy. Had actually *lost* him. Their son and brother. The kid had been swimming in the ocean when the riptide came out of nowhere. It sucked him away and, just like that, he was stolen by the sea.

The Coast Guard was there. A medic, too, and a big group of people trying to help. The Guards held on to a rope as they waded into the water, trying to feel around for a body, but they never found one. Not that day, at least.

I have always been a really strong swimmer. Even back then, I was able to swim the mile at meets. Swimming in the ocean was never quite the same for me after that day. Every time I got into the water the riptide was in the back of my mind.

What would you do? If it took you away? Would you even bother to try to find a way out?

My father saw me watching the family on the beach. He came over and sat down on the sand beside me.

"If it ever happens," he said, "don't fight it. Just let it take you out. You'll know the moment you get free of it. And then you can come up for air."

Kyle ran anger for half an hour, screaming incomprehensible things about wanting to live.

"You're doing great," David said. "Really great. Get it all out."

His voice had gotten softer. He seemed almost pleased, or at least satisfied. He walked over to Kyle and placed his hand on the boy's head. "Good job, Kyle."

It was the moment my dad had told me about. When the riptide relents and it's safe to swim out. David had decided the ordeal was over, that Kyle had done enough emotional work for the day. And Kyle began to pull himself back together because he knew exactly how the whole experience was supposed to play out.

That first afternoon shocked me completely. It's frightening to realize just how quickly I'd come to see what happened with Kyle as run-of-the-mill. The anger, the abuse, the cascade of tears—all of it was real. But at the same time, running anger was a sort of a ritual. An exorcism, even, and everyone had their part to play.

I have no doubt that the demon Kyle was fighting was very much alive. I also know now that he didn't really have a choice when it came to casting it out. David knew exactly what he wanted to see, and Kyle knew enough to give it to him.

But it was an unfinished exorcism, that much I know. Kyle didn't win the fight against his demon—not that day or any other. But for now, he could stop fighting so hard. He could enjoy the rush of euphoria that comes with the release of so much emotion.

I was too overwhelmed to get up and walk to dinner. So I lingered in my seat, pretending to tie my shoe while everyone else filed out of the room. When I looked up I saw that Maya, the girl from my dorm, was lingering by the door. She smiled and I realized she was waiting for me. I was cautious as I walked over, remembering that we were on bans, but Maya threw her arms around me.

"Hugging's allowed," she said, "after tough groups."

I didn't cringe this time, like I had with Beatrice. Instead, I hugged Maya back.

Later that night, when Maggie was brushing her teeth, Brittany broke bans to talk about Kyle.

"He tried to kill himself," she said.

"Here?"

"Yeah. Like a month ago. He ran off into the woods with a razor blade."

"What happened?"

"His friends saw him take off," Brittany said. "They chased after him and convinced him to come back."

"Does that David guy know?"

It seemed impossible that David could have said what he said, knowing what Kyle had gone through.

"Of course."

I must have looked queasy because Brittany laughed.

"That's kind of the thing here," she said. "They like to tear you down to build you back up."

"Oh. Okay."

It was all I could muster. I had Kyle's tormented screams playing on a loop in my mind.

It didn't seem like they did a whole lot of building him back up.

Chapter 17

AT CARLBROOK, THERE was a rigid schedule in place to facilitate our "emotional growth." In fact, the promise of structure was the very reason a lot of parents sent their kids to the school. Every weekday began at 6:00 a.m., on the dot, with inspections at 6:15. Since we showered at night, that gave me fifteen minutes to make my bed, straighten my row of shoes, and make sure the hangers in my little closet were spaced evenly apart. For the first few weeks I had to fight the impulse to stand at attention while Maggie bounced a quarter off my bed.

Ma'am, yes, ma'am!

After inspections, we had another fifteen minutes to "complete our modular chores"—a fancy way of saying it was time to clean the trailer. We rotated assignments, including vacuuming the floors, cleaning the toilets, and washing down the sinks. Vacuum duty was everyone's favorite, including mine. For most of my peers, scrubbing shit stains from a communal toilet was the worst possible way to start off the day.

For me, sink duty was actually the worst fate. Even now, I have a hard time looking at globs of other people's dried toothpaste without gagging. I shudder when I recall the experience of reaching my hand into a clogged drain to pull out a hairball made up of multiple textures and colors. Luckily there was a bartering system I would learn about soon enough, and that made chores much more tolerable.

Sink: spotless. Closet: hangers spaced two fingers apart. Acceptable clothing: to be determined.

Before I could leave the double-wide, Maggie had to sign off on my outfit. It was a total bore getting dressed in the same conservative J.Crew stuff every day, and as time went on my options only got more limited. Everyone gained weight at Carlbrook. It was so common it fueled a rumor that the kitchen staff added starch to the food just to mess with us. We all had the same experience of waking up one day to find that half of our limited wardrobe was suddenly too tight. But someone, somewhere along the line, had come up with a brilliant solution.

We'd gather pillows and stuffed animals and shove them down the waistline of our pants. Then we'd proceed to do squat after squat until the fabric loosened enough that it no longer cupped our butts. On any given morning you could walk down the hall and see at least one girl with a stuffed animal petting zoo hanging out of her pants. Never Charlotte, though.

"Fuck that," she said once. "I hate what I'm wearing anyways. Who cares if I buy my clothes a size bigger?"

With our clothing checked off, we'd head to the dining modular for a breakfast of Frosted Flakes, cold buffet food, or a sad-looking banana. As a breakfast lover, these options bummed me out so much that I'd try to finish eating as quickly as possible. Unless, of course, Luke happened to be there. I'd developed a full-blown crush on the boy I'd locked eyes with during that first night of smooshing, and catching a glimpse of him was one of the few highlights of my day.

Next on the agenda was a long walk across campus. We'd leave one set of trailers, stroll past the pond and the mansion, and all those beautiful snow globe things, only to arrive at another cluster of double-wides. This was where our classes were held, if you want to call them that.

At Carlbrook, everything, including high school, came second to the all-important therapeutic work. Our schedules were set up to allow for those long group sessions every Monday, Wednesday, and Friday afternoon.

It wasn't like we totally bypassed traditional education. We had report cards and transcripts like every other high school. (Although they were often inflated with AP class credits we most definitely didn't earn.) The bigger issue was that Carlbrook tended to deprioritize thinking in general, especially when it was an obstacle to the miracle that was *feeling*.

For every hour of history class spent on the Constitution, another one was dedicated to playing the social deduction game Mafia. A science lesson might involve chemical equations, just as it might involve an episode of *CSI*. There were some teachers who seemed to have been hired simply because they happened to have a teaching degree and lived in Halifax, Virginia. There were others who became genuine allies to us. Some of these teachers stayed on at the school just to make sure we were okay.

As for the books we read, they certainly weren't the same standards my friends were reading back at home. I don't remember reading *Of Mice and Men* or *The Great Gatsby*. But we were assigned self-help books from time to time, like *The Four Agreements, Love Is Letting Go of Fear*, and, on the more literary side, *The Alchemist*. But it wasn't like we had a whole lot of downtime for reading.

The real joke, though, was study hall. We spent Tuesday and Thursday afternoons sitting in the dining mod with our standard-issue laptop, which had a word-processing program on it and very little else. We were expected to write the occasional paper, but we didn't have any internet access. So we were usually handed the exact research we needed to type up in a slightly different arrangement.

As much as that might sound like a lazy high schooler's dream, it's one of my biggest grievances. My academic learning basically stopped after my freshman year of high school, which has been a pretty big handicap and something I've had to overcome on my own.

When I did have extra time during study hall, I found myself using this time to write letters to my parents. I wanted to recount every horrible thing I'd experienced since arriving at Carlbrook, but I knew that would be a waste of time. The staff read through every single letter with a black Sharpie, ready to censor anything that exposed the reality of life inside the snow globe.

I bet I can't even tell my father those tennis courts he was so excited about don't exist.

The need to be positive left me with very little material. I could write about the ducks. Or dinner, when it was pizza. Or I could tell them more about the school store.

The store was one of the only true Carlbrook highlights. Every Tuesday and Thursday those of us not on disciplinary programs took a trip to the school store. There, we could each select one piece of candy and a single can of soda—unless, of course, we were Beatrice or a member of her little army. The school flag raisers were rewarded for their rah-rah attitude with entire cases of soda and armfuls of snacks.

Nevertheless, I cherished my weekly rations. Not because I desperately craved soda and candy, but because I finally had something I could barter with. Some people love M&M's. Some people hate cleaning the sink. Whenever I could, I traded my snacks for the privilege of staying far, far away from other people's toothpaste.

Dinner came right after group / study hall. It was more of the same—tasteless, greasy food I didn't want to eat. Once a week, we'd get breakfast for supper—scrambled eggs, sausage, bacon, toast—but no chocolate chip pancakes, sadly. Nevertheless, that was my favorite meal of the week.

After dinner we had something called "appointments." This meant an hour of sitting with another student, checking in. We were supposed to share our "life stories" with each other, the most forced way I can think of to get to know another person. The only way to get out of appointments was by getting put onto a crew, a form of peer-on-peer punishment that combined manual labor with pointless humiliation. When faced with a choice between running across campus while holding a twenty-pound jug of water and sharing the same prerehearsed speech about my life with yet another person, honestly, I'd have to say it was a toss-up.

Appointments usually went the exact same way.

"So, how do you like it here?"

"I don't. My parents are forcing me to stay."

"Oh. Okay. So anyway, tell me your life story."

At this point I'd launch into my speech, recounting it with zero emotion.

"I was born in South Carolina. A few months later we moved to California. My dad was in the Navy and we lived in San Diego first, then moved to Oakland. I ran away for the first time when I was five. I loved sports and GI Joe and I wanted to be a fighter pilot. Someone brave who might save the world. You know, when I wasn't too busy playing with all my American Girl dolls."

"That's fucked-up."

I looked up, startled. My appointment that night was with Kristen. Even though she was my roommate, I hardly knew her. Most of our time together was spent asleep.

"What?"

"American Girl is just creepy." A moment later, Kristen added, "I had Molly. It was a Christmas present I didn't want."

"Did she order the outfits?"

"Yeah. All those plaid dresses and shit."

"She would have fit in perfectly here," I said.

Kristen laughed. When it was her turn to talk, two things from her story stuck out. The first was that she came from an aristocratic family, which I never would have guessed from her rebellious, earth-child persona.

The second was that Kristen was turning eighteen soon. She was two months away from becoming a legal adult. Two months from being able to walk off the Carlbrook campus and never look back. The staff could follow her—and they probably would—but they couldn't force her to return.

Kristen was counting down the days.

Chapter 18

MOST OF MY life I believed that turning sixteen was supposed to bring me freedom. I figured I'd get my driver's license and maybe even a car to go along with it. I'd have more independence from my parents, a later curfew, and fewer rules. But there has never been a time I've felt less free than on my sixteenth birthday.

There was a "party," I guess, but the only people there were my adviser, Catherine, and other members of her team. I hadn't been at Carlbrook long enough to make any real friends, and I was still on pre-Integritas bans with Brittany and Charlotte. I did receive a sweet handmade card from Maya, though. She couldn't say happy birthday to my face, but she placed the card down on the table in front of me.

There was one good thing about that day. Everyone got a cake on their birthday, made by the Carlbrook Cake Committee. It wasn't the cake itself that was so great. Those were all the same: a confetti base from a box and vanilla frosting. The committee itself, which I joined not long after that day, was something special.

Mostly this was because of Nelly. If anyone at Carlbrook came close to being a "fill-in mom," it wasn't Catherine, it was Nelly. She was a warm mama bear of a woman who ran the kitchen and headed the cake-baking group. She looked after us in a way that was so rare for

Carlbrook. She would sneak me snacks and treats and tell me to have a good day. If I seemed down, she would always try to cheer me up. Nelly had no interest in my therapeutic growth or calling me out "for my own good." She was a rare example of someone normal, and she made life at Carlbrook a little bit easier.

My other "present" was a five-minute phone call home. It would be my second one since arriving at Carlbrook. My first hadn't gone very well at all.

I started asking about phone rights pretty much as soon as I arrived. The first time I met with Catherine, we sat on the couches upstairs in the commons and she explained the ins and outs of my new life. I kept getting distracted by the strange scene across the way, inside a room with one wall made entirely of windows.

There were a few dozen desks, but only five or six of the seats were occupied. There didn't seem to be a teacher present, and it certainly wasn't a group. In fact, the kids were all completely silent. They didn't even look at each other. I half expected to see a casket and a photograph of some smiling dead person at the front of the room.

"What's that room for?"

Catherine followed my gaze.

"That's the program room. If you see someone carrying a red binder it means they're on a program. The entire school is on bans with anyone on a program."

"How do you get on a program?"

"It's a punishment. Just do your emotional work and follow all the rules, and you'll be fine."

So just do everything they want, no matter how stupid, all of the time. Sounds great.

I looked at the program room again and shuddered. It would make anyone think twice about this place, including, I realized, my parents.

They must not have seen it. Right?

"Hey, Catherine? When can I talk to my parents?"

"Every two weeks you get a twenty-minute phone call home. It's a privilege, which means you can lose it."

"Two weeks? What if I need to talk to them now?"

"If you have a message, I'm happy to pass it along," Catherine said. "I speak with them once a week to update them on your progress."

I did eventually get that first phone call home, and I had every intention of putting my best foot forward. I would use my sweetest voice and show them how much I'd changed, asking them to please bring me home. But when I realized that the calls took place in a tiny room with cubicles and a staff member monitoring my every word, my heartbeat started to surge.

The nice act lasted approximately three seconds.

"Hi, Mom. Dad."

"Hey, sweetheart," my mother said. "We miss you."

Bullshit.

I hadn't heard their voices in almost four months, and it triggered the hell out of me. All the anger I was trying to contain rushed up like a tidal wave. It was completely unstoppable, and within a minute I was sobbing and telling them how much I hated everyone and everything.

"I didn't want to be at this fucking school. It's like fucking prison. Everyone who works here is insane and you're the worst parents in the fucking world if you make me stay."

Usually, the guy monitoring the call will give you a tap on the shoulder just before the twenty-minute mark. Then you can say your good-byes before hanging up. Sometimes, though, he'll hang up for you. That happens when you get too aggressive or start making accusations about the school. But neither of those things happened to me on that first call because I was the one who hung up with ten minutes still to go.

The next time I saw Catherine, she told me I had lost my phone privileges. The monitor must have reported back to her. The next call on the schedule had been canceled.

"Spend the next few weeks working on yourself," she said. "And we can try again."

My birthday came before I could prove myself one way or the other. This call was different; we got only five minutes, but it went much more smoothly. Basically, I said nothing.

"Hi, Mom."

"Happy birthday, Elizabeth."

"Thanks."

"I can't believe you're sixteen."

"Yep," I said. "Neither can I."

What I meant was, I can't believe I'm spending my sixteenth birthday like a prisoner. Permitted a single phone call and a birthday cake baked by a committee.

Loneliness hit me hard that night. Lying awake in my tiny bunk bed, I actually started thinking about home. There was a time when my mom and I used to talk about making a quilt from all of my old tournament T-shirts. Between soccer and swimming I had entire drawers full of them, so many more than had been packed for Carlbrook. They were from tournaments held all over, where I often did quite well. Each shirt was like a snapshot, a piece of evidence that a life had been lived. Sewn together, they would make a full portrait.

We were subject to hourly bed checks by the "Securitas," the locals Carlbrook hired to watch over us at night. When I heard footsteps in the hall, I shut my eyes and waited for the swoop of light to cut across my bed. When the room went dark again I knew I'd have a bit of time before the next check. I wanted to run away or make a desperate phone call to Melanie or Nick, but I didn't. Instead, I crept to the bathroom and stared into the mirror.

For the first time in almost four months, I was completely alone. I had a true moment to myself, and I'd almost forgotten what that felt like. In the woods I didn't see my own face at all except as a warped reflection in a bowl. Since arriving at Carlbrook, I hadn't done more than glance in the mirror before six other girls came clamoring in for bathroom space. It occurred to me that I had been afraid to really look. I honestly didn't know if I would recognize myself.

Do I still have my freckles? Is there still a dimple in only one of my cheeks?

I was worried that everything unique about me had been erased. That I'd become as vacant on the outside as I felt on the inside. When I finally looked in the mirror and saw a face that hadn't changed at all, it made me angry. I looked completely normal, I could just as well have been at my old high school.

I should look blank. I should be unrecognizable. At least that way I wouldn't feel like such a fraud. How can I be in this hellhole and still look okay?

My mom and I never actually made the quilt. I guess it just didn't seem all that urgent. Not to a kid with an open future and endless tournaments still to come. As a newly sixteen-year-old girl, lying awake in a cramped double-wide trailer, I would have given anything for a sense of identity as concrete as a homemade quilt.

Chapter 19

WE WEREN'T ALLOWED to talk about workshops with students who had yet to go through them. There were rumors about each one, whispered words like *funeral* and *hypnotized* that filled me with dread. *Workshop* is such an unremarkable word. Dull and corporate. It didn't seem to fit, but maybe that was the point.

At CEDU they weren't called workshops, they were *"Propheets."* In their very first form, they were "Trips," a word chosen for its association with psychedelics. Chuck Dederich wanted to induce an altered state of consciousness. An acid trip without the acid. Because there could be no drug use in Synanon, he created a mocktail from ingredients like sleep deprivation, repetitive music, and group hypnosis.

In the hands of Mel Wasserman, they became even more insidious. His plan? *Add another cult!* Many of the workshop exercises were taken straight from the large-group awareness trainings that were a controversial part of the Human Potential Movement. Programs like est and Lifespring—which themselves developed from *Dianetics*—would bring groups of people together for several days of intense personal growth work. Techniques included hypnosis, guided meditation, and referring to people as "asshole"—an est specialty that fit in nicely with the CEDU model.

But of course I didn't know any of that back then. All I knew were the rumors and whispers. After about a month at Carlbrook, still on bans with my entire peer class, it was finally time for my first workshop. The night before Integritas, I gripped my baby blanket tightly. I'd hardly slept at all when I heard my alarm go off.

Time for Integritas, peer group Pi.

Workshops began at dawn. That part I knew, but I couldn't tell you when they ended. Time played by different rules inside the workshop trailer, which had blackout shades over every window. All I knew was that it was dark when we walked in and dark when we walked out. If the sun even rose at all, it was news to me:

"Get in a single-file line. Eyes down, group Pi."

Two so-called student supports, kids who'd already been through Integritas, gathered us from the sleeping mods. Brittany and I joined the line, falling between Charlotte and Maya. We marched across campus in total silence, past the pond and the mansion. By the woods where it was even colder and darker. It felt like heading off to war.

But are we comrades or are we enemies?

I was on bans with everyone in my group, but I had a few vague impressions. Rose was a kiss-up. Conrad was a troublemaker. Benjamin and Dash seemed sweet. Lindy didn't. While Levi was a goofball posing as a tough guy.

Platoon Pi, reporting for duty.

The first assault came in the form of a song. Specifically, a song from the *Les Misérables* sound track, which held an importance at Carlbrook I'll never understand. I could hear Jean Valjean's voice crooning from a hundred feet away. It pulsed out from the trailer and boomed against the trees.

It's way too early for this shit.

When the song ended, it began all over again. We reached the trailer and made our way inside. The noise was deafening and all the lights were off. It really did feel like walking into battle. I half expected to be handed an AK-47. Or at least a bayonet.

"Welcome to Integritas."

It was Alan's voice. The music faded and the lights came on. Everything looked shockingly normal. Just a regular Carlbrook classroom other than the blacked-out windows. Instead of weapons, staff handed out pens and paper.

"Before we can get started," Alan said, "I want you all to write honor lists. And remember. This workshop is about *Integrity*. It's about being honest with yourself and with other people. Remember: *If it looks like a duck, swims like a duck, and quacks like a duck, then it probably is a duck.*"

Writing an honor list was like going to confession, receiving no forgiveness, and waiting for the priest to tell the whole congregation about your sins. We were expected to write down every single thing we'd done that was out of standard or against the rules. Mine went:

I stayed up in the bathroom after lights-out.

Maggie told me my pants were too tight, but I wore them anyway.

I skipped breakfast once. Just pushed the food around on my plate and threw it away.

I broke bans by smiling at Charlotte in the hallway.

I paused. I'd also broken bans with Brittany pretty much every day since I'd been at Carlbrook, but I didn't want to get her in trouble. I also didn't want to *be* in trouble, and if she wrote about our nighttime chats and I didn't, that's exactly what would happen. I decided to compromise. I'd confess, but I wouldn't get specific. I jotted down "I broke bans with Brittany" and hoped it would match whatever she wrote.

"Are you sure that's everything, Elizabeth?"

Alan was reading over my shoulder. I felt his hot breath on my neck and his hand on my back. I tried not to cringe.

"Don't get caught lying," he said. "Remember, we always know more than you think."

I stared at my paper. Other than my half-truth about Brittany, I really had listed everything. Or at least I thought it was everything. Carlbrook had this way of making me feel like I had done something wrong even when I knew I hadn't. Was there some grand crime I was forgetting? I'd thought about running away; did I need to write that down?

They can't read your mind, Elizabeth. Chill out.

I honestly wasn't convinced. I felt like I was going crazy.

Should I write that down?

Thankfully, the student supports soon appeared to collect our lists. In exchange, we were each given a journal. There was an intricate design on the cover that felt vaguely Greek and/or Latin.

"Okay, peer group Pi," Alan said. "We're almost ready to get Integritas going. But first I want you all to write down your goals for the workshop in your new notebooks."

I saw Catherine walk to the stereo. She cued up more *Les Misérables*.

"And remember," Alan said again, "this workshop is about *integrity*. While we're in this room nothing is more important than honesty. So please be sincere about your goals."

Sincere about my goals, okay. Let's see. I want to survive this. How's that? My goal is to get out of Integritas without being hypnotized or brainwashed. And after that, I want to get out of this abusive hellhole.

Catherine turned up the music. It was suddenly hard not to laugh.

Great. I basically have the same goals as Cosette.

Why stop there? If they were going to make us identify with characters from *Les Misérables*, we may as well be the student revolutionaries.

My goal is to overthrow the government of Carlbrook. Alan, David, Randall, everyone in charge. Then I want to burn this place to the ground.

I didn't write any of that, obviously. The student rebellion in *Les Mis* was a failure, after all. Everyone who participated died. Instead, I wrote some crap about wanting to understand myself better. To figure out where all my anger came from and why it was so hard for me to accept love from others. I really had no idea. There was so much about my childhood I just couldn't remember. Basic things, like my first day of school or learning to ride a bicycle.

If I know how to ride a bike, someone must have taught me, right?

I racked my brain, but the only thing I could locate was a memory of my sister learning to ride a tricycle. I remember running beside her and pushing her down the hill from our house. We were gathering speed little by little until I suddenly realized she was going way too fast. I saw the tricycle flip over backward and my sister come crashing down onto her head.

I didn't mean for her to get hurt. Maybe I'm just a monster who hurts everyone I touch. If that's true, hopefully this workshop can help me own up to it.

We ate lunch in the trailer. I desperately wanted some fresh air but would have to settle for a stale sandwich. At least it meant I could take a break from being inside my own head, wondering who else was in there with me, and feeling generally paranoid and insane. I chewed my stale sandwich and drank from a small cup of water, which was all we were given.

Part of me wondered if keeping us dehydrated was just another way to mess with our heads. A control tactic, part of the acid trip. It didn't help matters that the first thing I saw after lunch was a pendulum, swinging from Alan's hand.

So the rumors are true. They do hypnotize us, after all.

Alan flicked the metal ball. It began to swing back and forth.

"I want you to take a good look at this pendulum," Alan said.

Don't do it. Look anywhere but there.

"Focus on the way it swings. How it goes all the way to the left and then all the way to the right."

Blink if you have to. Pretend you have something in your eye. Just don't let him get to you. Not today, Alan!

"The pendulum represents our relationship to pain and joy. As far as it

173

swings to the left, that's how much pain we feel. And to the right, that's our experience of joy. You can't have one without the other. One will always influence the other."

Wait. It's just a metaphor?

Maybe, but now Alan wanted us to lie down and close our eyes.

"Just take a deep breath and relax."

He asked us to imagine ourselves as little kids. What did we dream of becoming back then? When the whole world was full of possibilities.

"Pick up that childhood dream and really look at it," Alan said. "I want you to look at it so deeply that you're there again. Wearing what you used to wear, smelling all those familiar smells."

I've never been one of those people who can relax on command. "Just relax" is usually my cue to do the opposite. I closed my eyes because I had to and thought about my dreams. Back when I was all about becoming a fighter pilot, I used to run around the backyard in camouflage pants and an Annapolis Naval Academy T-shirt, catching snakes and shooting BB guns. I was fearless and maybe a little bit crazy. When a BB pellet ricocheted off the wall and hit me in the stomach, I didn't cry. I laughed. I was proud of the bruise it left. I thought it was cool.

Then there was soccer. At one point I truly thought that would be my life. I'd win a World Cup or two, my face would be on a Wheaties box. *No big deal.* The next exercise was about childhood heroes, and there was only one person in my mind. *Mia Hamm, of course.*

"My hero was Babe Ruth," Dash said.

"Jem," Charlotte said. "From *Jem and the Holograms.*"

Benjamin's hero was Superman. Levi's was Al Capone. Brittany's was Superwoman, or maybe she just ripped off Benjamin.

"My hero is my sister." Maya was sniffling as she said it, a wad of crumpled tissues already in her lap. "She's so brave and confident. I wish I was more like her."

"That's great, Maya," Alan said. "Really feel whatever's coming up."

I was next.

"Mia Hamm."

"Were you a soccer player, too, Elizabeth?"

"Yes," I said. "It's basically all I ever did."

"That's great," Alan said. "Let's get you back to Mia Hamm."

Hearing him say those words made me wish I'd lied. I wanted to yell in his face.

Fuck you. I'll never be Mia Hamm. Or anyone like her. That's a dead dream, Alan.

To add insult to injury, the names of our heroes were written down on index cards and Alan taped them to our shirts. Back in the woods I had sort of enjoyed being Number Nine. Now, looking down and seeing "Mia Hamm" clinging to my J.Crew sweater like a name tag made me feel like I was being mocked.

Maybe I was, because the next exercise involved giving each other compliments—which wasn't exactly what I'd come to expect. Alan put Charlotte in the hot seat and asked the rest of us to list the things that made her just like Jem.

"Charlotte wasn't born a drug addict," Alan said. "She was born pure and beautiful. You all were and that piece is still in there. Charlotte just hardened around it."

He touched Charlotte's hair and I shuddered.

"Elizabeth." Alan must have heard my movement. "Why don't you go first. What do you think is true, deep down, about Charlotte?"

My throat felt dry and tight. I was relieved I didn't have to say anything shitty, but I still felt put on the spot. None of us even knew each other. We'd been on bans this whole time, and now we were suddenly expected to see everyone's true selves?

Plus, it was Charlotte. The girl I met in the dining mod on my first night, when I knew instantly that we were destined to be friends.

"I think Charlotte seems strong," I said.

Charlotte smiled, and I knew I'd said the right thing.

"That's great," Alan said. "I agree."

"You're definitely a leader," Rose said.

Everyone took a turn saying something nice about Charlotte. Since we didn't actually know much about each other, a lot of us echoed the same idea. Charlotte seemed relaxed, like she'd let her guard down a little. Maybe workshops weren't really so bad after all.

"I was in the woods with Charlotte," Maya said. "And I know she's strong and doesn't give up. But she's kind and vulnerable too."

After Charlotte had received her compliments, Alan asked her to pick the one that resonated most. That would be her "truth," a label summing up her essential identity.

"Maybe it's something you usually hide. Something people don't often recognize in you."

Charlotte was silent for a moment. I didn't blame her. It seemed like a trick question, and who wants to give themselves a compliment?

"Vulnerable," she finally said, echoing a sentiment Maya had shared.

Alan nodded at Catherine, who scribbled *vulnerable* on an index card. This one went right over Charlotte's heart.

Sensitive. Honest. Trustworthy. Kind. One by one, my classmates went around the room branding themselves. When it was my turn, David said he could tell I was fearless.

Since it came from a staff member, there was no way it was going to be my truth. Maya told me I was sensitive, which I appreciated, but it didn't feel quite right. It wasn't how I wanted to see myself.

"She's powerful," Brittany said.

I nodded. It sounded good—and if it wasn't my real truth, at least it was something I wanted to be true.

"I'm powerful," I said.

"Great choice," Alan said. "It suits you."

When another round of catering arrived, we broke for dinner. It was mystery-meat cold cuts once again. Which hardly mattered when my mouth was too dry to know the difference, and it all tasted like starch anyway. I wasn't eating, I was fueling up. I just needed enough energy to make it through the rest of the night.

After dinner it was time for my very first disclosure circle. This meant going around the circle again and again, sharing dark secrets about our pasts. We'd have to reveal traumas and crimes. Everything we'd ever done and even some stuff we hadn't.

Months later I was a student support for another group's Integritas, and it gave me a little insight into the disclosure circle process. Before we started, the staff asked the supports to decide on an initial disclosure to set the tone for the group. They said that if we picked something "basic," like an eating disorder or smoking weed, the other kids would choose basic disclosures of their own. If we landed on something harder, like rape or abuse, the circle would take a very different tone.

Alan took the reins on this one. He told us all about how he'd been abused as a child, which led to years of confusion and acting out. In later workshops he would divulge the specifics of those lost years: drug addiction, anonymous sex, various combinations of the two. Every word he spoke set off another alarm bell, like my brain was trying to drown him out in an act of self-protection.

I really, really don't want to hear about you having sex.

"It had me under its thumb for a little while there," he said. "But I beat it."

Fine. Good. Please stop talking.

"And now I get to help kids like you."

It was the student supports' turn to share next and after that, it would be us. I sat paralyzed with fear and prayed I would somehow get skipped over or be granted a pass. I had no idea what I was going to say. All I knew was that I didn't want to use my made-up story from the woods. Writing about the first week that never happened was one thing, but actually saying those lies out loud was a line I couldn't cross.

On the other hand, I didn't want to share too many real things either.

I ended up just talking about a blow job. I didn't even have to get into the details. I just explained my religious upbringing, how I was raised knowing sex was something you saved for marriage. I *was* still a virgin, so it hurt when people in my hometown called me a slut. Little did I know I was setting myself up to be labeled much worse than that at Carlbrook.

We continued to go around the circle. Rose also had a blow job tale to tell. Charlotte shared some insane drug stories. Levi confessed to shoplifting. Lindy talked about throwing up after eating.

We went a few more times, running out of things to say just as the staff was demanding an escalation. The third round seemed to be when the lies started coming out. So the only options were making something up or sharing something really dark and personal.

I noticed that Benjamin seemed especially nervous during the third round. When the circle finally got to him, he broke down crying. His voice sounded broken and scared, and his mouth appeared contorted in pain. He told the group that he'd touched a family member once. A girl, younger than him, though he was still a child himself.

"Let it out," Alan said. "Get it all out."

Benjamin started sobbing, which was usually Alan's cue to offer one of his infamous back rubs. Instead, he simply passed Benjamin a box of Kleenex. No one else moved to comfort Benjamin either. In fact, the rest of us all looked a little sick. We had no idea what we were supposed to do—or even how we were supposed to feel.

Alan exchanged a long look with David, then kept the disclosure circle chugging along.

He wrapped up the disclosure circle, and I silently prayed that would be it for the night. My whole body felt like one raw nerve, swollen and exposed. I had been poked and prodded all day, and I knew I couldn't take much more before I broke.

Alan knew it too. He was like a predator catching a whiff of fear. He pulled a chair into the middle of the room and looked directly at me.

"Elizabeth," he said, "why don't you go first?"

Thanks a lot, God.

I walked to the hot seat on spaghetti legs. They continued to shake as I sat down. What happened next, I could have done without. The trailer door swung open and a group of more-senior students entered the room. They looked like hunters, thirsty for blood, and I felt like the deer they had sighted in their scopes, ready to shoot.

Before I could catch my breath I was in the thick of it. I was being roasted by the older kids and my peer class alike. My disclosures were being thrown in my face. I was a slut all over again. A dirty slut who gives blow jobs. Because I have no self-worth and the men in my life don't love me. Fifteen people I'd never spoken to in my life told me I was a pathetic whore, desperate for attention.

I knew the actual content of my disclosure didn't matter. I could have talked about burning myself with salt and ice and I still would have gotten it just as ruthlessly. They told me I was pathetic, that I didn't deserve to live.

"What kind of worthless girl just sucks dick like that?" David said.

"You're disgusting."

"You should be ashamed of yourself."

I could have counted every bad thing that had ever been said about me up to that point and multiplied it by ten, and it wouldn't have come close to what happened in that trailer. I tried to breathe through it, squeezing my hands together, telling myself not to cry. I didn't want to give them the satisfaction. But holding out just meant enduring the horror.

No guy is ever actually going to love you.

You're just a pretty face with an open mouth.

No wonder your parents didn't want you.

The accusations hit so close to home, like a broadcast of my own dark, internal monologue. All the worst things I'd ever thought about myself in my lowest moments now echoed inside the trailer. I started crying, feeling cracked apart. I closed my eyes and recalled a photo that hung on the wall back at home. A photo I'd seen a thousand times.

It was a picture of my brother the day he killed his first deer. He stood over the carcass, the animal's blood smeared on his face. It was a hunting custom, the traditional way to mark a young marksman's first kill.

When I opened my eyes, everyone in the room had blood on their faces. It was my blood and they'd earned it. A successful hunt, they shot me right in the heart.

It wasn't even over yet.

"Okay, Elizabeth," Alan said. "It's time to pick your lie."

The lie was like the shadow side of our truth. The way we cover up our essential goodness.

"Come on. Tell us who you've become."

I had no idea what I was supposed to say. I just sat there sobbing and bleeding out. I wanted to disappear.

"Come on, Elizabeth. Tell us your lie."

"I don't know," I whispered.

"You have to say something."

"I'm worthless," I said. And in that moment, I meant it.

"That's a start, but there's more. Tell us what really lives inside that heart of yours."

I looked up at Maya and Charlotte, pleading for an answer. Maya had tears running down her cheeks, but Charlotte just looked angry. She shook her head, pissed off on my behalf, her expression saying what I felt: *This is so fucked-up.*

"Elizabeth . . ."

Alan was walking over. I didn't want him to come near me.

"What's it going to be?"

The whole day flashed before my eyes. Every horrible moment and the moments that had become horrible because I'd been naive enough to think they were kind. I thought about the goals I'd written down in my journal. I remembered pushing my mom outside Lynn Anne's office. So I was a monster after all. A worthless abuser.

I had my lie.

"I'm a worthless abuser."

We stayed up until four in the morning, railing on person after person. Each of us walked away with a new word or phrase on an index card. Charlotte's read *Stone-Cold Bitch*. Maya was a *Pathetic Slut*, Brittany a *Manipulative Liar*. Levi was a *Wannabe*. Even so, no one got it worse than Benjamin. He had to walk back to the sleeping mods with *Molester* written across his shirt.

We could hardly look at one another that night. We were each other's destroyers. And we were all destroyed. We had only a few hours to rest, and I spent most of them thinking about the worthless abuser I had become. The slut, the bitch. If I could have gotten my hands on salt and ice, I would have burned myself until I went numb. I wanted to kill pain with pain. Instead, I folded myself into my tiny bed and cried silently into my pillow.

I must have fallen asleep because all of a sudden, I was inside my nightmare. The faceless man is there as well; he has come for me just like on a thousand other nights, but something's different this time. He's outside the workshop room, lurking in the woods. When he sees me he starts moving toward me. His hands reach up and pull down his hood. For the first time, I can see his face.

It's a face I recognize.

It's Alan's face.

Whatever I had been scared of had been subsumed by a bigger fear, a real-life villain who tormented me day in and day out. His identity wasn't blurry in the least. In fact, I knew far too many sordid details about Alan's life.

The morning air had a chill running through it. We trekked back across campus, reversing course, though we'd only just left. I felt the slap of wind on my cheeks. I hadn't gotten more than another hour of sleep, and I was so emotionally drained I felt delirious.

"We did important work yesterday." Alan began talking as soon as we entered the trailer. "Hard work. We tapped into the part of us we hide from the world. And that isn't always pretty."

As he spoke, Alan handed out silver marbles. One for each of us, shiny and new.

"These marbles were just born," he said. "They're perfect, beautiful. Completely untouched. But the more you use a marble, the more scratched up it gets. Maybe you drop it on the concrete. Maybe you throw it in your toy box without any care."

He went to his easel and drew a circle. His own marble.

"Maybe you forgot about your marbles completely, left them on the floor for weeks."

Alan drew a scratch on his paper marble.

"Maybe you took your anger out on your marble. Threw it against the wall."

Another scratch.

"Maybe your marble was adopted. Maybe its parents got a divorce."

Scratch, scratch.

"Its brother calls it ugly. Dad yells at it for singing too loud. Maybe your marble has sex with a boy and the boy isn't very nice."

Scratch, scratch, scratch.

"Sometimes the scratches are on the surface and sometimes they go deep. Those disclosures we opened up about yesterday are the deepest kind of scratches."

Alan put down his pen ceremoniously.

"But today," he said, "today we get to scratch back. If we don't confront our wounds, they'll never heal. But if we face them head-on, we have the chance to wash those scratches away. We can be those shiny, new marbles again."

The student supports entered the room carrying armloads of pillows.

There were stacks and stacks of them, as though they'd just robbed a Bed Bath & Beyond and needed to stash the merchandise.

"Is it naptime?" Alan said. "No. It's time to fight our demons."

So we're marbles. And the pillows are demons. Got it. Totally.

"Everyone partner up and find a space to work. Think of the pillow as your deepest scratches. The things that hurt you the most."

Catherine demonstrated the pillow-demon-fighting technique. We were to sit on our knees and interlock our fingers. Raise our hands above our heads and bring them down to attack the pillow again and again.

Orchestra music came on, so loud I could barely hear myself think. But maybe that was for the best. Maya and I teamed up and found a corner. We got down on our knees and placed our pillows on the floor. Alan suddenly thrust his hands into the air and brought them down sharply.

"Begin!"

No one moved. None of us wanted to be the first to start beating up a pillow. But that wasn't about to stop the likes of Alan and David. They walked around the room taunting us with our disclosures.

"Come on, Elizabeth," David said. "Don't be so weak. Is this how you act around all those boys?"

I wanted him to get the fuck away from me, so my only choice was to attack the bedding. I pounded down, once, twice, and then I couldn't stop. All around me I heard screams as feathers went flying. Some of my classmates really seemed to be fighting their demons. While some of us had realized that the louder you screamed, the more the staff stayed away. Each punch kept them at a distance. Suddenly I realized I was fighting the staff. They *were* my demons.

Fuck you, Alan! Fuck you, David! Go to hell, Lynn Anne Moore! I fucking hate you all and I hope you can feel every single punch.

Like everything else, this exercise wasn't going to end until there were tears. But I didn't have to fake it. I was so exhausted. I was sick of this workshop, of this place—the fucking marbles and pendulums. I looked around and everything was feathers and tears and . . . smooshing.

Oh no, not smooshing.

We were battle-weary and broken, totally spent from two days of hurling insults like weapons, forced to go in for the kill. Now we had to lie around on top of one another. In workshops, boys and girls could smoosh together, and of course Alan and David joined in.

Surely there's something against this in the Geneva Convention.

I got through it, somehow. I had made it through to the other side. There was a term for a group reappearing after a workshop, looking older if not wiser, or at least that much closer to death. It was "the return." Our Integritas return was set to "Superman" by Five for Fighting. We walked down the stairs and sat down with our arms around each other, waiting for the song to end.

One by one we stood up and said our truths. It seemed insane that after all of that, we were somehow expected to think of ourselves as honest and kind again? I sure as hell didn't feel like I had any strength or power inside me whatsoever.

But no one had to know that. After all, I was a Southern girl. Even though I was the furthest from okay I'd ever been, I knew how to pretend.

"I'm powerful," I said.

A few days later I was walking across campus when I saw the black SUV pull up to the carriage house. Two men dressed in black stepped out. *Escorts.* It meant one of two things: Either someone was arriving or someone else was being taken away.

The escorts were there for Benjamin. I watched him get into the car, his head hanging low, and I never saw him again.

In that evening's Last Light speech, all Alan said was that Benjamin would no longer be attending Carlbrook. He was being sent somewhere "better suited to his particular needs."

What does that mean? A different kind of school? Back to the woods?

But I feared the worst: that Benjamin was being sent to lockdown for the things he'd said in the disclosure circle, and that was something else entirely. Obedience, cooperation, those were things we could control. But how could any of us navigate this new situation?

We were being mined for deeper and darker disclosures all the time, and we had to deliver or we'd be accused of lying. But say the wrong thing and it's off to one of those dreaded lockdowns to stay a prisoner until you turn twenty-one.

Great. One more thing to be afraid of.

Chapter 20

AFTER INTEGRITAS, I was finally off bans with my peer group. It was a relief to actually be able to make some friends, and almost immediately Maya and I became attached at the hip. We were both from small Southern towns and there was a familiarity and ease that made me feel like I'd known her forever. She was in my sleeping mod, and we walked to breakfast together every morning. At the student store, we each picked out a different candy bar and split them in half so it felt like getting two.

Before long I was part of an unofficial clique. It included me, Brittany, Kristen, Charlotte, Maya, and a girl named Valerie who I was just starting to become close with. Valerie was the president of the Cake Committee. She asked me if I wanted to join, and saying yes was one of the best decisions I made at Carlbrook. Nelly actually let us listen to music and dance around the kitchen. She never said anything when we stole a spoonful of frosting.

Eventually, the clique would come to include a few more girls from the peer class just below mine. There was Shelby, from Texas, who reminded me more of home than anyone else I met at Carlbrook. She always wore large pearl earrings and seemed to thrive in those J.Crew sweater sets. She was the only girl I knew who brought a Bible with her to school, and besides God, her primary interest seemed to be landing a wealthy husband.

Lina was the polar opposite of Shelby. She was the one person who could actually make the dress code seem cool. She wore beaded moccasins and headbands and combined colors in ways that shouldn't have worked but always did. She was tough but had a good heart and would end up being one of my best friends.

Then there were the boys, a group of nonconformists. This crew included Luke, who I was developing a real crush on; Bryan, a brilliant kid with an anarchist streak; and Levi, the would-be mobster from Detroit.

Luke's roommate was a kid named Owen, who was so quiet and unassuming I often forgot he was there. Though if Owen was trying to blend in, to stay beneath the staff's radar, you could hardly blame him. By the time I met him he'd already become a cautionary tale.

I got the story from Brittany, who seemed to know everything about everyone—an impressive feat when you considered that her arrival preceded mine by only about a month. The way she explained it, the whole thing was a total accident. When Owen's parents shipped his belongings to Carlbrook they included a backpack along with clothes and bedding. Unbeknownst to them, the backpack happened to contain a bottle of pills hidden in an interior pocket. The contraband slipped past the staff and sat untouched in the backpack for weeks.

Of course, as soon as Owen realized he had drugs there was only one thing he could do. He shared them with Luke and another roommate, they told a couple of friends, and from there it was only a matter of time until Owen got caught. When he did, the whole "It was an accident" thing didn't exactly land. They made good on their threat and sent Owen back to the woods while figuring out what to do with him next.

At Carlbrook there were levels of punishments. Mild infractions meant running crews, our peer-on-peer punishment. That meant scurrying around in front of the entire school scrubbing toilets and carrying water jugs pointlessly around the lake. Next was a program, which meant a month or two in isolation. Do something really bad and Carlbrook would send you back to the woods for observation. It was a sort of test, where passing meant going back to Carlbrook and failing got you sent to lockdown.

He must have had either a guardian angel or parents with especially deep pockets because Owen was back at Carlbrook the following month. It easily could have been lockdown instead, and Owen knew that if anything ever happened again, it most certainly would be.

The backpack incident gave the group of boys quite a reputation. They were known around school as the troublemakers and it wasn't exactly untrue, but weren't we at Carlbrook? Wasn't everyone here one kind of trouble or another?

Well, not exactly. This place had its overachieving kiss-ups just like every other school in the world. I don't know where the word came from, but we called them Ponies. Beatrice was a Pony, of course. As was a girl named Molly, along with Rose from my peer class. There were male members of the species, too, and these boy Ponies tended to be the most overachieving of them all. Paul was our student body president, and he walked around like a hall monitor. Seeing Paul always made me freeze in place.

Am I doing anything out of standard? Did I finish everything on my breakfast plate? Can you see my ass through my jeans?

I was constantly on guard, especially on group days. One morning, I saw my name right below Rose's and just had an instinct she had requested me. It was an Alan group, which meant he would be crying along with everyone else. Halfway through, Rose switched chairs to sit right across from me and I knew my instinct had been correct.

"Elizabeth, I requested you for group today," she said. "I've noticed you've been spending a lot of time with negative people like Luke."

Are you fucking kidding me?

"I really care about you. And I think you flirt with negative people to avoid dealing with your emotions."

I was stunned. I had no idea how to respond. But I didn't have to because apparently half the group had an issue with my supposed flirting.

Shelby jumped in. "I agree. I've also noticed you spend a lot of time with Luke."

"Other boys too."

"You're always laughing and smiling at them."

"Flirting really triggers feelings from back home," Shelby said. "I don't feel safe when you do it."

This is fucking bullshit.

I locked eyes with Maya. I was on the verge of tears and I think she could tell I was genuinely upset.

"I know you've struggled with feeling like a disappointment," Rose said. "Especially since your parents sent you away. You know I deal with the same thing. I just don't want to see you bring another toxic relationship into your life."

Alan could see I was close to a breakdown. He knew it was time to dig in.

"Do you have anything to say? How does it feel to hear you're making people feel unsafe? Are you a flirt, Elizabeth?"

"No," I said. "They're overreacting."

"Elizabeth, don't be defensive."

"But it's not even true. It's not like I'm some slut all over everyone at school."

"Your *behavior* is slutty," Rose said.

I started to cry. But I honestly couldn't tell if I was genuinely hurt by what was being said or if I was just doing what I needed to do to make everyone stop. Maya moved across the room and sat down next to me. She wrapped her arm around my shoulder and hugged me while I cried. After a moment I realized Maya was crying too.

"Maya," Alan said, "what are you feeling right now?"

"Sad," she said. "Sad for Elizabeth. And for myself."

"What's making you feel that?"

"I know what it's like to want to feel loved," Maya said.

She was crying. Alan brought over a box of tissues.

"My whole life, I've just wanted to be good enough. Good enough to be loved."

Maya put her head down and started sobbing uncontrollably. I placed my hand on her back like she'd done for me.

"You are," I said, whispering in her ear.

I don't know if she heard me. She was fully in it now, engaged with her demon. Her tiny body was slouched over, and tears ran onto the floor.

"I just want to be me. But better."

Hearing her say those words made me want to cry more than any of those accusations had. Maya was so earnest and raw, something I could never be. So I continued to keep my tears at bay. Crying for real would have been too honest.

"I deserve love. I know I do."

Maya was crying for real. She didn't do what I did, what so many of us did, lying and exaggerating to protect ourselves. She really believed in Carlbrook. She trusted the place and the people much more than I could ever have imagined doing. She wanted to heal, to do the work, no matter the toll it might take.

If anyone here deserved to be loved, it was Maya. I wanted to tell her that she was strong and beautiful, worthy of all the love she'd been missing in her life. Instead, all I could do was rub her back while she ran anger, hoping she knew how special I thought she was.

An Alan group always ended with hugging. I tried to leave, but he stopped me and wrapped his arms around my shoulders.

"You got cut off there," he said.

"That's okay."

"I think there's more work to do. Why don't we meet tonight at appointment time?"

I went through the rest of the day with a knot in my stomach. That evening, I met Alan on the couches outside the med bay. I was shaking as soon as I got there and I hardly heard anything he said. I could feel myself begin to check out of my body.

He patted his thigh, a signal for me to sit on his lap.

"It's all going to be okay," he said, stroking my hair.

I nodded. I felt sick. Nothing seemed okay in the least.

"You're so beautiful, Elizabeth." Alan had tears in his eyes. "You're beautiful and everything's going to be okay."

I realized I was crying too. It was out of fear, the feeling that I was trapped. I wanted to scream and run away, but I couldn't. I didn't want to end up in lockdown or wherever Benjamin had gone. I sat there frozen like a little girl while Alan whispered in my ear and rubbed my shoulders.

"Let it out. You'll be okay. You just have to do the work."

After the appointment was over, I didn't want to see anyone. I wasn't sure if Alan had actually done anything wrong, but I did know that I didn't want to feel that way ever again.

I would, though, many more times during my time at Carlbrook. Alan's questionable behavior wasn't talked about back then, but it came up a lot in the years after I graduated. It would turn out that most of my friends had a story about a time a staff member's physical affection made them feel uncomfortable.

I walked to the sleeping mods as quickly as I could. At lights-out, I buried my head in my baby blanket and silently sobbed for most of the night. When I woke up my eyes were rimmed with red. I was so tired that eating breakfast felt like too much effort. I pushed my food around on my plate and rubbed my eyes.

"Hey you."

Nelly was standing over me, peering at my plate. "Why aren't you eating? What's going on?"

I looked up with my puffy eyes.

"I just hate it here," I said.

"I know you do. But cheer up. This is just one day in a very big life."

"I guess so."

"Here," Nelly said, pulling out a chocolate bar. "I snuck this for you. Eat it and smile, okay?"

"Thanks, Nelly."

It worked. I did smile. I pocketed the chocolate bar and picked up my tray.

"Hey, Elizabeth?" Nelly said, dropping her voice to a whisper. "I would hate it here too."

Chapter 21

Dear Parents:

It is a special pleasure to extend holiday greetings to the families of Carlbrook School. In keeping with new traditions underway, we plan to have a HUGE HOLIDAY TREE about fifteen feet tall, one which will have over 1200 lights! We, the faculty, want this tree to represent ALL of the students at Carlbrook.

If ever there was an example of the hypocrisy that ruled over Carlbrook, it was every single thing about the Christmas season. A huge holiday tree did indeed go up, with all the trimmings listed in the letter that was sent to our parents. It appeared a little after Thanksgiving, right around the time our families were scheduled to visit.

Accordingly, we are asking parents to select an ornament that you feel particularly represents your child. This decorative gift will become a permanent part of your child's legacy at Carlbrook. Each holiday ornament on the tree will be a colorful and lasting symbol for every child who has ever attended Carlbrook.

I had always loved trimming the tree. Back in my old life, it was one of my favorite parts of the holiday season. My mom would bring down boxes of decorations and carefully unpack them, pulling out nutcrackers, wreaths, and all the hand-painted ornaments from Christmases past.

The best ornaments came from the holiday market. Every year, my siblings and I would return to the same stand for a new custom figurine. My collection included a soccer player with a #9 jersey, a diver wearing my swim team's colors, and a fighter jet complete with a little blond captain looking out the window. I would hang them on the tree one by one, adding the popsicle-stick reindeer I made in kindergarten and finger-painted snowflakes. There was even a little paper angel who had my face, a Sunday school original.

Maybe they'll send that one. It would really complete the whole Christmas facade.

I was nervous about my parents' upcoming visit to Carlbrook. I hadn't seen them in more than five months, and I had even more anger toward them now than I did before they sent me away. Every phone call home was some version of the same thing. I'd put so much effort into suppressing my rage, stopping each angry thought I had from coming out of my mouth, that I ended up saying next to nothing. The conversations were either petty fights or trivial talk about my sister's horseback riding lessons.

At the same time, they were still my parents. Somewhere behind that cloud of anger, a part of me really did miss them. I also knew pleasing them was my best chance at getting out of this place. I secretly began to hope that if I saw them face-to-face, I could convince them to take me back to South Carolina.

While I fretted about this family visit, Maggie and her peer class were getting ready to say good-bye to Carlbrook. Graduation happened three times a year. There was a spring ceremony, like a normal high school would have, a summer ceremony, and this one in the winter. All went pretty much the same way. The boys put on suits and the girls dressed all in white—like child brides or sacrificial virgins. Alan would make a speech that would inevitably lead to crying, and every graduating student would get up and say a little something about the school.

I sat through the ceremony without paying much attention. It seemed wholly unimportant, just more of Alan's bullshit. There was plenty of nonsense, but that day also had a weird sort of significance I'd become aware of only many years later.

Before Maggie left she let me pick what I wanted from her wardrobe. She gave me her little candy stash and hugged me like she really was my big sister.

"Promise you'll stay in touch," she said.

"Promise."

"And you have to come visit me."

"Of course."

"At college. You can stay with me. It'll be so much fun."

"I can't wait," I said. "I'll see you soon."

I did keep in touch with Maggie for a little while. We exchanged a handful of letters while I was still at Carlbrook. Maybe that would have been the extent of our relationship even if she hadn't died. I don't know that we were destined to be friends for life or anything, but when I hugged her good-bye I truly didn't think it would be the last time I would ever see her. That in less than two years she would be dead.

"Thanks for everything," I said.

So would Kyle, whom I had watched battle his demons. Owen, with that backpack full of pills. I waved as he walked away, looking awkward in his suit.

Trevor came up to me and wrapped his arms around me in a hug. He was just as warm and friendly as the first time I met him, when he helped me out during my first request group.

"You hang in there, kid," he said.

I hugged him back. I wouldn't see Trevor again, either, except in a casket three years down the line.

The parent weekend fell between graduation and Christmas, and the school never looked spiffier. That fifteen-foot tree was all lit up, aglow with the souls of "every child who has ever attended Carlbrook."

As if that's not creepy. Are they trying to trap us here forever? I always figured I was living in a horror movie.

Parents started arriving in the morning, and cars continued to pull up throughout the afternoon. Some parents came running in with open arms, others seemed more tense and even hostile. From the tenor of our recent phone calls, I had a feeling I knew which end of the spectrum my reunion would fall on. I could feel myself getting angry just waiting for my parents to show up, and part of me hoped they wouldn't even bother.

As I waited, a boy who had issues around being adopted greeted his family with a strained smile. I saw Maya come into the commons with her own family, looking so happy just to have them there. She showed them around, pointing to the chairs where we smooshed and the glass program room as if it were all somehow normal. I knew this place hurt her just like it hurt me. Maya swallowed all that pain and managed to keep it hidden somewhere deep, where her family would never have to see it. I admired her for that, but it also made me angry on her behalf.

So I figured I'd make up for it by being pissed off for both of us.

My parents' visit began like a replay of our first phone call. I promised myself I'd be even-tempered and restrained, the version of a daughter they'd want to take back home. Just as before, actually seeing them sent all those lofty goals right out the window.

I could tell my mom was nervous the moment she walked through the door of the commons building. She scanned the room and when she spotted me, I waved. Two stiff hugs later, and my blood was already beginning to get hot.

"This is nice," my mom said, looking at the Christmas tree.

"I guess," I said.

"Look, there's your ornament."

It was the soccer player, the ceramic girl with the nine on her jersey.

I want to smash that fucking thing to pieces.

I was about to say something snarky, but Alan's voice called for everyone's attention. He gave a little speech welcoming the parents and announced it was time for our first group. We were sent off to join family groups, led by our advisers. I took my parents to the classroom where Catherine's group was meeting. We sat down in a circle along with four other families.

The group was an absolute disaster. When it was my turn, Catherine wanted to focus on the so-called issues that landed me at Carlbrook. My anger, the drinking, sneaking off to parties. I just wanted to say something that might convince my parents I was ready to go home.

"I don't feel like I'm that person anymore," I said.

Catherine, the kids on my team, and even my parents wore a look that said the same thing: *Bullshit.* No one was buying it. Not even me. I was grasping at straws and everyone knew it.

"Elizabeth." My mom sighed. "Don't do this again."

"Do what?" I doubled down. "I'm saying things are different now. I've learned my lesson. Can I please just come home?"

"You're not ready," my dad said. "Even if you think you've changed, your wild friends haven't."

"Okay," I said. "Then I won't hang out with them anymore."

"That's not true and you know it," he said. "Can't you please just be honest with yourself?"

Okay, sure. I'll be honest. You're right, I haven't changed. In fact, I'm pretty sure I've only gotten worse. This fucked-up place doesn't fix people, it breaks us. And I've never wanted to go out and party more than I do right now. And guess what? Thanks to Carlbrook, I know more about drugs than I ever would have in my life if I'd stayed in South Carolina.

I could feel rage building like a fire. Catherine noticed and saw it as an opportunity.

"Elizabeth," she said, "are you ready to discuss your anger issues?"

The very question was like fuel for my temper. I started to yell, taking my rage out on my parents. Though I was mad at both of them, I was especially upset with my mom. Usually she at least attempted to defend me, and when that didn't happen it seemed like a betrayal.

"I hate you," I said. "I hate you for sending me here. For being so stupid that you did exactly what Lynn Anne Moore told you to do."

I felt myself boiling over.

"She tricked you," I said. "She just wanted your money. What a coincidence that I happened to be the perfect candidate for her SON'S FUCKING SCHOOL," I screamed, my face flushing crimson. "You let her RUIN my life."

"Elizabeth," Catherine said, "do not speak to your mother like this."

No one protested. After that, Catherine kicked me out of the session.

"Fine," I said and stomped out of the room.

After group, my parents found me and tried to make peace. But I was so upset I couldn't see straight. My mom was supposed to be on my side. She was supposed to pick me up and take me home, just like she'd made Dad turn the car around last summer. I knew I couldn't change my father's mind. He was the disciplinarian, but I had always been able to win my mother's sympathy.

I had no power, no leverage. When I realized she wasn't going to take me home I finally just asked her to leave. "Can't you just go back to the hotel or something?"

To my surprise, she actually did. I spent the rest of the day playing board games with my dad. Neither of us said very much, and it was clear we weren't happy. It was less exhausting than fighting, and I had no energy left.

When I got back to my room that night I felt empty. Brittany and Kristen seemed to be in a similar place. If we were sad about anything, it was that our families had left without taking us with them. It would have been easier not to have seen them at all.

At least Kristen had a card up her sleeve. Her birthday was getting closer and she was still determined to run away. Everyone seemed to know about her plan to leave Carlbrook. Even the staff had questioned her about it during group. Now she was storing up food, sneaking an extra granola bar or banana every once in a while.

As Christmas approached there was a sad attempt to get us into the holiday spirit. We made cards for each other using glitter and markers, and I felt like I was back at Sunday school.

There was no need to write a letter to Santa—we were all on the naughty list and coal wasn't even on the list of acceptable gifts. We could get J.Crew sweaters, blankets, and photobooks and that was about it.

Christmas morning was everything I hated about the school. It was lots of smooshing and Alan holding court. Back home, we always had cinnamon buns for breakfast on holidays. Here, I ate the same crap I always ate. The only thing that made this day any different was that a couple of snowflakes and candy canes had been hung in the dining hall.

I was worried I'd find Alan in a Santa suit, asking kids to hop onto his lap. Instead, he wore a red-and-green plaid vest and a candy-cane-print tie.

"Were you a good little girl this year?"

No, Alan. I was a worthless abuser this year.

"Yes," I said. "I think so."

"Merry Christmas, Elizabeth."

Someone handed me a box. My name was written on the label in the elegant cursive I recognized as my mother's. I opened the box without much enthusiasm and pulled out the contents. My parents had sent me a scrapbook from home, a new blanket, and photos they had developed from those disposable cameras we had in the woods.

Thanks. As if I needed that reminder.

Charlotte got a blanket too. It was bright pink and featured the grinning faces of the Care Bears. She didn't keep it, though. Secretly, she passed it on to Kristen. It was cold in Virginia, and Kristen would need whatever extra warmth she could get. As far as anyone knew, her entire plan was to make her way by foot to a phone and wait for her boyfriend to make the multistate drive.

It was the saddest Christmas in the history of Christmases. We spent the rest of the day watching Santa cartoons and writing thank-you notes to our parents. I found it a lot easier to be nice in letters and managed a brief but earnest-sounding message.

The next morning I found out I had one more present coming to me. Catherine handed me my red binder and a paperback book.

"Congratulations. You're on your first program."

I wasn't exactly surprised. I knew there would be consequences for getting kicked out of group and asking my mom to leave campus. Thankfully, my time in isolation was short. It was designed around finding better ways to communicate with my parents.

"Start by reading," Catherine said. "I think you'll find a lot of useful tools in there."

I looked at the book resting on top of my binder: *The Five Love Languages* by Gary Chapman. It's a self-help standard, though probably not something on a normal high school reading list. According to Chapman, there are five ways people express and receive love, and everyone has a different dominant "language."

1. Words of Affirmation
2. Quality Time
3. Acts of Service
4. Receiving Gifts
5. Physical Touch

Well. I guess I know what Alan's love language is.

Chapter 22

KRISTEN WASN'T THE first person to run away from Carlbrook and she wouldn't be the last. There was even a term for it: "walking the road," which occurred when a kid got so fed up they'd simply walk off campus and continue down the long road leading into town.

Walking the road usually ended pretty quickly, though. Someone would hop in the school van and drive alongside the student until they eventually gave up and got inside. Instead of heading back to Carlbrook, however, the runaway would be taken back to the woods.

For most of us, this was enough of a deterrent to keep us on the grounds. Those of us still months or years away from turning eighteen didn't really have a choice. Legally, we had to get back in the van. If we refused, it would only mean dealing with the cops. The only way a minor could escape was to leave when no one was looking, and that was not something that happened too often at Carlbrook.

Kristen was a legal adult now, and she was determined. She had no money and no ID. Just some hoarded food, a winter jacket, and that Care Bear blanket. It was the middle of winter in Nowhere, Virginia. On the day of her eighteenth birthday, she walked off campus, started down the road, and never came back.

She was done with groups, she was done with crews. She was done with all the bullshit.

She's my hero and I wish I was right there running off beside her.

Kristen's disappearance was announced at Last Light. Alan told us she had made the unfortunate decision to walk off campus, giving up on her emotional work. Then he asked Charlotte and Brittany to stand so they could announce they'd been put on programs.

Fuck. This is gonna be bad.

I'd seen the two of them sitting in the program room on my way to Last Light. My stomach dropped instantly. Nothing went unpunished at Carlbrook—someone always had to be made into an example. Since they couldn't punish Kristen, her sentence was going to come down on her friends. I looked at Charlotte and Brittany. Their heads were down and they were writing what could only have been honor lists.

A storm was brewing and my gut told me I was going to end up right in the middle of it.

It took only a few days. One morning, a request group list went up that let me know the trouble had begun. It was the longest list I'd ever seen, and it included anyone who'd been friends with Kristen to any degree. My name was right there in the middle of the block, between Lina and Levi. And, of course, Charlotte and Brittany.

The worst part was the name at the top of the list, letting us know who had put the group together. It was Randall, the founder of the school. To the best of my knowledge, this was the first group he'd ever run.

It was like a dark cloud had formed above the campus and hovered all day long. I felt sick to my stomach as I sat through my classes. At lunchtime I was unable to eat with all the dread already in my stomach.

In all the time I'd been at Carlbrook I'd met Randall only once. It was my second or third week when he strolled over and introduced himself. He was also from my town in South Carolina, he said. In fact, he was part of the very same country club my family belonged to.

"I know about you," he said.

"Me?" I was genuinely confused. "What do you mean?"

But he had already walked away, leaving the stale smell of cigarette smoke to linger in his wake.

The same scent now filled the commons, the only place big enough to hold this group. His face was red and his eyes were bloodshot, the effects of too much anger and what seemed to me like too much booze.

"Everybody sit the FUCK DOWN."

Oh shit. This is gonna be even worse than I thought.

"We've got a serious problem," Randall said. "All of you in here? You're in deep shit. I don't even know where to begin."

He did, though. He went right to Charlotte. In his mind she was some sort of ringleader. We were all bad apples, but she was utterly spoiled. He called her out for being entitled and selfish. A monster who looked down on other people and thought she was better than everyone else. None of it was true and the rest of us knew that, but Randall seemed intent on tearing her apart.

"I know you think you're a debutante, Charlotte, but you aren't. You're a *dilettante*."

He seemed proud of that one, like it was something he might have thought up in advance. There was something personal about the attack. It felt like Randall resented Charlotte simply because she came from wealth, like he wanted her to feel guilty for the life she was born into.

"Kristen never made it home," he said. "Did you know that?"

Charlotte shook her head. Of course she didn't know that. None of us knew anything at all.

"She's missing. Could be anywhere."

I felt sick to my stomach. Charlotte's expression told me she did too.

"When the cops find her dead body, left in a ditch on the side of the road," he said, staring right at my friend, "that's on you."

I was half expecting Randall to pull out an index card and write a new lie for Charlotte: *Worthless Murderer.* And honestly, maybe that was a label we all deserved. I was dizzy and nauseous, overwhelmed by guilt.

I replayed Randall's words in my head. He hadn't actually said that Kristen was dead. It's not like the cops had *actually* found her body in a ditch. In all likelihood, Randall had no idea what happened after Kristen left that day. She was hardly about to give Carlbrook a call to let them know she got home safely. Randall could have told us she was off sunbathing on a tropical island and it would have been just as much of a fiction, but that wasn't the game he was playing. It wasn't manipulative enough. In his version, Kristen was an inevitable tragedy. She was dead, or would be soon, and we all had blood on our hands.

"You know what I think?" He turned to address the whole group. "I think you're all ungrateful little shits."

His face was red.

"You have no idea what kind of hellholes are out there," he said. "Places for bratty fuckups like all of you."

Randall paced, looking for a target. He zeroed in on Brittany.

"Don't think I'm gonna take it easy on you just because you ratted everyone else out."

Fuck. What did she put on her honor list?

Brittany looked ashamed, but that didn't keep Randall from telling her she was a scumbag and a snake. That some people are just shitty and it was no wonder her family sent her away. I had no idea if Randall was reacting to something Brittany wrote on her honor list or just being mean for meanness' sake. As her roommate, the only other person who shared space with Kristen, it made me really nervous.

"Alan wanted to expel you and all your little friends," he said, looking around the room. "Some of the other staff too. How'd you like to go back to the woods?"

No one said a word, but I knew a lot of us were on the same page: *Right now the woods seems pretty appealing.*

"I'm showing fucking mercy," Randall said. "Believe me. If something like this happened at my school? There would be hell to pay that you brats can't even imagine."

Randall was speaking about Cascade, the CEDU spin-off he'd gone to as a teen.

"If they'd discovered a whole underground operation like you little shits are running? You'd all be in lockdown."

An underground operation? What the hell is he talking about?

Randall kept talking about this underground. He was starting to sound paranoid. It was like he thought there'd been some big conspiracy to help Kristen run away. An operation to make sure every Carlbrook student had a Care Bear blanket and stash of granola bars.

It wasn't exactly a secret. Everyone suspected Kristen was planning to take off on her birthday. Even if she'd never said it out loud to the staff, there were several times when her intentions were questioned during groups.

It felt like Randall was punishing us because he couldn't punish Kristen. She was eighteen, free from his control, but the rest of us weren't. So he screamed at us for six straight hours, spewing his venom and basically accusing us all of murder.

"I dedicated my life to this," he said. "And I'm not going to let a bunch of brats like you dismantle it. You have no idea how lucky you are."

He decided then that Brittany and Charlotte should be on out-of-school programs. He wanted them digging up old tree stumps with a pickax. It would take at least a month, but Randall made it clear he didn't care if it took three.

It was like he was in some sort of vengeful trance. He yelled out insults almost at random while picking out his next target. He landed on a boy named Charlie who probably shouldn't even have been in this group. Charlie was shy and awkward, a wallflower who happened to be room-mates with some of my friends. He was guilty by association at worst, but something about him set Randall off. I guess he just didn't like the way the kid looked.

"Hey you, what's your name?"

"Me?" He was stuttering. "Um, Charlie."

"*Um Charlie.* I have a question." Randall sneered at the kid. "What the fuck is wrong with you?"

The boy's face turned bright red.

"No, I'm really asking. Why are you such a loser?"

"I don't know," Charlie said.

"God. You're not even a person. You're a fucking wet blanket."

He turned to the nearest Securitas and asked the man to bring him a wet blanket. It took only a minute, but the wait was agonizing. I prayed that the blanket was actually just for Randall, to cool him down before he exploded. But when the Securitas returned with a dripping blanket Randall grabbed it and threw it over Charlie's head.

"There. Now you can't pretend anymore. That's what it feels like to be a wet blanket."

Randall wasn't done yet. In his grand finale, he threw a water bottle at a boy and called a girl a cum dumpster. My stomach was in knots. I had been sitting frozen in place for hours. I kept expecting Randall to attack me next, and I knew that one wrong look, one accidental nervous smile, could spell disaster. I was terrified of inciting his rage and ending up on stump duty or in lockdown simply because of spite.

He never got to me. I think he simply ran out of time. Dinner was long over by the time we were released. I knew more was coming, but I'd have to sit with that anxiety for a few more days. We made our way to the dorms, stumbling beneath the weak light of a crescent moon.

You're not a real moon. You're a wet blanket.

Pathetic.

That night my room was the coldest, loneliest place in the world. Maggie had graduated, Kristen was gone, and Brittany wouldn't even look at me. Suddenly it was like the whole world was her enemy and she hated me along with everyone else. Whatever she put on her honor list must have been pretty bad. I just wished I knew what she'd said about me.

I wasn't angry so much as I was frustrated and scared. I had that little-kid feeling of knowing I was in trouble, just not how much. At the same time, I understood that whatever Brittany said, any dirt she came up with, wasn't done by choice. She was just trying to make it through.

So was I and that was the problem. We were pitted against each other with the gaslight logic that it was for our own good. I felt so trapped and alone that I prayed for the first time in months.

Dear God,

I don't even know why I'm praying to you right now. There's no way you're real. Honestly, if you are, I hate you. My friend is dead in a ditch. Or maybe she isn't. Maybe she's off somewhere having the time of her life while I rot in this prison.

I'm so scared. I know I wasn't always great to my parents, but do I really deserve all this? I've never felt so hopeless and alone in my life. So why have you abandoned me just like everyone else?

I thought you loved all of your children equally, God. Clearly that isn't true because you don't love me. I have nothing left to believe in at this point, not even you, so I guess this is good-bye.

The next morning, I watched Brittany out in the freezing cold digging up a giant stump and almost wished I was there with her. At least then I'd know my punishment. I was living in a weird sort of purgatory, and there was nothing to do but wait.

Charlotte had managed to get off pickax duty with a doctor's note about her injured back, but her new assignment wasn't much better. She had to clean the entire length of the fence using nothing but a bucket of soapy water and a toothbrush. She was on bans with everyone and wasn't allowed to speak to me, but I made sure to catch her when I walked past her. In those moments, we communicated silently, both of us thinking the same thing.

How the fuck do we make it through this? Kristen was right to run away.

A few days later, another Randall group went up on the list and my name was at the top. It included mostly the same people from the first one, every one of Kristen's friends he hadn't gotten to yet. This one was held in the dining mod, which at least meant it couldn't go past dinner. Any hope I had that Randall might have cooled off with time was dashed immediately. If anything, he seemed even more worked up, red in the face and out for blood. He didn't waste any time getting started and he began with me.

"Elizabeth," he said, "you know I've been waiting to talk to you for a while now."

My blood froze. There was something about Randall that terrified me to my core. Alan and David were creepy, but Randall was a loose cannon. He had a charming aspect, a sort of venomous sparkle, and that made his anger so much more frightening.

"Me?" I said. "Why?"

"My mother gave me a heads-up about you before you even got here. She said you were a mean, angry bitch. You know, she wanted to call the police on you when you pushed your mom."

Fucking Lynn Anne Moore. I bet she loved that I pushed my mom. It was just what she needed to convince my family to send me to her son's school.

"Brittany," Randall said, "let's hear it. Stop being so spineless and tell Elizabeth what you really think about her. To her face this time."

"I think you're weak," Brittany said. "And you deserved to be ratted out because you think you're better than everyone else, but you're not. You deserve to be on a program just like me."

"No one cares, Brittany," Randall said. "I just wanted her to know what a bad friend you are."

He continued on this way, asking people to say shitty things about me and attacking them as they did. But I barely heard any of it. I was inside the riptide where the roar was deafening. I knew this was the moment I'd been dreading since I saw Kyle running anger that first week.

"Charlotte. Tell Elizabeth what it feels like to have blood on your hands."

Whatever she said drowned alongside me. I wasn't even looking for a way out. I just let the tide take me under and it was better that way. I didn't have to feel the tears that ran down my face or hear my own voice come out strangled by sobs. I let my body do the work of producing mucus and tears and screamed incomprehensible nothing words at the floor.

To my surprise, running anger was almost a relief. I didn't have to do any of the hard work. I didn't have to keep track of my lies or get into any specifics at all. I just had to perform, to scream and sob. Language disappeared, dulling the jagged contours of my pain, and my head filled up with white noise.

I must have given a pretty good performance. It was clear that Randall was satisfied, that he thought I'd done real emotional work, because my punishment wasn't nearly as bad as I'd feared. He put me on a program but it was in-school, which meant no stumps. I was about to go into Amicitia, the friendship workshop, so I figured there would be a lot of overlap in my assignments.

The only person sentenced to stump duty was Lina. I hardly ever saw her interact with Kristen, so it seemed like a move out of left field. But Lina was in our friend group, and I still didn't know what kind of dirt was on Brittany's honor list. It didn't help that she froze when Randall attacked her. When it came time to run anger, she didn't go all in like I had. She didn't perform, so Randall made an example out of her too.

To this day, I still wonder if Randall actually believed he created a better kind of school. He certainly built an expensive one. Was that the point all along? Maybe he was another Mel Wasserman. Just a guy who saw an opportunity to monetize the pain of adolescence. His mother was right there next to him, helping things along.

Wasserman, though, was just a businessman. He was an outsider, a *square*. But Randall was a part of the thing, trapped inside the cycle of trauma and abuse.

I don't know what the teenage Randall did to end up at Cascade. Or what kind of adult he would have turned into if he hadn't. One look into his bloodshot eyes and it was clear that place had a real effect on him. Maybe Carlbrook was his attempt to control the uncontrollable. To square the cycle.

Maybe, like all of us, Randall was just doing what he needed to survive.

Chapter 23

I HAD A very different nightmare the night before Amicitia. I was on an empty street in a rural town, somewhere close by that could have been anywhere. There was a body on the side of the road. A dead girl in a ditch. I knew exactly who it was before I saw her face.

Kristen. She had been raped and murdered. Discarded like a piece of roadside litter. I heard someone yelling and I turned around. It was Randall, taunting me.

Look what you did. Do you see? She was your friend. Now she's your dead friend.

I started running, but there was nowhere to go. Randall's voice followed me no matter where I turned.

This should be you.

I woke up in a cold sweat. I was almost glad to be heading into a workshop with Alan and David. At least they weren't Randall. I shivered all morning, trying to shake off the dream. I knew this workshop would be especially brutal for me and Charlotte and Brittany. Everyone knew the reason we were on programs: what happened with Kristen, our supposed roles in the nonexistent underground. I was marching across campus with a giant target on my back and a cracked egg in my hand.

About that: In the days leading up to Amicitia, we were given a warmup assignment to test our ideas of friendship. It was one of those classic egg-baby exercises, where students are supposed to keep a hollowed-out egg "alive" as a stand-in for a real human baby. Of course, there was a Carlbrook twist. Instead of carrying around our own egg baby, we had to trade eggs with someone else. So I was tasked with keeping Maya's egg baby alive and she was responsible for mine.

I didn't know how my child was faring, but Maya's was a little worse for wear. I hadn't shattered Lily or anything (of course Maya named her egg), but there were a few cracks I was hoping to keep hidden.

As we got closer I heard music coming from the trailer. "Lean on Me" was playing on a loop. We all filed inside and sat down in a circle.

"Welcome to Amicitia," Alan said. "This workshop is about friendship. Last time we learned about integrity. Unfortunately, some of you really struggled to honor that."

I locked eyes with Charlotte. We both looked down immediately.

"Amicitia will teach you what it means to be a friend," Alan said. "To others and to yourself. I know a few of you in here who could really benefit from that lesson. But first, let's check in on those eggs."

Fuck.

My face went hot. Sheepishly, I held out Maya's egg baby, with all its cracks.

Thankfully, my egg was hardly the worst one. Several of them were totally shattered. Not Maya's, though. The egg baby she took care of for me was thriving.

"Interesting," Alan said, looking around. "Those of you with cracked eggs really need to think about how you treat your friendships."

Alan paced the room as he spoke. "Because friendship means being both a giver and a taker. And taking? That's easy. A lot of you are in this room right now because you got very good at taking. But I want you all to become givers."

"Let's start out by telling each person all the ways they're a giver. Walk right up to each of your peers and tell them what you admire about their giving."

I heard some nice statements. That I was a leader. Someone who could accomplish big things. A good listener when I wanted to be. But none of it mattered one bit when we got to the next part. The taker part. My peer group had a lot more to say about all the ways I was bad.

"You take because you can. That's selfish."

"You aren't even capable of being a true friend."

"You care more about being liked than doing the right thing."

"Yeah. You're a follower who just wants everyone to like you."

"That's why you didn't try to stop Kristen."

"You were never a friend to her, not really."

I tried not to let it get to me. In a way, knowing what was coming actually helped. I couldn't even blame my classmates. After all, I was eventually forced to do the same to them. Anything to keep the sharks circling in another part of the sea, tasting someone else's blood.

After the exercise, we broke for lunch and the *Les Misérables* sound track made a reappearance. There truly is no satisfactory way to explain Carlbrook's obsession with that musical. Were we meant to see Jean Valjean as a role model? I bet our parents would have gotten a real kick out of that one, especially when it came time to pay the tuition bill.

I finished my cold cuts and took a seat on the ground for the dreaded disclosure circle. I thought about Benjamin, whose confession now served as a cautionary tale. It was a helpful reminder that this wasn't a simple game we were playing. The rules for making it through Carlbrook were complex, and it felt like they could change at any time.

The very first disclosure dropped us right into the deep end with a story involving bestiality. One of the student supports confessed to a situation involving the family dog and a jar of peanut butter. I stared at the ground as he spoke, feeling unsettled. I was genuinely shocked, and there was no way that didn't read on my face. I mean, I'd been raised to believe that sex before marriage was a sin. Same for masturbation. Of course I didn't follow the rules completely—but if there was any truth to those biblical ideals, then what kind of mortal stain was on this kid's soul?

The worst part was the casual way he talked about it. As if enticing an animal to lick peanut butter off your junk is just a normal, everyday thing. At first, I decided that one of two things had to be true: Either the kid was really sick or he'd made the story up. There could be a third explanation of course, this being Carlbrook and all. Between the school and the woods, the kid had probably been forced to tell this story so many times it had *become* run-of-the-mill.

I wanted to forget the disclosure as soon as I possibly could. I felt violated, filthy by association. Unfortunately, a boy in my peer class had a very similar confession to make about his own dog. He broke down crying, and I wondered if there was a time the student support had sobbed through his own story.

Those men were vampires. They fed on our pain like it was the only thing keeping them alive. They were ravenous and insatiable, always searching for another vein. Some buried trauma or unspeakable shame, fangs at the ready. They'd say whatever they needed to in the moment in order to get at those darkest disclosures, and then they'd suck us dry.

I didn't even have what they required. I had my same old recycled stories. Two blow jobs. A few unremarkable weed experiences. The one time I did Molly. I didn't even have an ace up my sleeve like the one a lot of my classmates pulled out when they needed to satisfy the mostly male staff.

When all else fails, go girl-on-girl.

Lindy confessed to experimenting with a female friend back home. Variations on this particular theme tended to pop up during disclosure circles. It wasn't hard to figure out that this was David's favorite topic. His excitement was obvious. A Sapphic kiss at a sleepover, a lingering glance in the locker room.

I didn't even have any of those stories to share either. It wasn't like I hadn't *thought* about kissing a girl—who hasn't? Just thinking about something isn't enough to be a disclosure, though. So I ended up revealing that sometimes I would make myself throw up after eating. It wasn't about body image so much as it was a way to stay in control. It was like my salt-and-ice burns, a way to sublimate the pain I felt when Nick ignored my calls or my brother said something shitty to me.

I didn't like to talk about those things—not at Carlbrook and certainly not back home. For me, self-harm was inextricable from my deepest inner pain—the part of me that didn't feel safe or loved. If I was throwing up or burning myself, it just meant that I was having an extra-hard day.

At Carlbrook, most of my days were of the extra-hard kind. I constantly felt the urge to self-harm or make myself throw up. I didn't, because the stakes were so high, but the feeling rarely left me. This disclosure circle wasn't any different. The whole workshop had been an exercise in degradation, and I wanted nothing more than to purge it from my system.

"Every single person in the room has made bad decisions," Alan said. "We've been liars, cheaters, thieves. We poisoned our bodies with drugs, alcohol, sex."

His eyes traveled around the room as he talked, locking us in with his gaze.

"Why'd we do it? Just for fun? Did we fuck up our lives for the hell of it?"

I wanted to look away but found it was impossible.

"We did it," he said, "because we're our own worst enemies. So it's no wonder we can't be good friends to other people. We have to be our own friend first."

The student supports went around the room passing out supplies. We each got a handful of markers and a red paper heart. Arts and crafts, it seemed. A grade school activity that would undoubtedly come with an NC-17 twist.

"This is your heart," Alan said. "It's yours and yours alone, but it's not the heart you have today. It represents the pure version, the heart you had as a little kid."

I was momentarily confused. What happened to us being marbles?

"I want you to cover your hearts with the things you loved when you were young and innocent," Alan said. "People, places, imaginary characters. Maybe it's a word like *love* or *hope* that hung above your childhood bed. Maybe it's a picture of your favorite game. Anything that meant something to you back then, no matter how small, put it on the heart."

David stood over the CD player to cue up some creative inspiration. As he bent down to fiddle with the stereo his khakis rode up in a way that could not have been comfortable. I looked away, wishing I could unsee that image. David could have been a decade younger than Alan, but you'd never know it from the way he dressed.

Thankfully, he got the stereo working. It was now time to rouse the artist within, and what but *Les Mis* could be up to such a task? "I Dreamed a Dream" began to play on a loop.

There was a time when men were kind / When their voices were soft / And their words inviting.

There was a time when love was blind / And the world was a song / And the song was exciting.

I zoned out and began to scribble. I drew a soccer ball and an Olympic gold medal. A fighter jet soaring over the Pacific Ocean. I wrote Hotshot, my childhood nickname, across the middle of the heart. I sketched a garden and filled it with flowers and blackberry bushes just like the ones near my grandma's house.

There was a time. Then it all went wrong.

I added a rainbow to the sky. Some puffy clouds. Everything was happy and innocent...and easy to draw.

I dreamed a dream in time gone by / When hope was high and life worth living / I dreamed that love would never die / I dreamed that God would be forgiving.

Charlotte had her head down, scribbling intensely. I could tell she was avoiding the rest of the group. I tried to catch her eye, but she was totally focused on her drawing. I spotted musical notes, a microphone, and the pink-haired Jem.

Then I was young and unafraid / And dreams were made and used and wasted.

Dash had drawn a baseball diamond and written the names of his favorite players.

There was no ransom to be paid / No song unsung, no wine untasted.

Maya had drawn her family. It was a version of the classic little-kid picture: mom and dad on either side, two kids in the middle, triangle house behind them. Everyone was holding hands and smiling big, loopy grins.

But the tigers come at night / With their voices soft as thunder.

"Okay, guys." Alan was pacing the room, examining hearts and massaging shoulders. "Take another minute or two to finish up."

As they tear your hope apart.

"I hope you had some fun with that," he said. "Because now we get to do the hard work."

As they turn your dream to shame.

I knew a twist was coming, of course, but I didn't expect it to be quite so cruel. We got back into a circle while Alan explained the rest of the exercise he called "pieces of my heart." There was nothing clever or ironic about that name. Basically, it meant going around the circle saying the meanest possible thing about each person.

"Every time you hear a judgment about yourself," he said, "I want you to rip off a piece of your heart and let it fall to the floor in front of you."

The taker exercise felt like a warm-up compared to the barrage of insults that were about to echo across that trailer. Again, I told myself it was a forced attack, so it didn't really count. I wanted to stay as detached as possible—like I was in a movie, playing a role. That lasted only so long before I began to break apart. I don't know which hurt more, the judgments I gave or the judgments I received.

"You're a pathetic slut with zero self-esteem."

"Your daddy didn't love you. That's why you're so desperate."

"You spineless, stupid coward."

I ripped my soccer ball in half and tore up my fighter jet. I was suddenly ashamed of everything I'd drawn. I wasn't Hotshot, I was a worthless abuser. I was stupid and spineless. My heart deserved to be torn apart for refusing to forget all those dreams that were now out of reach.

"Of course your daddy didn't love you. You're a terrible person. And a bad friend."

"You should be sent to lockdown for what you did to Kristen."

"Stupid bitch. Starting an underground in the only place willing to help you."

I shredded my heart until there was nothing left but a mound of red pulp. It wasn't like I needed another stupid metaphor to feel like there were pieces missing from my life. I felt like my own identity had been turned into a weapon and used against me. The holes in my heart were already there. I had felt their absence my entire life, but whatever had been merely empty before was now hollowed out completely.

I had a dream my life would be / So different from this hell I'm living / So different now from what it seemed.
  Now life has killed the dream / I dreamed.

The first day of Amicitia finally came to an end after what felt like an eternity inside the stale trailer. David cued up "Everybody Hurts" by R.E.M. while Alan joined us on the floor for some good old work-shop smooshing. We exited the trailer and walked back to the dorms in total silence.

What could possibly be left to say?

I breathed in the crisp air. It was a clear, cool night and the stars were shining. I looked up at them and thought about Kristen. I hoped she was somewhere great, surrounded by people she loved. Wherever she might be, she was certainly better off.

She's safer there. No matter where she is, it's safer than here.

As soon as the thought entered my mind I was absolutely certain it was true, and that meant my dream hadn't been a bad omen at all. I wasn't seeing a premonition of Kristen's future, I was seeing the fate she avoided. Whatever happened next, whatever path she was on, at least she would be living a life that was her own.

There was peace in that, and it was enough for that moment. I closed my eyes and fell right into a deep and dreamless sleep.

The next morning, walking into the workshop trailer felt somehow different. It took me a moment to realize that music was playing on the stereo that had nothing to do at all with *Les Mis.* The specific song was "Break on Through (To the Other Side)" by the Doors, and I was about to hear it approximately fifty times.

The Circle of Exclusion was a simple but vicious exercise. Basically, it was like the version of Red Rover that would be played at the X Games. Alan instructed us to form a barrier, linking our arms together as tightly as possible.

"There shouldn't be an inch of space between any of you," he said. "There's no such thing as too close together."

One by one, we each took a turn outside the circle. The idea was, quite literally, to *break on through to the other side.* The excluded kid had to ram his body up against the human circle again and again, trying to force a way in, while the rest of us did whatever we could to make sure we stayed impenetrable.

Needless to say, I can no longer listen to the Doors.

It was awful. Being the barrier was bad enough, but when my turn came I wanted to give up before I even began. Instead, I started ramming my body up against my peers again and again. Trying not to get hurt, physically or emotionally, as they did whatever they could to keep me from getting in.

If I stopped for even a moment, the staff just screamed at me to keep running. There were only three ways this would end. I could break on through, break a bone, or break down completely.

I actually found comfort in the physical pain. I liked it when it hurt because that numbed the sounds in my head. Each smash and I was transported back in time. I was flying into a windshield. I was burning myself with salt and ice. I was getting my lie. I felt like such a disappointment. But at least I'd have the physical bruises to prove it this time.

I went from sad to angry to dead-set on breaking through that fucking circle. I kept going, slamming myself up against shoulders and backs again and again. I didn't stop, not even when the music cut off and Alan was yelling my name.

"Elizabeth! That's enough! You can stop now."

Alan knew what I was denying: I was never going to break through the barrier. He seemed to be saying that I had humiliated myself enough and should just give up.

So I did. I didn't have anything left anyway. My entire body hurt and my heart was broken. I started sobbing, and all I wanted in the world was just to be left alone.

That was never going to happen, though. I had to take my place back in the human circle and wait for the rest of the group to each take a turn. Some of them cried the entire time, some screamed obscenities, and some of my friends seemed like they were already dead.

I couldn't tell you who said what, though. Something happened that day, and maybe it was just in my mind, or maybe it had been a long time coming. After Amicitia, I suddenly felt like there was no difference between any of us. We weren't individuals any longer, we were part of a hive. Too tired to fight, though we would be forced to do it anyway.

Chapter 24

BEING ON A program was as close as I've ever gotten to feeling like an animal at the zoo, but I wasn't an exotic one—a red panda, say, or an anaconda—nor was I one of the marquee draws like a tiger or a giraffe. Now that Amicitia was over, I had to spend my days in the glass program room, where I felt both on display and completely alone. Everyone could see inside, but they didn't always bother to look.

We're the meerkats. The flamingos. We're those giant tortoises so slow and static that everyone always mistakes them for rocks.

The rules of a program were straightforward. You were on bans with the entire school, with the exception of two student supports. It was just my luck to get a pair of Ponies, Molly and Paul, the student body president. They checked in on me every day, making sure I was on track with my therapeutic assignments. Every time I saw them trotting toward me I wanted to scream *FUCK OFF!* But somehow, I managed to hold it together.

Since mine wasn't an out-of-school program, I still went to class. I had to carry my program binder around like a scarlet letter. A reminder that I was on bans with everyone and couldn't actually communicate with them, not during class, in the sleeping mod, or anywhere else. In a way, it was even worse than digging up stumps. I felt like a shadow, sort of there and sort of not, just a shapeless presence lurking in the corner.

I had to run crews every night; and I still slept in my room, which had a very different setup now that Kristen was gone. Brittany was moved to another dorm and Rose, one of the Ponies, took her place. Every other second of my day was spent in the glass room. Meals came to us, brown boxes of cold cuts, and we sat in silence, doing what they called "emotional work." My first assignment was a list entitled 100 Things I Hate About Myself.

I would have preferred to list one hundred things I hated about the school. But it turned out that I had nearly as many problems with myself as I did with Carlbrook. As soon as I started writing down negative things about myself, I realized I could have gone on forever.

1. I hate that I got myself here.
2. I hate my anger and how it makes me full of hate.
3. I hate my legs.
4. I hate that I have stretch marks from the woods.
5. I hate my stupid life.
6. I hate that I don't know who I am.
7. I hate that I don't know what I want to be.
8. I hate how I'm not sorry about certain things.
9. I hate that I can be mean.
10. I hate how hopeless everything feels.
11. I hate that I stopped caring about soccer.
12. I hate that I let men treat me badly.
13. I'm a slut. I'm desperate and easy.
14. I'm pathetic and attention seeking.
15. I hate that I want to hurt myself.
16. I hate how scared I am all the time.
17. I hate that I try to seem strong and brave when I'm actually weak.
18. I hate that I'm nothing but a worthless abuser.

By the time I was finished I honestly couldn't tell how much of it was real and how much was for show. I knew that the more self-hating I seemed, the more I'd be praised for doing good work. So I called myself pathetic and desperate, mean and slutty. They were all things I'd heard, after all, so why shouldn't I believe them?

I was getting more and more despondent inside the glass room. It was like being under a microscope. Every minute of every day, the whole school knew exactly where I was. I was sitting at my program desk with my red binder. At first I didn't mind when people like Maya or Luke would walk by and sneak in a wave, but soon that only made me feel worse. I began to keep my eyes glued to my binder at all times so I wouldn't have to see life still going on outside the room.

I was as lonely as I'd ever been, and yet I was never alone. That was hard enough, but I didn't have any of my old tools or defense mechanisms to make me feel better. I couldn't burn my arm with salt and ice or make myself throw up. There were no pills for me to swallow, no boys to distract me. All I had was bullshit therapy and a bunch of stupid assignments.

Plus, one tiny silver lining. One Saturday night, I was assigned to trash duty during crews and that meant running pizza boxes from the dining hall to the dumpsters across campus. On my last trip I was delighted to find Charlotte crouched behind a dumpster, chowing down on pizza remains.

"Shit," she said. "Caught me."

I laughed and sat down next to her. "Give me some of that," I said.

For a whole two minutes we got to sit there like life was normal, eating pizza and looking at the stars.

"Can you believe those are the same stars we'd see if we were back at home?" she said. "That it's the same sky our friends might be looking at right now. I wonder if they still think about us. If they ask if we're okay."

"I hope so," I said. "I don't know how much longer I can do this."

"We have to." Charlotte looked me directly in the eye. "Do not let this awful place win."

That night I thought about our conversation. I knew she was right, of course, but I couldn't find the motivation to care. Especially when I was back inside the glass room.

My next task was totally humiliating. I had to go around the entire school and ask every staff member and student to list two things they liked about me and two of their harshest judgments. If Carlbrook taught me anything at all, it was this: When someone calls you a pathetic whore, any compliments they might throw into the mix don't mean very much at all.

I was getting used to all the insults. It wasn't that they had stopped bothering me completely but more like my body had figured out a way to shield me from their impact. I stored them in my bones and muscles like hundred-pound weights so that I could at least go on living without being consumed by negative thoughts.

There was only one person I truly didn't want to ask for judgments, however, and that was Luke. Just thinking about it made me nauseous. It wasn't like we had some torrid romance going on, but we were there for each other in small ways that, taken altogether, felt like a kind of support I rarely got at Carlbrook. Even just a smile in the hall that felt like sharing a secret was enough to get me through an afternoon. I felt safe around Luke. He was nice to me—or at least he wasn't openly mean.

I guess the bar's set pretty low when a boy refusing to call me a slut counts as chivalry, but hey, that was Carlbrook. They didn't make it easy in groups, but Luke managed to avoid pointing out my weaknesses and doubling down on things I was sensitive about. Even if he secretly thought those things about me, just like everyone else, we both got to pretend he didn't.

That is, until I was forced to press the issue. I avoided Luke all week and made my way through the rest of the school. I didn't want to turn him into just another boy who didn't respect me. I was scared that once he gave me judgments there would be no going back. Finally, I had no choice but to face my crush. I walked right up to him, holding my red binder and a pen like I was signing people up to save the whales.

"Hi." I tried to sound as casual as possible. "Can I please have your two harshest judgments of me?"

I was smiling, but I could feel tears welling up behind my eyes.

"You forgot about the compliments," he said. "How about I just give you those and you can make the other things up?"

Luke told me that he liked me because I was smart and he respected me because I was a fighter. It was exactly what I needed to hear, and I think he knew that. Then Luke leaned in and whispered in my ear:

"Don't worry. This place isn't forever."

I returned to the glass room just a little bit lighter. My muscles and bones could relax ever so slightly from the pressure. It was barely anything, but I could tell the difference.

My program lasted about two months, which wasn't very much time at all compared to what Brittany, Charlotte, and Lina were saddled with. It was, however, long enough to serve its purpose—Randall used me and my friends to send a message to the school. It was enough to fuck with my psyche once again. I had gotten used to being a shadow. Which didn't mean I liked it, only that a strange half existence was my new normal. It shocked my system to suddenly be off bans and expected to participate— even communicate—like a full human being.

There was a general shake-up of school structures in the aftermath of Kristen's escape. For a lot of us, that meant swapping advisers. I was taken off Catherine's team and handed over to Monica, which was its own sort of punishment. Monica was notoriously harsh, which was probably why she ended up with nothing but difficult kids on her roster. Lina and Brittany were already on her team and now she was stuck with little old me.

Interacting with Catherine felt a little bit like dealing with my mom. She wasn't especially confrontational, and as long as I was reasonably pleasant and well behaved, I could keep her off my back. Monica, on the other hand, was a lot more like my dad. She was totally no-nonsense and even militant at times. There would be no sneaking out in pants that were slightly too tight with Monica's eagle eyes trained on my every move.

Monica was trying to mold her little band of outcasts into perfect examples of reformed Carlbrook students. I was to wear my J.Crew with a smile and do my therapeutic work without hesitation. I was expected to buy in completely, and if Monica saw anything other than total compliance, she'd have another program ready to go.

There was one perk to being on Monica's team: She came with an adorable three-year-old son named Aidan. He was a cheerful little kid with a big, sweet smile, and he played happily with anyone who'd have him. I was always torn when I walked into an appointment and saw little Aidan. Carlbrook was no place for a toddler, and we were a poor excuse for child care. Selfishly, I loved getting to entertain him. It made me feel normal, even happy. I just hoped that all the weirdness of the place didn't rub off on him somehow. It wasn't like he was sitting in on group or carrying around an egg to keep alive.

I wasn't thrilled to have my new adviser, and I still felt shell-shocked about my entry back into school society. On top of that, I was consumed with guilt every time I walked by Lina and her pickax, forced to tack index cards to her that listed every single thing she hated about herself. Seeing Charlotte with her toothbrush and half-frozen bucket of soapy water made me want to disappear.

Really, there was only one thing keeping me from descending into full-on despair, and that was Luke. He'd been away on his home visit for the last few days and was set to return at any moment. In fact, we had an appointment scheduled for that very night. It wasn't like we got to hold hands and kiss or anything, but it still felt like a schoolgirl crush. I was looking forward to an hour of feeling something other than dread and maybe even smiling in his presence.

Our last appointment had been so nice and distracting that I was actually disappointed when the hour was over. Mostly we talked about Luke's upcoming home visit—the boating trip his dad had scheduled, all the restaurants he was planning to hit. Luke was excited to have his own room for a few days where he could listen to music and just *be alone*. When we set our next appointment for the evening he returned, it felt a little like he was asking me out on a date.

All day, vans had been shuffling back and forth between the school and the airport. Kids trickled back in looking exhausted from their home visits, but none of them had been Luke. When everyone was gathered in the commons for appointments, he was nowhere to be seen.

I figured he had a late flight. Or maybe it had been delayed. But when Last Light arrived and he still hadn't appeared, some part of me knew he wasn't coming back. I looked around at everyone smooshing and felt sick to my stomach. If he'd found a way out of all this, he was gone for good. Luke hated Carlbrook so much that he didn't care if he had to sacrifice his high school diploma in order to be free.

Free he was, diploma be damned. Alan gave his standard "today was a beautiful day speech," but it ended on a serious note, confirming what I already knew.

"I have some news," he said. "You may know that Luke went home for his visit. Well, he didn't come back. As far as we can tell he never boarded his flight. We're in contact with his parents, but for the moment all we can do is keep him in our thoughts and hope he's okay."

If Luke didn't get on that flight, then he was gone for good.

No more Luke. There goes my last vestige of hope.

Deep down I understood that he was just saving himself. He might have even been trying to tell me something the day I asked him to give me his harshest judgments. When he told me that Carlbrook wasn't forever.

Chapter 25

FOR THREE WHOLE hours, we thought Carlbrook was about to be shut down. Alan called a special meeting for that night and emphasized that every student and staff member was required to attend. To the best of our knowledge, this had never happened before. Everything was always discussed at Last Light. Housekeeping issues, new students, the fact that my crush had missed his flight and was never, ever coming back to Carlbrook. No topic ever required a special meeting of its own.

We're free. We're fucking free! My knight in shining armor has come at last.

"Okay, guys," Alan said. "Quiet down."

The air in the commons felt charged and everyone chattered, unable to stop.

"Seriously, that's enough."

I closed my mouth and crossed my fingers.

Please, please, please.

"I have something kind of big to share with you. It's about David."

David? Did HE get the school shut down?

"I know David's been a big part of life here at Carlbrook," Alan said. "Both in workshops and in groups. A lot of you probably consider him a friend or even a father figure."

Wait. Is David dead? Is that what this is about?

"And I have no doubt that he feels just as close to all of you. But unfortunately some things have come up . . . in David's personal life . . . and we've come to a mutual agreement."

So David's not dead. And he didn't get the school shut down. Then what the fuck?

"We've decided to part ways. David will no longer be a member of the Carlbrook family. We wish him the best, of course, and have no doubt that he has a bright future in front of him."

I could feel the energy deflate all at once. Alan continued to talk about David's departure for a little while, letting us all know that we could come to him with any feelings we might have. He was still there for us. With open arms and an empty lap.

I assumed Alan's diplomatic story about a "mutual parting of ways" was total bullshit.

It's not that David was *just such a good guy* or anything—because he definitely wasn't. David was an asshole, through and through. He berated us in workshops, yelling the most horrific things until we were broken down and sobbing. He would target certain kids.

I remember one group, early on, during which David latched on to Luke and wouldn't let up. His wrath seemed to come out of nowhere. He swore and taunted Luke mercilessly for the better part of an hour.

His behavior was horrible, no doubt, but it wasn't any worse than what I'd experienced from other Carlbrook staff.

David's sudden and mysterious departure struck me as oddly similar to Benjamin's. Carlbrook's rules had always seemed so arbitrary, its boundaries ever-shifting. It was a strange comfort to think that not even the staff was immune to the chaos.

Chapter 26

SOMETHING STRANGE HAPPENED right before the next workshop. I stopped having nightmares because I'd stopped dreaming completely. Animus, like the previous two workshops, had a theme. It wasn't anything as tangible as integrity or friendship. Animus was concerned with "passion," as modeled, absurdly, by Don Quixote. The night before, we watched *Man of La Mancha*, that musical adaptation with the famous song about the "impossible dream." Clearly, my subconscious had taken those words much too literally.

We filed into the dismal trailer once again. Alan looked us over and grinned, as though this workshop was a treat and we were lucky to be there.

"Congratulations," he said. "You've made it to Animus."

Great. How long do I have before you call me a whore?

Like always, the workshop began with honor lists. Only this time we had to do them out loud. We stood in a circle for hours, going around and around, confessing our sins. Reaching Animus meant that after about eight months at Carlbrook, I was about to become an upper-school student. As such, my peer class and I were expected to be extra accountable for our bad behavior. Each time we confessed we had to come up with a punishment that fit the crime and would get us back into standard.

I borrowed a pen from someone I was on bans with. I will go on bans with the entire school for a day to get back into standard.

I talked about wishing I was eighteen so I could leave. I will make appointments with lower schoolers on programs who are struggling.

I ate a piece of pizza while taking boxes to the dumpster. I will run crews for a night and be on cleaning duty in the dining mod.

I wore pants knowing they were too tight. I will go on bans with boys for a week.

We circled around again and again until there was truly nothing left to say. We had exhausted every possible infraction, copped to every rule that could be broken. Regardless, the staff and student supports still weren't satisfied. They began to rail on us for lying, hurling accusations in every direction.

"Hey, Lindy," Alan said. "You're looking really skinny these days. Are you throwing up again? Worried the boys won't think you're pretty if you get too big? Just like your dad always said would happen?"

I looked at Lindy. She seemed to weigh what she always had. If anything, she'd gained a few pounds, another victim of the Great Starch Conspiracy.

"I want to talk to Dash and Levi," Monica said. "Pretty convenient that you're right next to each other. Aren't you always together, though? What's that about? You aren't plotting to run away or anything. Are you?"

The boys shook their heads.

"No way," Levi said.

"Well." Monica was smirking. "Maybe there's something more intimate going on. Is there any news you'd like to share with the group?"

Monica called Conrad a thief. Alan called Rose a bitch. It went on like that for a while until everyone had a brand-new insult of their very own.

When the exercise started losing steam, Alan switched gears. Music that I could describe only as *triumphant* played on the stereo.

"It's time to learn just what we're fighting," Alan said. "Is your life what you imagined? Are you everything you want to be? If you're here, I'd say the answer to that question is no."

And to that, I'll add "no shit."

"Let's be knights," Alan said. "Pick up your swords and fight for your lives."

He meant it. He actually wanted us to hold out imaginary swords.

"Maya," he said, "what are you fighting for? Yell out what you stand for."

"I stand for living," she said.

"Is that all you have? Louder!"

"I STAND FOR LIVING!"

Rose stood for being strong.

Levi stood for honor.

I stood for having a purpose.

I'm not sure why I said that. I didn't have much purpose at all. I was a lost kid with no direction and no dreams at all. Maybe deep down I longed for something to be passionate about, even if it meant tilting at windmills like Don Quixote.

Suddenly, the door opened and a group of older students ran in. They seemed energized and excited to be there.

"All right, Knights," Alan said. "It's time to battle. This is FIGHT NIGHT!"

Alan went around the room giving everyone a fighter's name. Charlotte was "Sucker Punch," Conrad was "the Bomber," and Maya became "Body Shot."

I was Elizabeth "Fights the Good Fight" Gilpin.

More like Elizabeth "Ready to Give Up" Gilpin.

Alan instructed us to lie on our backs. The supports handed everyone a towel. Fight Night was structured like a boxing match with three rounds lasting three minutes and fifty-eight seconds, the amount of time it took for "Eye of the Tiger," from the movie *Rocky*, to play. There was no jabbing or throwing left hooks, only a pointless, incredibly painful exercise.

It went like this: As soon as we heard those first notes kick in, we'd put the towels in our mouths. We simultaneously bit down and pulled up, creating tension like our jaws were about to pop out of their sockets. Of all the physical exercises we'd done, this was the most baffling. At least the Circle of Exclusion had a plausible metaphor to justify the violence. This was pain for pain's sake.

It was really fucking excruciating.

The older kids were our "trainers." They moved around, yelling at all of us one by one. Instead of advice or motivation, they were just assholes. Of course, Beatrice was leading the charge.

"You call that a good fight, Elizabeth?" Beatrice said. "Pathetic. You might as well just give up now."

I pulled harder just to get her to leave me alone. Alan was really in his element. After three rounds he decided Brittany and Dash hadn't tried hard enough so he made them do the exercise a fourth time. Halfway through, Dash sat up and promptly vomited on the floor.

A look of absolute misery fell across his sweet face. He slumped over and put his head between his knees. Alan hunched down next to him. He put his hands on the boy's thin shoulders and squeezed.

"This is a breakthrough," he said. "You should be proud."

Dash wasn't proud, he was miserable. He was slumped over, totally defeated. He looked the way Don Quixote should have looked, if he hadn't been such a goddamn fool.

"It's all part of the purge." Alan was rubbing Dash's back. "Your trauma was ready to move on, and pain leaves the body any way it can."

Alan didn't waste any time getting started the next day. We were fighting for our lives, after all. Staff separated us into pairs for the next exercise, which was as simple as it was cruel. We were supposed to make statues out of our partners' bodies, freezing them at their lowest point, the place they'd end up if they ignored the lessons of the workshop.

We could put someone behind bars, we could hang a noose around her neck, we could stage a rape. The choice was all ours as long as it was something awful. Then we gave the statues corny names like "Falling Star" and "Snow Day."

I was partnered up with Brittany. I looked her over and tried to decide her fate. Given her history, I decided it should involve cocaine, so I had her bend over at the waist with her hand pressed to her nose to hover midbinge. For her part, she placed me on my knees and told me to keep my mouth open.

Is this a trailer? Or are we in the Carlbrook Museum of Contemporary Art?

I glanced around the room as much as I could from my frozen position. Charlotte was slack and crumpled, dead from a heroin overdose. Levi had been shot to death; and then there was the pièce de résistance—Rose, perched on all fours to accommodate two guys at once. Unlike me, she didn't only have to keep her mouth open, she had to spread her legs apart as well.

Alan moved through the room, appraising the statues like they were works of fine art. I felt his hot breath on the back of my neck again.

"Does that make you feel good, Elizabeth?"

I cringed when he touched me but tried to stay still. Monica came over next. She lingered for a moment, observing.

"This isn't how you want to die, is it?"

No, you bitch. You're enjoying this, aren't you?

He kept us frozen in place for what felt like an eternity. When Alan finally announced that we could move I felt all the muscles in my body twitch. I needed a break, or at least some fresh air, but the staff had already moved on to the next exercise.

Alan cleared his throat and scanned the group for a victim.

"Lindy. Tell me something. What are you afraid of?"

Lindy seemed at a loss.

"Come on, what's your biggest fear? What keeps you up at night?"

"Um," she said. "I mean, I'm really scared of Animus."

"Oh, Lindy," Alan said. "No, no, no. Your nightmare is that no one is ever gonna love you."

Lindy looked down and shrugged.

"Am I wrong? Is there some *other* reason you'll sleep with anyone who shows you the slightest bit of attention?"

"I don't know."

"Yes, you do. You know you're a slut. What about you, Conrad?"

Conrad looked defeated. "I'm afraid my adopted family is going to give me up too. Well, I guess they already did."

"Good." He tossed Conrad a box of markers. "Draw it."

Alan turned to face the rest of the room. "Maybe your nightmare is an overdose. Maybe it's ending up a violent alcoholic like your mother. Maybe it's that boy you couldn't fight off. Whatever hell looks like to you, I want to see it pictured on that piece of paper."

Music came blaring through the speakers. It was "Meant to Live" by the Christian hard rock band Switchfoot. As I uncapped the marker, my first impulse was to sketch the Carlbrook grounds, with its deceptively picturesque lake and mansion surrounded by trailers. Being trapped in the snow globe forever truly was the worst thing I could imagine. It was my *actual nightmare,* I realized, so strong it took over the recurring dream that had haunted me for years. My real life had become worse than anything I could imagine, and that was why I'd stopped dreaming completely.

I pictured the last nightmare I could remember having. The image of Kristen's body lying in a ditch was still vivid enough that I could draw it as if from a photo. I sketched out an empty road and the body of a dead girl. It could have been Kristen, but just as easily it could have been me.

Alan collected the drawings and taped them to the wall. There were sketches of heroin needles and razor blades, a skull with a bullet hole through the middle. Charlotte had drawn the girl from *The Ring.* To me, it seemed like a self-portrait. Randall's abuse and weeks of isolation made her feel monstrous and alone.

Half of the wall was full of nightmares and the other half was left blank.

Alan emerged from a corner, holding a thick, coarse rope. I winced instinctively, hoping we wouldn't have to put it in our mouths.

"Over here is Death." Alan pointed to the cluster of nightmares. "And on this side, we have Life. How many of you want to live?"

Most of the hands in the room went up, but I couldn't bring myself to raise my own.

"Answer me. Who wants to live?"

"I do!" the group of us called out in unison.

"Prove it," Alan said, laying the rope on the floor. "Get up and fight for your fucking lives."

We scrambled toward the rope, pushing one another out of the way. The fastest of us made it to the Life side, while the rest of the group ended up on Team Death. We grabbed on to the knots and started to pull, swaying back and forth as dominance was traded. Every time Team Life threatened to win, the counselors came over to taunt us with our disclosures.

"Pull harder. Is this what you did when your boyfriend fucked with you, just let him do it?"

"You're fucking weak. This is why your brother hit you."

"You're a disgrace. Your family never wanted you."

It seemed like they were talking to me, but I wasn't certain. It didn't really matter. We were basically all the same to them, interchangeable problem kids they could scream at without recourse.

"Come on!" Alan was right at the center of the action. "Show me you want to live!"

My hands burned and sweat poured down my back. The lights were off, and it felt as though I was playing tug-of-war in that graveyard. Those buried were trying to pull me to the dark side, to join them in the ground. We were all supposed to be fighting for life, but I wasn't sure that life was what I wanted.

We wrestled back and forth, playing tug-of-war for our souls. Finally, the rope gave out and the other side fell down. I let go of the rope and collapsed, trying to catch my breath. All around, my classmates were panting and rubbing their blistered hands.

Collectively, we were exhausted, drained of adrenaline and emotional bandwidth. The humane response to seeing a group of teenagers in such a state would be to call for a break, but Alan wasn't done with us.

"Get up," he said. "On your goddamn feet."

Team Life winning hadn't been part of his plan. It was too generous and optimistic. He wanted us on the other side, in the nightmare zone where our drawings hung.

"This is now a Lifeline. Living's on one end and dying's on the other," Alan said. "I want you to stand in a line, wherever you think you should be. Closer to Life or closer to Death."

When we'd all chosen our spots, there were three or four people firmly on the side of Life and an equal number hovering in the vicinity of Death. The rest of us stood somewhere in the middle, halfway down the line, which just seemed like the safest bet.

"Really, Elizabeth," Monica said, "you think you belong this close to Life? I've been watching you all day. Get over on the Death side."

She wasn't wrong. I was in an awful place. There was no denying that my mood had been darkening for a while now. So why not embrace it? I stepped away from the middle of the Lifeline and walked the plank all the way to its unhesitant end.

It wasn't my first time traveling in the direction of death. That trail was littered with migraine pills and shrugged-off cat lives, signposts I had always ignored after turning back around. From where I stood, pressed up against the trailer wall, all I could see was the chaos of my current existence.

Alan and Monica were both screaming, berating the kids who still stood in the middle until they were chastened enough to pick another spot. It got harder to move as more and more of my classmates were sentenced to death, a wet-faced herd sent to join me at the edge of the Lifeline.

Alan kept yelling for everyone to move closer to the wall, corralling ten or twelve bodies so tightly I could hardly breathe.

It was four in the morning when Alan finally set us free. I could still feel the tightness in my lungs even as I stepped outside. I felt like I had truly pushed right up against death, closer than I'd ever been before, and for the first time I felt like there might not be a path back.

We were zombies the following morning: sleep-deprived, hungry, and emotionally depleted. I was over it and I didn't know how to hide that anymore. Not Alan; he seemed to have boundless energy when it came to this bullshit.

"Mayday, Mayday!" he started yelling as soon as we entered the trailer. "The ship's going down!"

Monica ushered us to the center of the room and we sat down in a circle.

"We're in the middle of the ocean," Alan said. "Hundreds of miles from land. We struck a reef and we're going down fast."

I took a seat between Levi and Brittany and rubbed my eyes. Alan paced, unable to contain his enthusiasm. I imagined him practicing his captain voice in front of the mirror, with *Titanic* playing in the background for reference.

"The good news is, we have a lifeboat," he said. "The bad news? It can only hold four people. And there are fifteen of you."

My classmates and I looked at one another, suddenly alert. It was definitely too early for what was about to happen.

"It's up to the group to decide who lives and who dies," Alan said. "So think hard. Who deserves to be saved? Is it the junkie? The self-harmer who wants attention? Is it the whore or the tease?"

One by one, we were forced to go around the circle, look each person in the eye, and say either "You live" or "You die." A student support made tally marks on the whiteboard, counting up our votes. It was a cruel task, a lose-lose game from every angle. It was smarter to choose Ponies over friends, a move more likely to fly under the radar, but that meant killing your friends. Some kids chose to keep a seat for themselves, but I gave all four of mine away. Saving myself would have been disingenuous when drowning just seemed so much easier.

I heard "You live" from only three people. Brittany, Levi, and Dash all gave me spots on their lifeboats, though I'm not entirely sure why. How could they want to save me when I didn't even choose to save myself? Maybe it was strategic in some way, or maybe they were just being nice. Either way, when both Charlotte and Maya looked me in the eye and said the words "You die," I knew I couldn't take it personally.

According to the final tally, I was one of the lives least worth saving. I tried to be okay with that fact, but Monica wasn't making it any easier.

"How does it feel," she said, hovering over me, "to realize you're expendable?"

"We all die eventually, right?"

"The words of a girl who doesn't value her own life." Monica's tone let me know my sarcasm wasn't appreciated. "Do you even matter, Elizabeth?"

I shrugged. "I don't know."

"Well, maybe that's why eleven of your peers just left you to drown."

"I'm a pretty good swimmer, though," I said. "Ranked and everything."

"And you just threw it all away." Monica shook her head. "What a waste. Your parents must be so disappointed, and your so-called friends don't care if you die."

I looked down at the ground, feeling the anger and shame Monica was trying to rouse.

"You need to figure out what makes you worth saving. Because I'm starting to think everyone else might be right."

Tears stung my eyes. Alan walked from the circle to a row of chairs at the front of the room, set up by the student supports. There were four of them, meant to represent the lifeboat.

"This is it. The raft's about to set sail." He looked us over. "If you want a spot on board, I want you to fight for it."

No one moved. Monica fiddled with the stereo and "Bridge Over Troubled Water" began playing at an alarming volume.

"Get up and go!" Alan said. "When the music stops, I want you to fight for your lives."

Quit telling us to fight for our lives. You just want us to fucking fight. Like we're animals. But this isn't real. It's just a fucked-up version of musical chairs.

We walked the perimeter of the lifeboat as a group, making tighter and tighter circles around the seats. The music stopped abruptly, and everyone just froze. Finally, Conrad made a break for one of the chairs. Levi was on him in a second, pushing him from behind. Dash fell to the ground and cowered.

"Dash," Alan said, "are you gonna let people push you around your whole life? I thought you had a breakthrough yesterday."

His face went red and he got back up. He lunged at Levi, who had just secured a seat. The chair crashed down with the two of them on it and they began to wrestle. The floodgates had been flung open and the rest of us all ran forward at once, shoving and clawing our way toward the chairs. Levi managed to capture one, but he was on the ground a moment later. I saw Charlotte in flashes, forcing her way through the crowd like an Amazonian warrior.

Every time someone managed to secure a chair, they were ousted moments later. There were no rules, just chaos, as much as each of us could take. One by one, my classmates gave up and sat down on the ground. I fought halfheartedly for a while, to keep Monica off my back, but I didn't actually want a spot on the lifeboat. As soon as I could, I took a seat on the floor along with the rest of the drowned.

When the game ended, Alan's voice took on a somber tone.

"A terrible crash off the coast of Virginia claimed the lives of eleven teenagers tonight," he said. "There were only four survivors. They say their lost peers showed great bravery in the face of the disaster."

I scanned the survivors. When I saw that Charlotte was among them I cracked a smile for the first time all day. Even with her hair in knots and scratches up and down her arms, she looked better than she had in months. The Charlotte sitting proudly in a hard-won seat wasn't the ghostlike girl who'd kept her head down and followed orders. She was her old self again, fierce and unbroken. Randall had tried so hard to snuff out her spirit by spewing accusations and treating her like a pariah. But Charlotte made it through the freezing cold days and the interminable isolation. Randall's campaign failed to break her down, after all. In fact, it seemed that all he did was make her even stronger.

"How do you feel, Charlotte?" Alan asked.

She smiled. "I feel pretty fucking good."

A word of advice: If you're ever offered the opportunity to attend your own funeral, decline. As we ate a dinner of cold cuts, the staff transformed the trailer into a funeral parlor. They dimmed the lights and lit candles. There was no more *Rocky* theme song, only the somber music of death.

Before we broke for dinner we'd written obituaries for ourselves, and now Alan was going to read them as if our funerals were real. One by one, we took turns lying on the floor inside invisible coffins. It was truly eerie. At the same time, at least we didn't have to do anything but listen. And when my time came, I was more than happy to close my eyes and pretend to be dead.

"When Elizabeth was a child, she was full of light and energy. Nick-named 'Hotshot' because of her love for sports, she had dreams of playing soccer in the Olympics. After that, she wanted to be one of the first female fighter pilots. Her heroes were Mia Hamm, Tara Lipinski, and Dominique Moceanu. Hotshot died tragically at the age of sixteen."

It was the opposite of an exorcism. Alan wasn't trying to cast out our demons, he was burying us along with them.

"Sadly, she'll never accomplish any of those things now that she's dead,"

Alan said. He was reading the last words of my obituary. "Regardless, we'll always remember Hotshot for the powerful person she once was."

The lights were still off when the door opened and the older students came back in. It was a candlelight vigil, and Alan actually started to cry.

"Get together," he said. "I want you all to hold your brothers and sisters."

We moved together. We had no other choice. "You've Got a Friend" by Carole King started playing.

"This is a celebration of life. It's your chance for a new beginning. That's right, Charlotte, let it out."

I noticed she was sobbing.

"We know you never meant to hurt Kristen, and you're doing such a great job now."

He looked at the rest of us.

"I know that all of you have what it takes to fight for your life. Today is the first day of the rest of your life. So let's make today the day that you choose to live! There's a saying I want to leave you with as the workshop comes to an end."

Alan took a deep breath for maximum effect.

"If you build castles in the air, your work need not be lost. That is where they should be. Now put the foundations under them."

With that grand statement, Animus was over. I had physically survived all three days, but mentally I was not okay at all. I hardly had the energy for our dramatic reentry into regular Carlbrook life. I knew from previous Animus returns that the commons would be decorated like a castle, full of paper flowers made by younger students. The thought of it alone made me want to run and hide. I wasn't Don Quixote, and Halifax was hardly La Mancha.

But that didn't matter to Alan. We were still expected to perform. Each of us had to stand in front of the whole school, pretending to draw our swords as we shouted some fresh Animus-approved lesson.

"I stand for having a purpose," I said. It was unconvincing at best.

I didn't have a purpose. Not even close. A pretend sword and a fake flower was about all I had in the world. I was exhausted and depressed, exactly the wrong emotions for what happened next. As the ceremony ended, upbeat music began to play.

It was dance party time. An opportunity to celebrate life. My friends all looked like they were having a good time, but I could hardly bother to pretend. I danced because I had to, but I wasn't really there.

In my mind I'd never left that invisible coffin. I was waiting to be buried because I felt about as good as dead.

Chapter 27

AFTER ANIMUS I had all but given up. I fantasized about dying in a shipwreck for real, or suffocating as my classmates pressed me up against the wall. But the Lifeline wasn't real—and that was the whole problem.

I was so depressed that even my demons felt apathetic. They were nagging at me to just kill myself already, but they didn't have any useful ideas of how I might accomplish that. The way I saw it, I had only a few options when it came to a Carlbrook suicide:

1. **Hanging Myself**

   I didn't know where to find a rope and all I had were J.Crew ribbon belts. That hardly seemed strong enough. Plus, where would I even hang it? We didn't have doors, after all. Our IKEA shelves wouldn't be up to the task. The bunk bed would hold my weight, but the logistics there were a little complicated.

2. **Drowning in the Lake**

   It was certainly deep enough. I was pretty sure my swimmer's instincts were so deeply ingrained in me that they'd kick in, like it or not. Then I'd just be cold, wet, and in trouble.

   There's always hypothermia.

3. **Toothpaste**

   I had free access to the toothpaste of every girl in my sleeping mod

245

and I figured if I swallowed the contents of all the tubes at once, it might do me in. Considering how hard it was for me even to clean up other people's toothpaste, the chances of me managing to ingest it were slim to none.

4. **Razor Blade**

This was the obvious choice for a Carlbrook suicide. It was the way Kyle had tried to do it, when he ran into the woods and tried to slit his wrists. But I was even more averse to blood than toothpaste. Once, in elementary school, I got a paper cut and fainted. Actually fainted.

5. **Cleaning Products**

Cleaning products were another option. The trouble would be in managing to round up enough to make it worthwhile. If I didn't, I'd end up with a tube down my throat, getting my stomach pumped. Then it would be off to a psych ward for me.

6. **Suffocating with a Pillowcase**

The problem with this one? It felt a little too much like a workshop exercise.

Ultimately, I didn't really want to die. I just couldn't keep on going the way I had been. Every time I thought I'd reached rock bottom, the ground beneath me would sink another foot. I was so exhausted just trying to keep up with all the lies I told to protect myself, always trying to think two moves ahead.

If I use this disclosure now, what will I say next time?

Do I use a real story? Or do I make something up?

Who do I call out to save myself from the hot seat? And who's about to call me out?

Is all this fighting even worth it?

There was no right move, not really. It was a rigged game. There was no getting ahead at Carlbrook. There was only falling further and further behind.

Chapter 28

GIVEN MY GENERAL mood, I knew there was another program in my future. I spoke in group only when I was asked a direct question, and my response was usually something along the lines of "I don't care." I kept to myself as much as I could, and I refused to smoosh during Last Light. I was headed for the glass room one way or another. It was only a matter of time.

I knew my time had come when I checked the request list and found my name right below Maya's. She'd been on my case since Animus, at first trying to cheer me up and then, when that didn't work, confronting me on our walks across campus.

"Are you still in a bad mood?"

"I'm fine," I said. "I don't understand how you're in such a *good* mood."

"Animus was so powerful." Maya smiled. "I just really connected to the message, I think."

"We must have gone through different workshops," I said. "Because I thought the whole thing was pretty fucking awful. Inhumane, really."

"I wish you'd stop being so negative about the school. You don't participate in group anymore. I know it may hurt sometimes, but it's for your own good."

I wanted to shake her. *How is writing your own obituary good?* I knew there was no talking Maya out of her conviction that Carlbrook was helping us, just as there was no convincing me it wasn't doing the opposite.

"I don't know, Maya," I said. "I think we'll have to agree to disagree."

As much as these kinds of conversations annoyed me, I never doubted Maya's intentions. I knew she was at least trying to help me; it wasn't some cynical attempt to advance herself or kiss up to the staff. Taking it to group, though, was another matter altogether. To make matters worse, Monica happened to be leading the session. The last thing I needed was to be called out in front of my own adviser. Just as I feared, that was exactly how the afternoon played out.

"All right, everyone," Monica said. "Does anyone with a request want to start things off?"

Maya raised her hand. "Elizabeth, I requested you because I wanted to check in. You've been so negative lately that it's kind of hard to be around you."

My eyes hardened as I looked at Maya.

"I'm worried about you," she said.

I bit my lip, starting to seethe. I couldn't help but feel betrayed.

"Elizabeth, do you have anything to say?" Monica's hair was in pigtails, which only made her seem even more smug. "Hearing this shouldn't be a surprise. You can't think I haven't noticed the way you've been acting."

"It's not a surprise," I said. "I just don't really care."

"It seems like you don't care about anything these days," Monica said. "You're in upper school now. You're supposed to be a role model. Is this really the behavior I can expect from you?"

"I don't know," I said. "I mean, I feel pretty mad at Maya right now. She could have just talked to me in an appointment."

"I tried talking to you," Maya said. "You just shut me down. I saw how much you struggled in Animus, and now you're trying to blame your own problems all on the school."

"Is that true, Elizabeth?" Monica said.

"Maybe," I said. "I just don't want to be here, okay?"

"Well, no, it isn't okay. You didn't even bother trying in Animus and you've stopped caring about your emotional work. Is it safe to assume you've given up on yourself?"

"I don't know how to answer that," I said.

"We need to get to the bottom of this," Monica said. "I'm putting you on a program. It's not a punishment. But I think you need some time to reflect."

Fuck you, Monica. And fuck you, too, Maya. How is this going to do anything but make me hate this place more?

After group, I reported to the glass room with my red binder in hand. My first assignment was to write a list of the things I felt were worth living for. I knew I'd be lying no matter what I said, so I just wrote the first words that popped into my mind. My second assignment was much easier. I was supposed to write down all the reasons I'd chosen death in Animus. Though I couldn't be completely honest on paper, I had no trouble composing this list in my head.

I chose death because life here is unbearable. I fucking hate every single moment of every single day. My family thinks I'm doing fine because every letter I write them is screened and every phone call is fucking monitored. If I could tell them what was actually going on here, they'd have no choice but to take me home. Since that's not going to happen, I guess I'll just keep choosing death whenever I can.

Is this ever going to end?

When SEALs are going through Hell Week and want to quit, they're told all they have to do is ring a bell three times. As Admiral William McRaven wrote, "Ring the bell and you won't have to get up early. Ring the bell and you won't have to do the long runs, the cold swims, or the obstacle course. Ring the bell and you can avoid all this pain."

If there had been a bell in the program room, I wouldn't have hesitated to ring it. I felt so hopeless. I didn't know what Luke or Kristen was doing at that moment, or even where they were, but that didn't matter. I would have given anything to be right there with either of them, even if it really was at the bottom of a ditch.

The work project for my program was to clean the long concrete path that cut across campus. I began down by the white picket fence and realized I was as close to the exit as I'd ever been, at least by myself. I watched two student government members head down the street for a run, one of the perks of being a Pony.

How was it possible that leaving was so easy, yet so hard? I was so confused about who I was and what I wanted. Did I actually want to live? I had no idea. The very idea of graduating felt somehow impossible. I could no longer tell the difference between reality and fantasy, between truth and lies.

Am I really a worthless abuser?

Maybe. But maybe not.

Am I a desperate cum dumpster?

I mean, I'm still a virgin. That I know for sure.

I scrubbed harder and harder, as if the truth would be uncovered if I could just get through enough layers of dirt. I thought about all the times I was called a taker and a bad friend, and I scrubbed. I heard Alan's voice screaming that my father never loved me, and I scrubbed.

"You're pathetic. You're a loser. You just take and take. You ruined your life. You'll never amount to anything so you might as well give up. You can't even clean goose shit off the ground, for God's sake."

Yes, I can. I'll get every last speck off this path if it kills me. How do you like that, Alan? You abusive asshole.

"Fuck you!"

I kicked my bucket and water splashed everywhere.

"Fuck you, fuck you, fuck you."

The bucket rolled to a stop in front of the fence. I had actually forgotten where I was for a moment. I looked around and composed myself. Thankfully, I was so far across campus that no one had witnessed my little freak-out. I had to laugh a little as I filled my bucket with soapy water. The chances of no one being around to yell at me or take notes for their group requests were so slight I almost had to feel lucky. I started scrubbing again, more calmly this time, and I felt just a little bit like I had brushed up against freedom.

My project extended to crews, which meant I kept going as the sun went down. It was cold, but that was okay. I worked my way up to the carriage house, a building I hadn't set foot in since the last time I was strip-searched. There was an energy around that stone house that I couldn't ignore. It was the same kind of energy I felt when I ran around the graveyard near my house, except this time it was dark and almost sinister. I was sitting alone, but I wasn't alone at all.

I continued scrubbing, and the sun disappeared completely. The darker it got, the more intensely I felt the disturbance in the energy around the building. I tried to ignore it, focusing on those stubborn stains illuminated by the lights of the carriage house, but that just wasn't possible. As layers of dirt and time fell away, the energy got stronger, breaking down some invisible barrier.

I thought back to that first afternoon in the carriage house. It occurred to me that before she sat there smiling on the couch, before she extolled the virtues of the school, Beatrice, too, had been strip-searched and degraded.

Like it or not, we all were connected through this place—probably forever. Me, Beatrice, and Maya. Maggie and Kyle. That first class of eight whose portraits hung on the wall. We were part of a long legacy of people held on this property against our will, trapped inside the snow globe where lies and secret horrors could flourish.

Even Polly and Carolina were off at their own versions of Carlbrook. They were stuck in the same web of "emotional growth" and therapeutic manipulation as me. Who knew what they had been forced to do to survive or even if they were surviving at all?

Had Beatrice, Maya, and the Ponies found a better way through? Maybe they had. Maybe the perks of jogging outside and an extra soda from the student store really did make life easier. Maybe being honest, really doing the emotional work, was worth it after all. I didn't know how they all truly felt inside, but I knew how I felt and it wasn't sustainable. I had sunk as far down into my depression as I'd ever gone, and what had that gotten me? Another program. My third. Clearly, my way wasn't working.

Carlbrook felt like a graveyard because it *was* a graveyard. So many lives had been stolen by this place, but our lives were only being borrowed. I still had a choice. I didn't have to ring the bell, and I think something was trying to tell me that.

After ten or eleven months of resisting, I finally made a decision that night. I wouldn't let this place kill me. I had a few more months to go and then I'd be free. My life wouldn't ever be the same, not at all. But it was still *my* life—and that meant I still had a chance.

As I read in *Man's Search for Meaning*, "He who has a why to live for can bear with almost any how."

Chapter 29

"Seventeen sucks a bit because you're waiting for eighteen. Or maybe I think that because I spent all of that year here."—Valerie

"Seventeen will probably be better than sixteen because you're graduating."—Lina

"I love you to death. One year closer to eighteen."—Levi

"At least me and you stuck around for each other, huh? No back to the woods or anything. We've been through it all together and I love you for it."—Brittany

"Happy birthday. We've had a damn long, hard time together."—Charlotte

I made it through my program in time for my seventeenth birthday. While it wasn't a dream birthday, at least it was better than my sixteenth. I actually had friends this time, and I wasn't on bans with any of them. Charlotte, Lina, and Brittany were able to come. By then we'd worked through any lingering problems and left the past firmly in the past. It was easier that way, and at the end of the day all we had was one another.

I got a special Nelly cake, of course. Confetti with vanilla icing, covered with fondant hearts and seventeen rainbow candles. Maya made me a scrapbook, as much a peace offering as a gift. I'm sure she still thought she had done the right thing by calling me out in group, but she could tell it had upset me. The book was full of pictures of the two of us along with cameos from people like Lina, Brittany, and Levi. She decorated it with glitter and magic markers, and she and my other friends had written notes about how grateful they were to have me as a friend.

It might have been the most thoughtful thing anyone did for me at Carlbrook, and that made my relationship with Maya feel even more complicated. Even so, it would have been the highlight of my birthday if it hadn't been for Bobby.

At some point I'd developed a crush on a gentle and unassuming guy named Bobby. Becoming closer with him helped fill the vacuum left by Luke. I didn't get my birthday kiss or anything, but Bobby walked me to class and waited for me at the end of the day.

Our relationship was just as chaste as my flirtation with Luke had been. At Carlbrook, being physical just wasn't worth the risk. (There were a few hook-up rumors in circulation and they all involved dumpsters, which wasn't exactly my style.) I still felt strangely connected to Bobby even if we couldn't so much as hold hands. He was someone I felt comfortable being silent around. Sometimes we'd walk around the lake without saying a single word, and I'd leave feeling like I'd just had a deeply meaningful conversation.

There was just something about him. He was magnetic but still low-key, and that meant I didn't have to worry about being seen with him. Maybe it was because Bobby flew under the radar and Monica just never noticed. It probably helped that Maya was usually there as well. Sometimes the three of us would sit on one of the benches and watch the geese, talking about life after Carlbrook.

"I can't wait to just go places," I said. "Paris or New York. Or the mall."

"I just want to be back home," Maya said.

"Yeah," Bobby agreed. "I miss my family's place in Mexico mostly. You guys should visit me there."

"Definitely," I said. "Maya, can we hang out with Bobby in Mexico?"

"Definitely," Maya said. "I love the beach. We'll have so much fun."

Chapter 30

TENEO WAS THE workshop that scared us the most. If there was even a theme, it got lost in all the rumors about brainwashing and hypnosis. I'd seen countless kids return from Teneo looking exhausted and life-less, totally blank behind the eyes as if possessed by the Carlbrook devil.

The workshop lasted four days. Four days of sleep deprivation and dehydration, on top of whatever mindfuckery they put us through, was enough to leave me with compromised memories of that workshop. What I can recall of Teneo is a haphazard collection of bits and pieces. Out of four days, I remember maybe four hours. There are brief moments that seem to pop up from the general hazy confusion of those days. I know it happened, and yet I could just as readily believe the whole thing was just a figment of my imagination. Maybe that was due to brainwashing, or exhaustion, or maybe it was my psyche shielding me from more pain than I could handle.

Probably, it was some combination of the three.

I remember a lecture from the first day on the subject of "I vs. ME."

"I thinks and ME feels," Alan said over and over.

The point, as far as I could tell, was to drill down on the idea that the thinking mind and the feeling mind are two separate entities. Feeling is true and good, while thinking is false and bad. Feeling belongs to the Little Me, the pure, unscratched marble. Everything bad that happened to our Little Me is due to the thinking I.

"Remember, what 'I' tells myself is what's wrong with 'ME,'" Alan said.

What?

"What's I saying to you right now, Elizabeth?" he said. "Is she saying that you're not good enough?"

No, she's saying, "Fuck you, Alan."

"It's time we fight back," he said. "Let's get all that shit that 'I' says to Little Me and kick it in the butt."

It might be worth noting that the "I and ME" theory of consciousness was originally developed by the psychiatrist William James in tandem with his work on hypnosis and dissociation. James just so happened to believe that schizophrenia, a literal split in the mind, can actually be induced with therapeutic work.

So I guess there's that.

The next memory involves running in place for what felt like an eternity. We weren't allowed to stop no matter how tired we got. Staff and supports walked back and forth screaming disclosures and general insults, like a greatest-hits record. Some of it was personal; some seemed to be directed at everyone. We had become a single hive once again, indistinct and equally broken.

"What are you thinking right now?"

"Is it that you are worthless?"

"Maybe if you'd been better, your daddy would have loved you."

"Maybe if you had done things differently, those boys wouldn't have used you."

"Maybe if you weren't so easy and attention-seeking, you'd be in a better place now."

We all felt rejected and unloved. We all felt scared. We all wondered why we were there.

We all kept running.

"Run so fast that the voice telling 'ME' she doesn't deserve to live is gone."

I managed to zone out by pretending I was on the soccer field. I imagined darting across the field. I was the center forward and the midfielder kicked a beautiful shot to the right corner of the box. A magnificent give-and-go. I outran the defender, kicked a beautiful shot, and...

GOAL!

When I came back to reality, I realized everyone had stopped running. The only other person not balled up on the floor crying was Brittany. Her face was drenched in sweat and she looked ready to throw up. Like me, Brittany didn't want to give Alan the satisfaction of letting him know he'd gotten to her.

"Your parents don't like you. Why do you think you're here? You're a fuckup. Run all you want. You're still gonna be just as unlovable."

We would hold out for only so long and could never win either; as always the exercise wouldn't end until we were all in tears. Brittany finally broke, and as soon as she did, all eyes were on me. Monica came over to deal the final blow.

"What are you trying to prove, Elizabeth? That you're better than everyone else?"

Monica turned to the rest of the group. "Who here thinks Elizabeth is better than the rest of you?"

I stopped running. It was time to give in; it just wasn't worth it. Monica and Alan could have this round. I collapsed to the floor with the rest of my peer group, my face dripping with sweat and the requisite tears.

Another memory flashback: lying on the floor while "Gravedigger" by Dave Matthews played on a loop. Alan began to talk about our "rock bottoms," but once again his speech seemed designed to confuse us. Instead of the traditional lowest-point meaning, he used the term to refer to the core part of us.

The innermost, purest part of that Little Me.

This exercise led into individualized guided meditations, another technique from large group awareness trainings said to induce hypnotic states. Each of us had a staff member sitting by our side, whispering in our ear. I was unlucky enough to get Monica. I lay in a fetal position while she ran through a scenario, so close I could feel her stale breath on my neck.

"I want you to remember your bedroom as a child. What did it smell like? What did it look like? Did you have a twin bed? A princess bed? Were your walls pink or flowery? Did you have glow-in-the-dark stars on the ceiling?"

I pictured my bedroom with my monogrammed sheets.

"I want you to remember every poster, every doll, every little glass animal in your room," Monica said. "Pick them up, feel them, and remember everything that Little Me loved about them. Hug your favorite stuffed animal. Hug it so tight you may never let go. Smell it and give it all the love in the world."

I thought about my baby blanket and imagined running my fingers through those loops.

"There were good memories in that room. But there were bad ones, too, weren't there? Now I want you to remember all the pain you experienced in the same room. Suddenly, Little Me is in her room crying. She's all alone crying. Those dolls and toys aren't protecting your Little Me right now. She's not the shiny ball she once was. She's watching out the window, listening to her parents fight about what to do with her. She's the problem child no one understands."

Don't listen to her. Block out the words.

"Outside the door, all she hears is someone yelling the word *slut*," Monica said. "'You slut. You fucking whore.'"

I bit down on my lip.

I'm not a whore. I'm not a disappointment.

"Back out the window her mom pushes her dad, she can only hear every other word. The argument is about her, she's the problem child. What are they going to do with her? She keeps crying. What does Little Me do to make herself feel better?"

She pours salt on her wrists. Takes an ice cube from the freezer. When the ice touches the salt she feels better.

"Okay, now the door opens," Monica said. "Big Me is there. Big Me gives Little Me a hug. Little Me is crying, but Big Me tells her it's going to be okay. She says, 'You're lovable and you're good enough. You aren't a problem child and you don't deserve to be yelled at. You don't deserve any of the things that happened to you. You're just a little girl and I love you.'"

Don't listen to this. It's a trap. She's trying to mess with you.

"Now I want you to turn around and see a tiny door you've never seen before. There's a light inside. Big Me carries Little Me through the door. The room opens up into a magical land of flowers and love. There's music everywhere. You're dancing with Big Me and your family is there. You feel whole. You feel worthy. You feel all the love in the world."

This is fucking insane.

The crazy exercise continued until I was told to become a caterpillar who transformed into a beautiful butterfly. Somehow the butterfly had to find three golden keys. Each key had a word engraved on it, a message for leading a successful life.

Forgiveness. Compassion. Love.

Once the keys were in Little Me's possession, the exercise finally ended. I was told to slowly open my eyes. "The Rose" by Bette Midler was playing on the stereo. I realized it had been playing on a loop the whole time.

Maybe I had lost touch with reality, after all. I don't know where the rest of those hours went or what else happened in that trailer. Somehow, I made it through Teneo and was one step closer to graduation.

Chapter 31

I CAN STILL remember my first concert like it was yesterday. The Spice Girls at the Blockbuster Pavilion in Charlotte, North Carolina. It was the summer of 1998, just before I turned ten, and it was the American leg of the Girls' famous Spiceworld tour.

I absolutely loved the Spice Girls. Sporty Spice was my natural counterpart, but I also had the blond pigtailed look of Baby Spice. I loved them so much I even saw their terrible movie in the theater. After my mom took me to that concert (the one where the band stripped down for the song "Naked" while hiding strategically behind chairs, much to her dismay), I was even more obsessed. I sang Spice Girls songs day and night for the rest of the summer.

Singing had always been a secret dream of mine. I never spoke about it, and I didn't hang it on my wall for everyone to see. Because singing didn't come naturally to me like soccer and swimming, it was a complete fantasy. It was something I'd really have to work at, and even if I did there was no guarantee I'd actually get good. So I kept my dream a secret from everyone but my friend Caitlyn.

Caitlyn had a beautiful voice. She hoped to be a professional singer one day, and she had the chops to make it happen. She was raised by a single mother who worked a lot, and for a period of time Caitlyn spent a lot of time at my house. We'd hang out in my room and sing together. Occasionally, I'd hit a note that was halfway decent and she'd look at me and smile.

"Hey, that was really pretty."

I loved music because it came from the heart. It was all about feelings, and your feelings couldn't be wrong. Unless, of course, you ended up at Carlbrook. Everything I loved about music, the way a single song could make me feel okay for having dark thoughts, was twisted inside out at Carlbrook.

Music was never simply something to be enjoyed. It was always tied to our therapeutic work, a tool to heighten our emotions so we'd lose ourselves completely. Songs played on a loop until they became automatic triggers for certain emotions.

Even in our free time, we couldn't just listen to music any old time like normal teenagers. There was a music committee for that, with total control over a single stereo and a book of CDs. It was the same collection used to torture us in workshops—Bette Midler, *Les Mis*—so I wasn't exactly vying for stereo time.

In fact, I had actually begun to fear music during my time at Carlbrook. My mind started to associate it entirely with trauma. Old trauma, relived. New trauma, created in workshops. The trauma, for example, of being forced to participate in a talent show.

After Teneo, we were each required to perform an "Ades Aces," as they called it, which apparently means "to stand on the edge." Talent shows are nightmarish enough when the participants want to be there. If you sign up by choice, ostensibly it's because you have some *talent* to *show.* Our specific performances were assigned regardless of any skill set we might or might not have had. Instead, we were made to perform whatever the staff thought would make each of us feel most vulnerable.

Music, dance, speech. Anyone could get any of them. While I never saw anyone forced to juggle or spin plates, that doesn't mean it didn't happen.

Once again, it was like the school read my mind. They peered inside and found my secret wish to be a better singer. They must have known I both loved and feared singing because when it came time to assign me an Ades Aces, I was given the song "Alive" by Jennifer Lopez.

The song's message relates the simple gratitude of being alive. It's about feeling okay in your own skin. The lyrics were a near perfect fit with my current state of mind—and that pissed me off. The decision to keep on living had been hard-won and Carlbrook hadn't gotten me there, I had gotten myself there.

To make matters worse, I hardly had any time to learn the stupid thing. We had only that one stereo to share, which meant practicing in groups—something I was way too self-conscious to do. I was insecure about my voice, but more than that, I didn't like the feeling of having to perform on command. I needed to be completely out of everyone's earshot. I would look for the quietest places on campus to rehearse sans stereo without anyone listening, but they were pretty much nonexistent, so most of my rehearsing was done in the five-minute showers I got each night.

Everyone sings better in the shower anyway, right? Still, I couldn't bear the idea of anyone hearing me. I whispered the words over and over, trying to get them right. I had no idea if I was in tune or even if I had the correct melody memorized. My showers got longer and longer every night as I just tried to get the thing to sound as not-horrible as possible.

"Elizabeth, what are you doing in there? There's a line, you know."

On the day of the show, I put on the dress my parents had sent for the occasion. I did my hair to the best of my ability, and we were even allowed to wear a little makeup. I sat upstairs in the commons waiting my turn but hoping it would never come. I felt a surge of empathy for the older students who had performed in the past. Once again, I felt like I was about to be strip-searched in front of the entire student body. I was about to be as naked as the Spice Girls, but it wasn't by choice and I didn't have a chair to hide behind.

The show began. Lindy cracked her way through "Somewhere Over the Rainbow." A girl with daddy issues quietly sang her way through "Not Pretty Enough" by Kasey Chambers. A kid named Tony, who was from South America, had to recite "The Road Not Taken" by Robert Frost in Spanish. Dash sang "I Won't Grow Up" from *Peter Pan*.

Levi was up next. He had been tasked with reciting Martin Luther King's "I Have a Dream" speech, and I must say he did a good job. It was an impassioned delivery, even if the original was pretty hard to live up to.

I moved to the side of the stage as my turn came closer. Charlotte was up next. She had a great voice and actually went on to sing professionally post-Carlbrook, so naturally Charlotte was assigned a dance. Not just any old dance. Poor Charlotte had to do an *interpretive dance*. To a *country song*, of all things. As the first notes of "I Hope You Dance" by Lee Ann Womack sounded, she began to flitter across the stage.

I could tell she felt ridiculous. Charlotte was dressed in a frumpy blue smock selected by the staff, and unlike the rest of us, she wasn't allowed to wear makeup or rehearse. As she jumped and pirouetted across the stage, really giving it her all, I understood why Charlotte had been given this particular Ades Aces.

It wasn't Charlotte up there dancing. It was the version of Charlotte that Carlbrook had created. A shiny new marble cleansed of all its scratches— even the ones she'd gotten by fighting for a spot on the lifeboat. Alan and Randall were molding a success story out of the upper-crust rebel from overseas. The girl who'd arrived at Carlbrook with escorts and a face full of makeup. They wanted Charlotte to see how fantastic she could be if she stayed pure, if she bought in completely. They wanted to strip Charlotte of everything that made her exciting and unique and turn her into an obedient puppet.

But although she danced her little heart out until the very last word, I knew the real Charlotte was still in there. She was only doing what she had to do. I saw her face relax the moment she could stop smiling. She had gotten past another obstacle and was one step closer to being done with Carlbrook.

Yet I was still behind the barrier. As I walked down the stairs for my fifteen minutes of Carlbrook fame, my legs shook and my heart raced. I was genuinely terrified. I felt so vulnerable that I had to glance down to reassure myself I wasn't actually naked.

I looked out into the crowd and only felt worse. The room was filled with people who'd called me a whore and a terrible friend. Peers who'd scapegoated me and adults who basically implied I was part of some murderous underground. Suffice it to say, these were the last people on earth I felt comfortable singing for.

I actually had to remind myself to breathe. That's how completely petrified I was. If Jennifer Lopez's delivery of "Alive" could be called "breathy," mine was more like "hyperventilate-y." As the first notes played, I nearly turned around and ran away. I saw Monica sitting alongside the stage, smiling in that smug way of hers. She truly did think she had me figured out. She thought she could sum up my whole life, all the pain I'd felt at Carlbrook, in a single song.

I guess I've found my way, it's simple when it's right.

She was right, I did want to live, but not for the reasons she thought. Carlbrook wasn't saving me. It had almost destroyed me, and living in spite of that felt like an act of defiance.

Feeling lucky just to be here tonight / And happy just to be me and be alive.

Chapter 32

CHARLOTTE HAD PROVED herself to be a model student with her dance performance, and she decided to run with the whole good-girl thing. But she did it in a way that would benefit her friends too. We were sitting around bored one weekend, lamenting the field trips the good kids got to take. Usually it was just a trip to a diner, but occasionally it was a basketball game or, bizarrely, a Mary Kay makeup party at a staff member's house. While we didn't want to do *that*, exactly, any chance to leave campus sounded pretty nice.

Charlotte was our ticket to Applebee's and she knew it. Luckily, she had the brilliant idea to start a committee that all our friends could join.

"A church committee!"

"Seriously?" I said. "You really want to do that?"

"Why not? Isn't church better than staying here?"

I thought about it for a second. "Definitely."

Just like that, the God Squad was born.

Once the staff approved our committee, they hung a list in the commons. If you wanted to join, you just had to sign up—pending adviser permission, of course. For me, just being from the South was enough to convince Monica that church had been a big part of my life.

Our little group really gained legitimacy when Shelby signed up. In her pearls and sweater sets, she might as well have been a preacher's daughter. I was pretty sure she even read the Bible every night like my mom, though whether she also kept a highlighter in her hand, I couldn't say. A few more people joined—including Levi, who claimed he was ready for a religious conversion. Who knows, maybe it was true.

When Sunday finally rolled around I was actually excited to get ready for church. I put on a loose skirt for the occasion, no stuffed animals needed. When I completed the look with a crewneck sweater and flats, I couldn't possibly have been any more the good Southern belle.

We piled into the Carlbrook van. Even though it reeked of cigarettes and stale hamburgers, something about it still smelled like freedom. As we took off down the road, though, I felt a wave of panic. The last time I got into a car that was ostensibly headed to Sunday service, it had been a trick, my parents' first attempt to send me to the woods.

"What church are we going to?" Charlotte said.

"Um," the driver said as he checked a note, "I don't know. Some local Baptist church."

"But I'm Presbyterian."

"Me too," I said.

"Do you want to go to church or not?"

The van continued driving down the road. Even though the land-scape was drab and empty, just a scattering of houses that appeared to be crumbling in real time, I found myself unable to turn away from the window. After so many months of seeing only Carlbrook, anything that wasn't a green lawn or a white mansion seemed impossibly exotic. Ordinary things, rusted trucks and barking dogs, struck me as utterly surreal. It was proof that there was still a real world out there, just as it was proof that I was no longer in it.

The van slowed down and I saw a wooden structure up ahead, set back a little from the main road. It was small but recently painted, with a telltale cross on the roof.

"I'm home," Shelby said, only half joking, as a serene look came across her face.

Though a collection of old sedans filled the tiny parking lot, there were zero signs of life outside the building. I glanced at the clock. We weren't late. Everyone else must have been early.

"Holy shit." Levi opened the door and hopped out. "Can you believe we're actually going to church?"

"Language," Shelby said.

This building was much smaller than the one back home. In fact, the whole thing probably could have fit inside the entryway of First Presbyterian. My old church had extremely high ceilings and a balcony like an opera house. The floors were red velvet, and there were rows and rows of pews, with huge stained-glass windows on either side. There were three sections of pipe organs and a huge choir that always looked perfectly put together.

This church was small and homey, a neighborhood congregation where everyone knew each other and had for years. It seemed like the type of place where not showing up one week meant getting half a dozen phone calls to make sure you were okay.

The biggest difference of all? People actually seemed happy to be there.

"I want you to hug your neighbor," the pastor said. "Shake hands if you've never met. And when you're done, well, hug your other neighbor!"

The congregation laughed. We stuck out like sore thumbs, but no one seemed to mind.

"I see we have new folks here today," he said. "Welcome. We hope you enjoy the service today and that y'all become part of our church family."

He was talking about us, of course, but it took a moment to realize that. It had been so long since an authority figure was actually *nice*, and the members were all so welcoming. They smiled and shook our hands. They didn't treat us like freaks or lab rats. They must have known who we were, of course. Everyone was aware of Carlbrook's reputation. Regardless of how crazy they'd heard we were, they welcomed us with open arms.

"It's a beautiful Sunday to be in the house of God!"

You know what? It really is.

"It's a beautiful day to give thanks to the Lord," the pastor said. "That is why we're here, after all."

He could have said anything at all and it would have been the best damn sermon I'd ever heard. I was so used to Alan preaching about shiny marbles and pendulums before whipping around and calling us all sluts that this was a breath of fresh air. On top of that, his pants weren't tight and he didn't offer anyone a massage.

"Do we get wine?" Levi asked.

"It's called communion," Shelby said. "And it's only a sip. Haven't you ever been to church?"

"I'm Jewish."

Shelby took the church part of things seriously and I had to respect that. But for the rest of us, it was all about freedom. We sang all the hymns with the choir, and after the service they shared homemade cookies and Rice Krispies treats.

Thank you, God. And thank you, Charlotte.

That week was a normal mix of school and group and bullshit appointments. It was so much easier to get through it knowing that when the weekend came there would be an escape. I laughed, thinking what my mother would say to see me this excited about church, and I even told her about it during our next scheduled phone call. It was a relief to have something I could actually talk to them about once we'd gotten past the weather and how my soccer team was doing without me.

When Sunday arrived, we were greeted like family.

"Welcome back. We're so happy to see you!"

It was like we belonged there. They'd even saved us the same pew we took last time.

"Hallelujah," the pastor said. "Everybody say Hallelujah!"

"Hallelujah!"

I yelled it loudly along with everyone else.

"You know it's my favorite time of the week when I get y'all here in God's house. This congregation is my family, and I can thank God for that. So thank you all for being my family."

When Alan talked about family it sounded like bullshit, and he must have realized that we had found a better version of what he was preaching somewhere else. Because after only a few weeks, something went horribly wrong.

The list wasn't posted. Because the church trip was canceled.

"Maybe in the future," they said. "There just aren't enough hands right now."

Chapter 33

A LITTLE MORE than a year after the night I was stolen from my bed, it finally came time for me to go home for a three-day visit. I had only one workshop left, and my peer group and I were supposed to be reacclimating ourselves to the real world.

Unfortunately, my home as I knew it didn't actually exist anymore. My parents had moved to a brand-new house in a brand-new city, about an hour away from my old town. Of course it wasn't personal—my dad had gotten a new job—but for some reason it still stung.

Maybe it's easier this way. Now they don't have to think of the daughter they sent away every time they see the last bedroom door on the right.

A few days before I was scheduled to leave, Monica called me in for an appointment.

"I just want to touch base with you before you go home. How are you feeling about it?"

"Good," I said. "Excited."

"And what about the move? You're touring your new high school, I hear."

"What?" This was news to me. "No, I'm not. I can't go to a *third* high school. Especially for one semester."

"I understand how you feel, Elizabeth."

"Then why do I have to go? I'm only one credit short, anyway. Can't I just get that here and graduate high school early?"

"I've spoken to your parents about this. You've just turned seventeen. That's too young to be out of school. Especially considering you'll be making a huge adjustment to life outside of Carlbrook."

"Well, then can't I just go back to my old school?"

"You can bring it up with your parents when you get home."

I tried not to let what Monica said get to me. I got a rush of nervous energy when I started packing, though I don't know why I even bothered. I wasn't going to wear my J.Crew bullshit if I didn't have to. I planned on spending my entire home visit in too-tight jeans and sweat-pants, going to bed whenever I felt like it. Technically, we were supposed to follow the Carlbrook rules on home visits, but there was just no way that was going to happen.

On the morning of my flight, I was too excited to eat breakfast. I just stared at my food until the vans arrived to take us to the airport. It was strange to look across the room at my classmates and wonder if I'd see all of them again in three days. Maybe someone would pull a Luke and disappear.

Are any of us brave enough to run away?

The problem with running away wasn't just that you were likely to be tracked down and sent back to the woods while the powers that be decided how best to deal with you. They also told us that all of our credits would be withheld. While I hated Carlbrook more than anything in the world, I didn't know if I could stomach being a high school dropout. I honestly wasn't sure which fate was worse, but part of me felt like I needed to find out.

I and my vanful of kids said our good-byes at the airport and went our separate ways. I went through security and found my gate, and then I just stood there. It was the first time in a year that no one knew exactly where I was and exactly what I was doing. I didn't even know how to comprehend that kind of freedom. At the same time, I couldn't bring myself to trust it.

I thought about making a run for it. Maybe I could convince the gate agent to let me sneak onto another flight. I spotted a pay phone and walked toward it instinctually. But I froze midstep before I even got there. Who would I even call? I was still in Virginia. I was still so close to Carlbrook, and I could feel the school looming over me.

How could I know for sure that no one had followed me? They probably had spies stationed throughout the airport. At the very least there could be a Pony lurking around the corner, ready to report on my every move. I knew I was being totally paranoid. But at the same time, I was convinced my fears were completely reasonable. Carlbrook had worked its black magic inside my head.

When it was time to board, I practically ran onto the plane. Maybe I just needed to get out of Virginia, to put some miles between myself and that school. If I could just clear my head of all the Carlbrook static, I'd understand what I needed to do next.

The plane pulled away from the gate and soon tilted skyward. As soon as we reached cruising altitude, I exhaled all the air from my lungs. I could breathe for the first time in a year, a big breath. I was free, free for the next two hours or however long it took to get home.

I had a layover in Charlotte—maybe I could just run away there. That would buy me some time; it would take a minute for my family or the school to get there. The devil won again, though, and I boarded the next flight as well.

I'll run away on the way back. I'm just getting myself ready.

The new house was actually quite beautiful, with marble floors and classic architecture. There was a hallway long enough that my dad could have target practice with his bow and arrow. There wasn't one thing about that house I could complain about, and under different circumstances I probably would have loved it.

However, my current circumstances made it hard to be anything but pissed off. I found my new bedroom, and it was like a Bizarro World version of the last one. The color scheme was similar but not exactly the same; the curtains were just a little bit off. While my bed was my actual bed—the one I'd hidden weed under, the place where I'd been lying when I said *fuck it* to life—it didn't feel like it still belonged to me at all.

I felt like I was borrowing a room from a ghost. It certainly wasn't a bedroom with any life to it at all. There was absolutely nothing on the walls. No posters, no trophies. No hopes or dreams. Even though my bed was still comfortable, it was even harder to get to sleep than usual.

Instead of snoozing, my mind went straight to building a case for myself. I played out the argument from all angles, looking for the words that would convince my parents to keep me in South Carolina. Never mind that this had never worked before—that every previous attempt to have this conversation had ended in disaster. It was like a weird form of amnesia took over every time I was in a position to speak to my parents. As long as I still had the capacity for hope, I would use it to try to save myself from Carlbrook.

Mom, Dad. I love you and I am so sorry. Please don't make me go back there. I promise you I've changed. Please just let me finish high school back home. I'll do anything you ask of me, literally anything. Just tell me what I need to do and I promise I'll be perfect.

I think I really meant it too. I knew how high the stakes were now. I could keep my mouth shut and my anger in check as long as it meant I'd never have to go back to Carlbrook.

"Good morning," I said, walking into the kitchen. "Hey, Emily."

I opened on a cheerful note. It was my first family breakfast. My mom had made my beloved chocolate chip pancakes for me and my sister. I smiled at her broadly.

"Hey, Mom?" I said. "There's something I want to ask you about."

"Yes?"

"Well. I want to stay. At home."

"Elizabeth . . ."

"No, I mean I want to stay because I think it's the best thing for everyone. Can't you see how much I've changed?"

"Honey." My mom sighed. "I can't have this conversation again. You know you have to go back."

Suddenly, the conversation was at a ten.

"You don't know what it's like," I said. "That place is fucking hell. Seriously, it's the worst place in the entire world. I'd rather die than go back there. You'd never send Emily to a school like that."

"Elizabeth, come on."

"Why won't you listen to me? I said I fucking hate it there. What's wrong with you that you don't even care if your own daughter is in HELL?"

I stormed out of the kitchen, leaving my pancakes untouched. I went straight to my room that didn't feel like my room and slammed the door. It had been so long since I'd had a door to slam that I went ahead and did it again. I didn't care that I was only making things more tense. My family would be rid of me soon enough.

When it came time to tour the new high school, I trailed behind my parents without saying a single word. I spent the rest of the day shut away inside my Bizarro bedroom, ignoring everyone. When I finally got hungry enough to venture out for snacks, I made sure the hallway was empty. Just like in our old house, the walls were covered with photos. Most of them were familiar, old childhood pictures, but there were a few I'd never seen before. It was strange to see my brother and sister on the wall, continuing on with their lives as though I didn't exist, and I couldn't help but resent them both.

I grabbed the phone as I headed back to my room. Suddenly, I wanted to break as many Carlbrook rules as I could. Since my dad was at work and my mom was trying to keep some semblance of peace in the house, it seemed unlikely that either of them would report me. I locked the door and stared at the phone in my hand. There was only one number I even thought to dial.

The phone rang twice.

"Hello?"

"Hi, Nick."

"…Elizabeth?"

"Yep. It's me."

Nick nearly had a heart attack. He hadn't heard my voice in a year. One day I was there and the next day I simply vanished.

"I don't even know what to say. Where are you? Where have you *been*?"

"I'm home. Well, not home exactly. My family moved, but I'm here for a few days."

"Where have you *been*?" he repeated.

I explained the whole thing to Nick. The woods, the escorts, Carlbrook.

"That's crazy," he repeated.

"Where did everyone think I'd gone this whole time?"

"I don't know. Some people thought you got pregnant and moved away to have the baby. People asked if it was mine. At some point I heard you were in Europe with your grandparents."

Nick stayed on the phone with me for hours. It was great just to hear his voice, and it reminded me why I liked him so much. Eventually, he had to get off the phone and my heart sank.

"I honestly didn't think I'd ever hear from you again," he said.

I didn't run away during my home visit, but I did land one success. After multiple heated conversations, I managed to convince my parents to at least consider letting me return to my old school. My idea was that I could live with Jenna. I hadn't actually consulted her about this plan, much less run it by her parents, but I leaned into wishful thinking. My own parents didn't reject the idea outright, which gave me hope that Monica wouldn't either.

The closer I got to the end of my trip, the more dread I felt collecting in my stomach. Despite everything, I was still holding out for a last-minute death row pardon. Unfortunately, when my time was up, my mom was there waiting to drive me to the airport. Once again, I had a quick layover in Charlotte. It was hardly enough time to get from one gate to the other and I knew I had to hurry. But the moment I got off the plane, every cell in my body screamed out for me to run the other way.

I knew it wasn't rational. But the thought of going back to Carlbrook was just too horrible to bear. I made a split-second decision that I wasn't going to return to Halifax. Not then, not ever.

Not for another five minutes.

I really did intend to run away. But there was nowhere for me to go. No matter what I did, I was certain I'd be caught in a matter of hours. Then it would be back to the woods for me. Another two months of hiking, then an extra six months tacked on to my Carlbrook sentence. It wasn't worth the risk and I knew it.

I made it to my gate just in time and then it was back to Carlbrook for the old spin, squat, and cough. Just like I had never left.

Chapter 34

Graduation was getting closer, and it was almost like the school was trying to cover its bases before sending us out into the world. One day there was a new list hanging outside the med bay. It was a drug-and-alcohol program for upper-school students. A last-ditch attempt to pretend that they'd been offering specialized treatment all along.

When the list for the group went up, I looked at it more out of curiosity than anything. It wasn't like I had any reason to expect that I'd be called in for this group. There were eight names in total. I read through the first six without noticing anything unusual.

Charlotte

Brittany

Levi

Bryan

Conrad

Lina

The seventh name on the list was my own. Everyone else had experience with serious drugs, but I was the kid who'd smoked pot a few times and drank on weekends. Maybe Carlbrook had progressed beyond simply reading my mind, though, and could actually see into my future.

The truth was, I found the drug-related disclosures to be sort of glamorous. It was always a welcome moment when the circle reached one of the druggy kids. A big part of that was simply knowing it meant a break from confessions involving pets and peanut butter, but I also found something exciting about those stories.

"So I was at a club on the Lower East Side doing coke with my cousin's friends..."

"That night I was on so much Molly I couldn't feel my face..."

"Yeah, I've done heroin. Dealt it too."

"And that's how I got kicked out of my second boarding school..."

In some ways I wasn't all that different from them. If I'd been from a big city and not my conservative Southern town, I have no doubt that my teenage experimentation would have taken a different form. After all, hadn't I gravitated directly toward those city kids? Everyone on that list was my close friend, and most of them made no attempt to conceal the fact that they were excited to return to their old lives. They felt the call of those sparkling nights and glamorous powders, and I was beginning to feel it too.

The drug group was pretty informal. We met on the couch just outside the girls' bathroom, and there was no real lesson plan or agenda. An adviser named Holly led the session. I had never really interacted with her except in the occasional group.

"So, you guys only have about two months left," she said. "Who still thinks about drinking and doing drugs?"

No one answered. We were all afraid that any admission would be used against us. We were so close to the finish line—what if they were looking for a reason to hold us back?

"I understand your hesitation," Holly said. "But it's totally normal to have those urges. Temptation is everywhere. And if you want to resist that temptation, the first step is to be honest with yourself."

"I still think about it sometimes," Charlotte said.

She got it immediately. The right answer was to admit it; otherwise, we'd only be accused of being in denial.

"Yeah," Conrad said, "I definitely have those old urges."

"I want to go over a few tools with you now," Holly said. "If you've got an action plan in place, it will be much easier to resist that temptation when it appears."

She handed out notebooks and pens.

"First, look around this group and pick a few people to check in with daily. I want you to hold one another accountable and use your workshop tools. That's how you're going to succeed out there."

Yeah, right. Like I'm going to make honor lists when I get out of here.

"Now I want you to close your eyes," Holly said. "Imagine your life three months from now. Then six months from now. Then go a year into the future."

I saw my old school, flashes of people like Jenna and Nick. I could form a hazy picture of the next six months. But after that my mind was a total blank.

"Can you imagine a life for yourself where you don't go back to those old, destructive ways?"

"I'd like to try," Brittany said.

"Trying is good," Holly said. "But it might not be enough. I want you to remember your workshop tools. Remember your truth from Integritas and your keys from Teneo. Take them with you wherever you go."

I had a feeling that would not be happening.

"Okay, turn to a fresh page. I want you each to list at least five potential triggers."

Holly watched us as we wrote in our notebooks.

"I want you to come out of here with a clear sense of who and what to avoid," she said.

I looked down at my list. It was full of lies. I couldn't write what I wanted to, the thing I already suspected would prove to be true.

My trigger is Carlbrook.

The group never met again. Our drug-and-alcohol program took up all of one afternoon. Clearly, they never cared much about our action plans in the first place.

Chapter 35

I HAD JUST one workshop left: Veneratio. Since it was our last, they really made the most of it. Veneratio was five days long. Five days of little to no sleep after long hours spent crying. Five days of cold cuts. Five days of checking in with my assigned buddy, Lindy, who had already started asking me if I was okay.

I actually was doing just fine. In fact, I was a little excited. Five days was nothing as long as it meant I'd never have to go through another therapeutic workshop ever again.

The night before Veneratio, I slept like a baby all night long.

> You are what you do, not what you say you do.
>
> —attributed to Carl Jung;
> used as a workshop tool in Integritas

Veneratio turned out to be something of a workshop retrospective. The first few days were spent recapping them all, Integritas through Teneo. Each one had its highlight reel. For Integritas, I was reminded of my lie, "worthless abuser," as if I'd ever forget. Next up was Amicitia, signaled by the Doors' "Break on Through (To the Other Side)." We needed to learn once again that running toward a circle of our peers at full speed was the definition of being a "good friend." Since we were already on our feet, why not jump straight into Animus's Fight Night?

Elizabeth "Fights the Good Fight" Gilpin strikes again, and this time she's going for the knockout. Will she take a win for Team Life? Or will it be a Team Death victory once again?

We were still fighting to stay alive and all, but now we had our tools for success. Because of Carlbrook, there was a chance we'd go on to lead long and prosperous lives. That meant writing a new, more positive obituary as well.

Elizabeth Gilpin died of old age after a fulfilling life. There was a point when she didn't think she was going to make it. But she found hope and got her spot on the lifeboat. She will be remembered as a positive, strong, and trusting woman.

I thinks; Me feels.

—used as a workshop tool in Teneo

Teneo's dreaded "I vs. Me" started off day two. We started running in place while Alan yelled insults as he paced across the room. I wasn't going to let the exercise get to me this time. Both Chelsea and I had the good sense not to be the last two standing.

If it looks like a duck, swims like a duck, and quacks like a duck, then it probably is a duck.

—used as a workshop tool in Integritas

The next exercise involved bringing in alumni, returned from the real world to tell us all about their awesome lives. I recognized some of them from my pre-Integ days and some I'd never seen before.

"These guys right here," Alan said, "are what it's all about. They're living proof of what can happen if you work hard and use your tools."

"Hi, I'm Evelyn."

The girl had dirty blond hair and kept a smile plastered to her face.

"I graduated in May of 2003 and now I go to college in Boston. When I first left here it was hard to adapt. I really missed my Carlbrook family. I relied on them a lot after graduating. I had weekly calls with my adviser and that really helped. I kept my workshop tools in mind whenever I wanted to fall back into old patterns. That was huge, I have to say, and so was keeping in touch with Alan."

Keeping in touch with Alan? I'm not talking to any of these psychopaths ever again and I'm not calling my peers so we can talk about our workshop tools. And you can bet I'm sure as hell not coming back to tell everyone how great Carlbrook was.

What a piece of work is man!

—*Hamlet*, Act II, Scene 2;
used as a workshop tool in Animus

Loud music played again as we approached the workshop room on the third day. The lights inside were low. On the floor was a sea of fake drugs, alcohol, porn, and a smattering of other illicit items. A TV was set up at the front of the room. It was like we had entered a legitimate crack house. Finally, after all those months of calling us whores and drug addicts, we were in our natural habitat.

"Come inside, everyone," Alan said. "Spread out and take a seat on your knees. I want you to sit as open as possible. Arms out and palms up. Open your bodies and your hearts so you can feel this to the fullest extent."

Even by Carlbrook standards, what happened next was insane. The TV came on and it was cued right up to the ten-minute rape montage from *Requiem for a Dream*. It was brutal and horrific. Ten minutes of watching a degraded and debased Jennifer Connelly fuck for drugs. I felt my cold cuts start to come back up.

"I want you all to watch this carefully," Alan said. "This is where your life is headed if you stay on the path you've been heading down."

What the fuck is wrong with you? You're an actual psychopath, I'm sure of it now.

"You see these items?" Alan pointed to the fake drugs and empty bottles. "Now you get to choose. You can either pick up this stuff and go back to your old life or you can choose to move on with all your workshop tools at your disposal."

I looked more closely. There were pills and fake powders. Bottles of booze. Razor blades and knives.

"What's it going to be?" Alan said.

We all sat there, stunned.

"Come on, Conrad. You know you want those pills."

I watched as Conrad made the decision to grab the fake pills.

"Come on, Charlotte. Pick up that tiny leather skirt. Grab that needle."

She shook her head.

"Go ahead, Elizabeth," Alan said. "Pick up that booze that you drink at home. Pick up that coke. We know the coke is what you want."

As usual, the exercise didn't end until everyone was sobbing, but it was a different feeling that filled the room this time. It was disgust and despair at a level we'd never quite expressed before.

"From this moment on," Alan said, "the people in this room will be your family and you must hold each other accountable. Use your tools. Remember what you learned here and don't go back to this dark and ugly place."

I was never even there in the first place.

> The deeper that sorrow carves into your being, the more joy
> you can contain.
>
> —Khalil Gibran, *The Prophet*;
> used as a workshop tool in Integritas

The fourth day was a blur of ridiculous, symbolic exercises. For the "baggage hike," as it was termed, we were each given a large cement block and led in an aimless circle. My arms hurt within seconds, which made sense as I was literally *carrying around a block of cement*. If it was meant to be a metaphor, it wasn't working the way Alan intended.

"I want you all to feel how heavy these bricks feel," he said. "Heavy, right? That's a lot of extra weight you don't want to carry around with you. When you hold on to past baggage—to shame or fear or regret—you're really carrying weights just like these."

Okay, fine. I'll put my baggage down now.

"Do you like carrying around this much weight?"

We groaned.

"I can't hear you," he said. "Do you like carrying this load around?"

"No!"

A few people dropped their blocks.

"Pick those back up. The exercise isn't over yet. You're gonna hold your own baggage for the rest of your life. So I want you to really feel all of that weight now."

To be or not to be: that is the question.

—*Hamlet*, Act III, Scene 1;

used as a workshop tool in Teneo

Another metaphor, this time with balloons. Which was better than blocks, but this one just made me want to laugh.

"This balloon is your vice," Alan said. "Think long and hard...what is that vice? Is it coke? Is it sex? Crack, cutting, video games. I don't care what it is, just make it ugly."

My face must have betrayed my thoughts about the exercise.

"Elizabeth, what are you making this balloon?"

Can I make it a balloon?

"It's smoking pot and drinking," I said.

"Good. Close your eyes. Imagine your vice, really see it. And let it go."

Today is the first day of the rest of your life.

—Charles E. Dederich, Synanon founder;
used as a workshop tool in Animus

On the final day of Veneratio, the metaphor went biblical.

We walked in to see a cornucopia of food set up on the floor, along with a tablecloth and candles. I felt like this was a scene taken from the Last Supper. There was an assortment of fruit including pineapples and grapes, along with cheeses and crackers Nelly had been sneaking us for days, which none of us realized were actually for Veneratio.

"Congratulations, peer class Pi," Alan said. "You did it. This is your Last Supper. A feast for us to share as a family while we think about gratitude.

"Levi, what are you grateful for?"

"I'm grateful my buddy looked out for me," Levi said. "Thank you, man."

We went around the circle.

"I'm grateful to have this family I can turn to in the real world."

"I'm grateful to be done with workshops."

"I'm also grateful my friends got me through this."

I'm grateful this fucking place didn't kill me.

Chapter 36

GRADUATION WAS ONLY a day away and our families were in town for the ceremony. We had one last ridiculous assignment: to pick a friend and switch families for the day. Charlotte and I swapped—she sat down with my family while I sat with hers. I mostly just chatted with her mom about Switzerland. We were supposed to be discussing my "transition plan," but that wasn't nearly as exciting as hearing about all the bungee jumping I'd get to do if I visited them next summer.

That night, Charlotte and I hung out in her family's hotel room while our parents were off meeting with our advisers. We sat with her brother Andrew and watched him drink whiskey. As he got drunker and drunker, he told us about how much fun his own boarding school had been. Meanwhile, Charlotte and I were paranoid that if we somehow got caught just *watching* Andrew, we wouldn't get to graduate.

We had to head back to the mods soon anyway. The Carlbrook van picked us up for one last night in the double-wide. Our last night without doors, our last round of bed checks, and like clockwork, the Securitas arrived.

She clicked her pen. "Lights out, girls. You have a big day tomorrow."

In the morning I got ready in my white dress. It was a floor-length gown from the bridal section of—what else?—J.Crew. I did my hair and swiped on a little bit of makeup. We walked to the dining hall, which was decked out for Christmas. I spotted my parents, and they were all smiles. They seemed proud of me, ready to believe that Carlbrook had worked. If only they knew the truth—of what I'd gone through and what was still to come.

"It's a beautiful day, and this is such a beautiful group of people," Alan said from the front of the room. "Look at these young men and women. It's been a long, hard road for them all. For some, harder than others. You know who you are." He winked.

Is that supposed to be a joke?

"We're so proud of you. You've made it through this rigorous program and are set up for success. You can now go out and achieve wonderful things. You finished this as a family and it's as a family you'll return to the world. I urge you all to really take this moment in."

He paused for effect.

"Okay, everyone," Alan said, "I want us all to put our arms around one another. Let's all sing the Carlbrook anthem."

Naturally, I hated the Carlbrook anthem. I mumbled quietly instead of singing. When we got to the last verse, I looked at Charlotte and we both started laughing.

Reach high for goals to guide us on our way.
That we might grow in courage day by day.
Keep firm our dreams to always be our best
So we may live in strength and happiness.

With that, it was time to graduate. Alan called out names, and we stood up to get our certificates. Most kids were actually graduating high school, which meant they were getting real diplomas. But since I still had a semester to finish back at home, I would just get a piece of paper saying I'd completed Carlbrook.

Is that even an accomplishment?

I'd gotten through something that had often felt impossible, but it wasn't like I was proud or anything. There was no room for that when every cell in my body was so full of relief. I had survived. I'd stayed as true to myself as I possibly could, and I hadn't let the school kill me.

Alan called out names. I clapped along with everyone else.

Charlotte. Maya. Brittany. Levi.

Elizabeth.

I walked up to the podium to receive my certificate. Alan handed it to me and grasped my hand. He looked into my eyes and I just wanted to run. All that relief curdled right back into fear. I didn't want to celebrate; I wanted to get the fuck out of there before something went wrong and I had to sit in his lap again. I needed to leave as soon as possible just to know I could. To prove that I wasn't trapped inside the snow globe forever.

As soon as Alan was done, I started to say my good-byes. I hugged Brittany and Charlotte, knowing it was just a temporary farewell. I said good-bye to Rose, hoping it was forever. Maya had tears in her eyes as we hugged and said we'd see each other soon. Some of the younger students were crying, too, but it wasn't just because they were going to miss us. Those were hopeless tears, and I knew the feeling all too well. It was hard to watch kids walk away from Carlbrook knowing you would have to stay. I hugged Lina extra tight, wishing I could take her with me.

"I'm really going to miss you," I said. "You can do this, okay?"

Tears ran down her cheeks as she watched us all walk away. I hustled my parents off, ready to get the hell out of Virginia. Monica stopped us at the door, going on about how proud she was. I nodded but hardly even registered the words. I needed to be inside my parents' car immediately. I was just about to slam the door shut when I heard my name.

"Elizabeth. Don't tell me you're going to leave without a good-bye."

It was Nelly. I jumped out and gave her a hug. I couldn't believe it, but even I had tears in my eyes.

"I'm so proud of you," she said.

"Thank you, Nelly. For everything."

I got back inside. My dad turned on the engine and I held my breath as the manicured grounds and the white picket fence receded from view. I didn't want to exhale until Carlbrook was out of sight completely, until I could finally fill my lungs with untainted air. What was a few extra seconds when I had been holding my breath for what felt like an eternity?

It's over. I survived. I'll never have to see my nightmare again.

We made our way through the tiny town. We passed the church where I'd spent those few happy Sundays and the hotel Charlotte and I had been in the previous night. My mother turned to me from the front seat, smiling, and handed me a small gift-wrapped box. Inside was a beautiful gold charm bracelet. It was just like the one my mom had, that I'd always admired. But instead of a charm for each of her children and one for my parents' wedding date, my bracelet was Carlbrook themed. There were six charms in all: five inscribed with the names of the workshops and one for the date of my graduation.

I didn't know what to do with it. I knew it was a well-intentioned gift, but that bracelet was truly the last thing on earth I wanted. It showed me just how deeply the school had conned them. My parents had given me a reminder of my prison set in lovely, shiny gold. It made me feel like they would never understand the truth even if I was willing to talk about it. Carlbrook had worked its dark magic on them, and they still believed the beautiful facade was all there was.

Soon enough, I was "home." We arrived at the big, unfamiliar house, where my brother and sister were waiting. It was decorated for Christmas, which only made the house look more perfect and only made me feel more alienated.

At least I knew I wouldn't have to stay there very long. I would be with my family for the holidays and then I'd return to my old school to finish the year, but even that proved to be too much time. I felt like a stranger in my own home, distanced from the family that had cast me out. I wasn't even sure what that word, *family*, meant anymore.

I returned from Carlbrook with even more anger than I had before. But I had even less sense of how to handle it. My tool kit was full of confrontational methods and strange sayings, and none of it was applicable to the real world at all. After a week of small fights and low, simmering anger, I finally exploded.

I was in the car with my parents and sister. My mother driving while I had the passenger seat. Emily shared the back with my dad. Since my sister was now twelve and no longer needed to be tiptoed around, my parents and I started fighting almost immediately—arguing about nothing and everything just as we'd done all week. When my voice raised to match my father's, Emily had finally heard enough.

"Elizabeth, shut up," she said. "I know you're a drug addict and an alcoholic. That's why Mom and Dad sent you away."

Something inside me just snapped. I couldn't believe that was the line my parents had fed her. I couldn't believe that was still the way my family saw me. To have gone through all of that—from sleeping outside in the rain to the humiliation of disclosure circles and the isolation of programs—just to return to the same bullshit?

"You don't know what the fuck you're talking about," I said.

I looked at my sister. She was silent so I picked up a cup of milk from the middle console and hurled it right at her. Emily screamed. She was covered in milk, dripping across the whole backseat, but I wasn't done.

"I'm not even a part of this family anymore, am I?" I said. "So why are we pretending? You hate me just as much as I hate you all."

"Elizabeth, we don't—" my mother started.

"Just take me to a hotel." I turned to face my mom. "I SAID, TAKE ME TO A FUCKING HOTEL."

If this had been a group, I would have been praised for screaming. The tears that accompanied my outburst would have been encouraged. At Carlbrook, being emotional meant being safe. In the car with my family, it just felt like confirmation of what I was convinced they truly believed: *There's something wrong with Elizabeth.*

There was no way to get them to see just how badly that place had scarred me. I don't think I even fully understood at the time. All I knew was anger and a deep, searing pain that knew no other form of expression than pure rage.

"I mean it," I said. "Drop me off somewhere. That's what you always do with me anyway."

They did end up taking me to a hotel, but I had no money for a room and my parents weren't about to get me one. I sat in the car crying for a while. Finally, I relented and told them to drive me home.

Somehow, I got through the next few days until it was time for my mom to drive me to Jenna's. The fact that my parents were sending me right back to the same friends in the same town that had supposedly been such a bad influence on me was never mentioned. I think that deep down, they probably felt like they'd punished me enough.

When I got to Jenna's, I was determined to make things seem as normal as possible—just as though I'd never left. It was the weekend and there was a party that night. I had my first drink in almost two years, which led to another. At some point I was handed a joint and didn't turn it down. The pot and booze made it easier to pretend that everything was just as it had always been. I was the same person I'd always been and nothing had to feel any different than before.

Part of that meant rekindling my pseudorelationship with Nick. I spotted him lying on the couch and drinking a beer and headed straight over. I hadn't told him I was coming to the party because I wanted it to be a surprise—and the look on his face made me light up.

He was happy to see me and I was happy to see him. I walked over and our eyes locked. Nick was in college now and he had his own house. He said that I seemed different, too, but he couldn't quite figure out how.

"I'm just older, Nick. You haven't seen me since I was fifteen. Remember?"

We flirted all night. When it was time to leave, I was drunk and smiling as I got into Jenna's car. We stopped at an intersection and I looked down at my cell phone. I saw a voice mail from a number I didn't recognize.

"Hi, Elizabeth. It's Monica. I just wanted to check in and see how you're doing. Are you settling in okay? Call me when you get this, please."

Not a fucking chance.

"Okay. Talk soon."

I hit Delete. Then I went ahead and blocked the number.

Monica no longer had any power over me. She couldn't discipline me or make me talk when I didn't want to. She couldn't force me to rat someone else out or write a list of reasons why I was a terrible person. None of them could, not ever again.

My mistake was assuming that made me free.

Chapter 37

I DIDN'T LIVE at Carlbrook anymore, that was true; but I lived *with* it every day. It had become a part of my DNA. As glad as I was to be back home, things just weren't the same. The town hadn't changed, but I certainly had. I often had trouble relating to my old friends because I'd gotten used to being in conflict with my peers about everything and anything. It turns out regular people *don't* resolve problems by writing "useless slut" on a name tag and sticking it on their friend's shirt.

For the next few years I found myself wanting to be in the company of my Carlbrook friends. Maybe we were trauma-bonded, or maybe it was just nice to have people around who *understood*. I saw them as often as I could, especially Charlotte. We were finally able to have a normal friendship without standards and request groups and bans.

Exactly a year after I got out, I took a trip to New York. Charlotte came, too, and we stayed at an apartment belonging to a member of her family. Some cousin or an aunt, I don't think I ever knew, but it was ours for the week. It was New Year's Eve, and we decided to have a little party with Carlbrook kids.

Brittany lived in the city and Levi was in town for the holidays. A few other kids came too. We had been drinking for hours when Brittany called her dealer. The next thing I knew I was leaning over a tray of white powder like an Animus statue.

It took all of a year for me to prove Carlbrook right. Because that first line of coke hit me like a revelation. I felt more awake, more alive, than I had in years. It was the feeling I used to get when I scored a goal. When I ran through graveyards late at night. Suddenly, it was like I still had a future. Like I could be everything I ever wanted to be, after all.

I'm a fighter pilot. I'm Mia Hamm. And I'm going to win a gold medal.

Hang on a second.

I smiled and did another line. I felt like *me* again for the first time since I'd left Carlbrook. It was an even better version of me and I knew I could stay that way forever. Just as long as I did another line, and one more after that.

When everyone else left, Charlotte and I met up with her friends from her old boarding school. And they had twice as much coke. The two of us went all night, talking about everything and nothing. We didn't make any sense and yet everything was profound.

When we finally made it back to the apartment, it wasn't because we were ready to stop. It was because the drugs were gone. All we had was a bottle of red wine that we immediately spilled all over the white couch.

"Fuck it," Charlotte said. "We'll clean it later."

"Yeah, I'm too tired to do anything right now," I said. "Except throw up."

I was starting to get sick and pretty soon, I felt about as bad as I'd ever felt in my life. I sat up on the bathroom floor for hours, feeling like I was going to throw up and wishing I were dead.

"Hey, Charlotte," I said, my voice rough and raspy. "Do you think we need to go to rehab? Am I a drug addict?"

"You've done coke *once*. You're not a drug addict."

"I want to kill myself. What do I do?"

"I want to kill myself too," Charlotte said.

"I think I need to go back to Carlbrook."

"You don't need to go back to Carlbrook, Elizabeth."

"I think I do, though," I said. "I think they were right about me the whole time."

I really meant it too. I was so confused. I was sick and shaking, trying to remember the clarity I'd had just a little while ago. That sense of being me again.

"You hate that place," Charlotte said. "You know it's a fucking prison."

"Yeah. You're right."

It was true, of course. It was a prison and I didn't really want to be back there. I did want something else in that moment, though. I wanted to know who I was.

Did Carlbrook turn me into someone I was never meant to be? A person who tried cocaine and then didn't stop for two days? Who was sick and depleted but already thinking about how to get drugs again? Or could Alan and Monica always see me better than I was able to see myself?

I was so disoriented, I had no idea if I was fulfilling a prophecy or acting out. Or if I was just being a teenager. I kept feeling the pull of Carlbrook even though I wanted to be free of it. I felt angry and confused, but I didn't know how to talk about any of it. Not even with Charlotte.

So I did the only thing I could think of to really try to break free. I put as much physical distance as I could between myself and Halifax, Virginia.

Chapter 38

*Few Details in Bloody Miami Murder: Student Trevor Malone Found
Dead in a Pool of Blood in His Own Home*
  Mother Grieves as Police Seek Clues in University of Miami Slaying
  *Twenty-One-Year-Old UM Student Brutally Murdered: No Updates
on Murder Case*
  Stabbed UM Student's Killer on the Run Ten Years Later

When I was a kid, I promised myself that one day I'd move back to
California. I wanted to live in Los Angeles, by the beach and the silver
screen. It was one of those things I'd talk about at soccer practice, almost
as if it were a done deal.

"I'm going back the first chance I get."

It wasn't a childhood dream like flying planes or playing in the Olympics, exactly. It was more like something I said when I realized the truth
about those childhood fantasies. That they were, in fact, just fantasies.
Maybe I wasn't Mia Hamm or fighter pilot material, but no one could
stop me from moving to Los Angeles.

I did it too. In the summer of 2007, I drove with a friend from
Carlbrook out to LA. We road-tripped from Charleston to Orange

County, where she had family. The GPS stopped working in Mississippi, and the car broke down the minute we parked on the West Coast. But that hardly mattered because we'd made it (almost) all the way to LA.

I heard through the grapevine that Luke and Bryan had moved to California the previous year. I had barely spoken to Luke at all since the fateful day when he left for his home visit and never came back, but I still thought about him sometimes. I called him from the side of the road, and he met us at the broken-down car.

From that moment on, we were a team. The other girl stayed only for the summer, but I was committed to sticking it out for the long haul. It wasn't like I had anywhere else to be. I was completely lost then and had only vague ideas of what I might want to do.

Should I model? Act? What about fashion school?

Before long, Luke and I were dating. When we were together trouble was never far away, and we were always together. We drank most nights and smoked a ton of pot. We took pills and more pills, whatever it took to get us numb.

Luke and I should have died several times over, but we never suffered any real consequences at all. The biggest incident was an accident on the 405. I had been out drinking with friends in LA, and at one in the morning I called him to come pick me up. I sat on the curb in my gold sequined dress and waited for him to arrive. I was so tired by the time he pulled up, or maybe just too drunk, that I didn't even bother with my seat belt. I curled up and went right to sleep.

When I woke up, Luke's car was facing the wrong direction on the freeway. Apparently another vehicle had flipped after hitting the median a few moments before. It had no lights and by the time Luke realized, it was too late. He hit the other car, another car hit us, and so on until there was an eight-car pileup.

They say if you've been drinking and your body is loose, you're actually more likely to survive a crash. Maybe that's what happened to me that night. Or maybe, once again, I had just gotten lucky.

I think I knew it this time. Because standing on the side of the road, still drunk, waiting for the tow truck, I felt compelled to call my mom.

"Hello?"

"Mom?"

"Elizabeth? Are you okay? It's five in the morning."

"We had an accident. Luke's car was totaled. But it wasn't his fault."

"I knew it," my mom said. "I felt it tonight, that something was wrong. I even had a nightmare that you'd been hurt."

It seemed for a moment that some strange force was pulling us together, but maybe my mom had nightmares about me all the time.

"What happened?" My mom's voice sounded pinched. "Are you hurt?"

"I'm fine."

I heard her exhale. "Why do you keep doing this to yourself?"

"I said it wasn't our fault!"

"Oh, Elizabeth. I just wish you could see what a dangerous path you're on."

I could tell my mom was crying and trying to hide it. I knew I should feel bad, but what I really felt was nothing. I was getting to be a skilled dissociation artist. I could turn off reality just like that. Blackouts and near-death experiences were becoming a habit, or maybe a hobby.

Somehow I still had all those cat lives and if I could have, I would have given them away. Especially when my friends started dying. Instead of engagement announcements and job updates, the Carlbrook network passed along obituaries.

I was out with Luke and Bryan one night not long after the accident, getting obliterated per usual, when all of our phones started going off at once.

"What the fuck?" Luke said. "Guys, you have to read this."

I forced my eyes to focus. Trevor, our easygoing, grinning friend, was dead.

"This can't be real," I said.

It wasn't just that he was dead. Trevor had been murdered—*fucking murdered*. Instead of an obituary, we were reading headline news.

"Jesus," Bryan said. "Stabbed seven times? In the neck?"

"Found dead in a pool of his own blood."

It was surreal, almost impossible to believe. Trevor had been such a bright presence at Carlbrook. He was the guy who got along with everyone, always looking for a way to be helpful. Like the day of my very first group, when he read the terror in my eyes and countered it with a giant grin. After that, he always made time to check in with me—and not in a bullshit, *tell me your life story* way.

He'd been there for Kyle as well—on that day and many others. He could tolerate his friend's pain without letting it consume him. The worse it got for Kyle, the more Trevor leaned in—but his smile was still there in case someone needed it. Despite being close, they always seemed so different. It made no sense that now both of them were dead.

Trevor was killed in Miami, not far from the college where he'd been finishing his senior year. But Los Angeles was his hometown. So the memorial was held not an hour from where Luke and I were living.

Luke and I arrived together and we walked into the church hand in hand. We were both so numb from shock that it felt like we were simply at a Carlbrook reunion. I saw kids I never thought I'd cross paths with again in my life—some welcome, some not. I saw a Pony and instinctively tensed up—until I realized there was nothing she could do to hurt me anymore. Even if other kids were still playing the game, I had opted out. For a moment, I actually felt okay.

Then I saw Alan and froze in place. My tormentor was standing twenty feet away, weeping in front of a dead boy's casket.

"Oh no," I said to Luke. "*He's* here."

"I know," he said. "We can leave whenever you want, okay?"

"Maybe we can just avoid him," I said.

But of course that was impossible. Alan spotted us before the words even left my mouth.

"Elizabeth! Luke!"

Alan walked over to us. The collar of his shirt was soaked with tears, and I could smell his hot, stale breath. It was the scent of déjà vu.

"Look at you two. How are you? I've missed you both, you know," he said. "Especially you, Luke. We never got to say good-bye."

Luke shuffled his feet. "Um, sorry about that."

I expected Alan to lay into him, but he just smiled. He looked around the room, sniffling. "Trevor was so beautiful."

"He was," I said.

"I'm going to miss him so much."

"Me too."

I wanted to tell Alan to shut the fuck up.

Stop crying, it's all your fault. You ruined every one of us. Even Trevor.

It was my one chance to say everything I really thought.

You're a pig. And I fucking hate you.

You ruined my life, you fucking creep. You made me feel dirty and disgusting. Like there was something wrong with me. But there's something wrong with you, Alan.

But I looked at him, standing there hunched and weeping, and I just couldn't do it. Alan seemed so weak without the force of Carlbrook behind him. He was just a pathetic old man. It suddenly made no sense that he had been able to wield so much power. How could this red-faced, blubbering man have caused us all so much harm? How was *that face* the face of my worst nightmare?

"You two really look great," he said.

Alan leaned toward me, pulling me in for that dreaded hug. My whole body went tense and I was flooded by a familiar feeling of disgust, but I wasn't frozen in fear like I used to be. Outside Carlbrook, Alan's hug was just a hug. I wasn't his prisoner anymore. I pulled back from his embrace, knowing there wasn't a damn thing he could do about it.

I hardly remember talking to anyone else that afternoon, or the things that were said about Trevor, stories and funny anecdotes. When the service was over, Luke and I walked out like we'd come in, holding hands and dazed.

I felt a surge of rage the moment we drove away. It confused me. On the one hand, I was angry that Alan had been there at all. I'd put more than two thousand miles between myself and Carlbrook and still, Carlbrook found a way to reach me in California. I was also mad at myself, though. I felt like I'd let Trevor down by failing to confront Alan. It didn't matter how pathetic he appeared, he was still the man who had hurt so many people, so many times.

"I hate him," I said.

"I know." Luke was shaking his head. "I hate them all."

For the rest of the drive, we talked about Carlbrook in a way we never had before. It had taken this long just to get past the subconscious fear of ending up on an honor list or being called out in group. It was the first time I opened up about how violated and unsafe the Carlbrook staff made me feel—both emotionally and physically. The words just poured out of me, long over-due. After keeping so much in, it was a hugely cathartic conversation.

At the same time, I never wanted to do it again. Thinking about Carlbrook was too overwhelming. I no longer wanted to understand my life. I just wanted to forget it. So I continued to block out the world with booze and drugs. I ran away without any particular direction in mind. I stumbled and blacked out, then I got back up and started running again.

As months passed, my relationship with Luke became about drugs more and more. I told myself we were just having fun. We were young and in love and making up for lost time, but most dates don't end in 5:00 a.m. comedowns or hangovers that last until the next bender starts. Plus, I don't think a romantic getaway is the right term for the night I snorted a line of crushed-up pills and woke up two days later.

A lot of the time, I was either too high or too sick to eat—but that was a good thing. In my mind I couldn't possibly be skinny enough. I was anorexic and bulimic, always googling new ways to lose even more weight. When I looked in the mirror, all I saw was a girl who wasn't good enough. A worthless abuser and a mistake.

When Luke and I broke up, things only got worse. I'd lock myself in my apartment for days, playing sad songs on repeat. *Just like Carlbrook taught me.* When I emerged from isolation, my only plan was to find the next party. I'd stay out all night long, fueled by alcohol and coke. When the sun was up and my friends were long gone, when the drugs had run out and there was nowhere else to go, I'd make my way home.

To the extent that you feel joy, that's how much you will feel sorrow.

I really understood the pendulum swing then. A great night inevitably meant a horrible morning. Some of those comedowns were so bad I would google the numbers of rehabs and call them up crying.

"I think I need to check myself in."

"Okay. Tell me what's going on."

I'd explain my problem and say I needed to check myself in. But instead I'd end up falling asleep for the rest of the day and when I woke up I always felt better.

I don't need rehab, I just need more drugs.

So I kept on running. I met a guy and ran away to New York to be with him. My new boyfriend helped me get an internship at *Vogue* that turned into a full-time job. I entered a world where there was always another party, then another afterparty, and the drugs didn't run out. At first I still kept in contact with my Carlbrook friends. I'd talk to Maya and Bobby on the phone every now and then, and I saw Charlotte whenever she came to New York. Eventually, I found myself wanting more and more distance. I wanted to forget about Carlbrook completely.

For a while, I actually did. There were several years where it was like that part of my life was erased from my consciousness. I had unraveled so much that even Charlotte and I stopped talking for a while. Most of my new friends had no idea I'd even gone to a therapeutic boarding school. Or that I lived in the woods for three months when I was fifteen. Every time a memory threatened to intrude, I'd push it away or drown it out.

I forced Carlbrook out of my own life story. It was there and it wasn't; everything that happened turned into nothing at all. I had split myself into two parts, and each half stayed alive by lying to the other. It was an exhausting way to live and I was dizzy from the effort of trying to keep up with myself.

Regardless, I knew it was worth it. Because this time—*this time*—I was actually free.

Chapter 39

THE KIDNAPPERS HAD come in the middle of the night and the call came in the middle of the day. A decade was spooled out between two moments that changed my life forever.

It was the summer of 2015 and I was back in Los Angeles. I had reached my breaking point with drugs and late-night drinking and was in the process of piecing my life back together. I finally found something to anchor me when I took my first acting class and fell in love. It felt like a safe way to express myself, almost like therapy for the darkness inside. Carlbrook was still buried in some distant corner of my psyche, and I wasn't quite ready to look at it head-on.

Then there was the phone call. When my cell started ringing with Bobby's name on the screen, it took me by surprise. I had just pulled up to my acting coach's house. I stared at my vibrating phone as I walked toward her front door. My first instinct was to ignore the call. I didn't want to be late or seem rude. I also knew in my gut that Bobby was bearing bad news.

"Hello?" I picked up. "Bobby?"

"Hey. Elizabeth. How are you?"

"I'm good," I said. "Back in LA. What's going on with you?"

"Oh fuck," he said. "You really haven't heard yet, have you?"

I heard the sadness in his voice and my heart froze. "Heard what?"

"Oh man," he said. "I guess I'm the first to call you. You two were so close at school and, well... This is gonna be a shock, okay?"

"Okay...," I said. "What?"

He hesitated.

"Bobby, just tell me."

"Maya's dead."

"*What? No.*" I could hear the panic in my own voice. "That's impossible."

"I felt the same way when I heard."

"What happened? Was there a car accident or something?"

"No," Bobby said. "Not an accident."

"What are you trying to say, Bobby?"

"It was suicide, Elizabeth." He took a deep breath. "Maya jumped off a bridge on Saturday."

Chapter 40

IT'S BEEN FIVE years since Maya died and about fifteen since I graduated from Carlbrook. That's half a lifetime that I spent running away from myself. Half a lifetime spent feeling broken and lost, confused about who I was or even *if* I was at all. But I'm not running anymore. In fact, I'm sitting.

I'm on a bench in Los Angeles, overlooking a lake. It's a place that reminds me a little bit of the one at Carlbrook. Where I'd sit with Maya and Bobby and talk about the future. I don't think any of us got the lives we'd planned. But I'm getting there. Little by little, day by day. It isn't always easy, but I'm rebuilding my life.

Although I'm alone, a workshop of one, I think I'm ready for my first truly honest disclosure circle.

Disclosure: I'm not free from Carlbrook. I never was and I'm not sure I'll ever fully get there. But I know now that avoiding it was never going to be the solution. I needed to run toward it, not away from it, and now that I have, I feel better for it.

Maya's death brought back my Carlbrook nightmares. I have dreams about the staff and others where I'm trapped in an endless workshop, but I recognize that this is a good thing. It's a sign I've stopped burying the painful parts of my life. I can look at Alan's face directly and know, even in my dream state, that I will wake up okay.

Disclosure: I suffer from depression. I'm not a drug addict, and my anger doesn't come from some unexplainable place. I just have trouble regulating my mood sometimes, just like so many other people I know. I didn't need to be sent away. I didn't need a full-time "therapeutic community." All I ever needed was for someone to take the time to really hear me. To interpret the cry for help that was at the center of every explosive fight or drunken night.

I didn't need tough love. I just needed a little extra help.

Disclosure: I've always been ruled by my emotions. As a kid it sometimes felt like my feelings were too big for me. As though I'd been given the wrong size by some accident of God or fate; and Carlbrook, that place of bullshit "emotional growth," made this problem so much worse.

After I left, I often had trouble figuring out what I really felt to the degree that I'd either explode completely or just shut down. I'd gotten so used to isolation that I unconsciously re-created it in my new life. Like that first year in Los Angeles, when I'd lock myself in my apartment for days on end.

My first boyfriend in New York had a storage room down the hall from his loft. It was filled with stacks of books and a single picture of Marilyn Monroe. Sometimes after we fought, I'd lie and say I was going for a walk. Instead, I'd lock myself inside the little room and stare at the picture of Marilyn, wondering what was wrong with me. Her eyes looked so sad and lost—but they were also completely familiar. Her eyes said the same thing that mine did every time I glanced in a mirror.

Someone hurt me once. And then everyone did.

My boyfriend was sympathetic to the bits and pieces he knew about my life. He really tried to help me, but I didn't know how to let him in. I was still hiding from myself, after all. I was more comfortable with drugs and parties—and that's what I returned to after we broke up.

Disclosure: I have a habit of getting in over my head when it comes to relationships. There was a night back in New York when I fell in love in a single instant. Whatever the reason, he made me feel safe and utterly content in ways I'd never experienced before.

He took me to Paris. Inside our hotel room, looking out at the city, he wrapped his arms around me and told me he loved me. He said he wanted to have kids with me—not one day, but soon. It didn't matter that I was so young, and so obviously traumatized, because I wanted it too. I had felt alone and lost for so long that once I finally had love, I didn't want to give it up, I wanted to double down.

I didn't expect to get pregnant so quickly, but I did. It felt just as sudden when I had a miscarriage. There were complications, and after days of constant pain and bleeding I finally went to the hospital.

I needed my boyfriend, but our relationship had started falling apart. Instead, I got Percocet. My first prescription was for thirty pills, and when that ran out, I got more. I couldn't handle the trauma of losing the baby, and everything fell apart in dramatic fashion. It was the last straw for my fragile psyche, which was already overloaded by the compounding trauma of everything I'd been through. I was a mess of crazed emotion, trying to soothe myself with whatever drugs I could find. Getting high and eating nothing but coconut popsicles for months. One day I even found myself crying in a church because I had nowhere else to go.

If there was ever a time in my life when I truly should have died, this was it. I wasn't saved by a cat life, though. I was saved by a friend. I barely knew Evan, but he took me in and pieced me back together. He helped me get off the opiates I'd become addicted to and forced me to eat real food. He was there for me at a time when it felt like everyone else in my life had written me off as a lost cause.

★ ★ ★

Disclosure: I still have a hard time with trust. I tend to keep people at arm's length, afraid of what might happen if I let those I love get too close. It's a work in progress, both in my relationships and with my family.

A few weeks after my miscarriage, I called my mom and asked her to fly out to be with me. I wanted her comfort; I craved family and connection, but I didn't know how to receive it. Instead, I took my pain out on her. This most recent trauma triggered all the old wounds and we got into it at a restaurant on the Upper East Side. I told her I hated her, that she'd ruined my life—that old refrain. I stormed out of the restaurant, unable to get past the betrayal I felt for even a moment.

I now understand they were victims too. When I finally began to unravel the tangled web of Carlbrook, I was able to see that things were more complicated than the simple narrative I fixated on at fifteen. My parents were scared for me. They didn't understand my moodiness and anger. When they were offered a magic fix, they took it.

I still wish they hadn't. I'd be lying if I said the thought of being sent away doesn't continue to break my heart. I'll probably always struggle with trust. But I don't blame them for trying to help me. Not anymore.

Disclosure: I didn't go to Maya's funeral. I had every intention of being there. As the date got closer, I just couldn't do it. I was too angry—not just at Carlbrook but at myself for letting our different views about our school get in the way of our friendship. I really loved Maya and I know she loved me too; but she never stopped defending the school, insistent that it had helped her heal.

Maybe that was her defense mechanism. Mine was to shut out any mention of the place, especially when it was positive. After all those years of repressing any thought of Carlbrook, Bobby's call opened the flood-gates. I was back in the snow globe, and it had been turned completely upside down.

I'd already had friends die—suicides, overdoses, a murder—and was still able to go on ignoring the root issue, but this time it was different. It was Maya. Always smiling, always willing to see the best in everyone and everything.

It was such a strength, but I can't help but wonder if ultimately her generous spirit was the thing that harmed her the most. I will never know why Maya jumped off that bridge, but I can't shake my conviction that Carlbrook had something to do with it. There were just so many deaths. As we learned in Integritas, if it looks like a duck, swims like a duck, and quacks like a duck, then it probably is a duck.

Losing Maya cracked me apart and all the pain I'd tried so hard to bury rose up at once. Suddenly I wanted answers. I wanted to know why and how. I wanted to know exactly what that place was, exactly the nature of what we'd been through. I wanted to understand why I'd survived it when so many others hadn't.

So no, I didn't go to Maya's funeral. I wasn't ready to face the past just yet. But her death was the catalyst for everything that came next. It's the reason this book exists. She deserved so much more from life than what the Troubled Teen Industry gave her.

We all do, every one of us. Maggie and Kyle, Charlotte and Brittany. Even Randall was a product of the cycle.

To those who didn't survive: You deserved a different ending.

To those who are still surviving: You deserve to be understood.

This book is for you. It's for us. It's for anyone who was touched by the long, cold arm of that terrible industry. It's for everyone who just wants the cycle to stop.

Afterword

Carlbrook has been permanently closed since December 2015. After fourteen years of operation, the school cited declined enrollment as the reason for its shutting. In 2010, a student named Forest Ferguson walked off the Carlbrook campus and was never heard from again. To this day, he remains a missing person.

As for Kristen, she did not end up dead in a ditch like Randall described. After we graduated, a postcard made its way to Charlotte's address. It was a Christmas greeting from Kristen, who was very much alive and well.

In memory of:

Adam, Alyssa, Arturo, Beau, Blake B., Blake J., Brendan, Brian, Cage, Carl, Cody, Cody C., Coleman, Connor F., Connor G., Daniel, Eddie, Elizabeth, Ford, Henry, James, Jennifer, Joe, Jonathan, Kate, Kelly, Laura, Lisa, Matt, Michael, Mike A., Miles, Molly, Neil, Rich, Rob, Sean, Sean W., Trevor, Walker, and Zack

Acknowledgments

To my family, who supported me in telling such a hard story. For reliving this time in our lives in order to make this possible. They were not only understanding of my desire to share it, but are also proud of me for doing so. These institutions prey not only on the children, but also scared parents and families. I am grateful to my brother, Thomas, for our trip to Montana. I was nervous about how everyone would react to my doing a book; he stood by me and walked me through the process. This journey has shown me that forgiveness is always possible.

Annabel Fay, who has become my family and whom I am forever indebted to. We survived this experience together and without her I don't know where I would be in life. Thank you for trusting me when it came to reliving your experience; I know how deeply personal and painful it is. To my other classmates who have kept in touch with me over the years, you did more for me than you know.

My deepest gratitude to Liana Maeby, my great friend and someone I deeply respect and admire. Thank you for the countless hours spent meticulously reading and reviewing the text and for offering invaluable notes, ideas, and suggestions. Your generous and thoughtful contributions helped me find the story I was meant to tell.

My managers at 3 Arts Entertainment: Molly Madden, who from the start encouraged me to write my story. She believed in me long before this was ever a memoir. Richard Abate, for taking me to breakfast that morning and making this all possible. Annie Gaspar, Martha Stevens, Desirae Stevens, Kristen O'Leary, and Rachel Kim—I appreciate your commitment. Special thanks to my editor, Suzanne O'Neill, at Grand Central, who treated this book like her own and gave me the confidence I needed to share it with the world. To Jacqueline Young, Ben Sevier, Staci Burt, Alana Spendley, Abby Reilly, Sarah Congdon, Carolyn Kurek, Lisa Cahn, Mark Steven Long, Chris Nolan, and the many others who played a part in bringing this to life, I am grateful for you. My lawyer, Tom Hunter, has been there for me through it all. His advice, knowledge, and friendship have been invaluable to me. Nicki Fioravante at Viewpoint showed me kindness, compassion, and generosity before she even knew me—thank you for going on this journey with me. Gayle Spitz, for giving me a safe place to grieve and heal during this process.

Sebastian Stan and Tyler Winther, for reading this in its many forms over the years and having an unwavering belief in me. Ali Kay, one of my best friends and biggest supporters, who even had to loan me a computer when mine crashed while writing this. To my friends who offered advice and lent me a shoulder to cry on or an ear to listen, I couldn't have done this without you. It takes a village—thank you to all of those who were part of this one.

About the Author

Elizabeth Gilpin is an actress, writer, and producer. She starred in and produced *Life Boat*, a short film directed by Lorraine Nicholson, which premiered at the 2017 Tribeca Film Festival. The film was nominated for the Grand Jury Prize for Live Action Short Film at AFI Fest and won the Audience Award at the Napa Valley Film Festival. Elizabeth also starred in *Endings, Inc.* and *Guerra*. *Stolen* is her first book.

Elizabeth currently splits her time between Los Angeles and Nashville.